Tropical I

Tropical Interludes

European Life and Society in South-East Asia

GRAHAM SAUNDERS

With a Foreword by
VICTOR T. KING

KUALA LUMPUR
OXFORD UNIVERSITY PRESS
OXFORD SINGAPORE NEW YORK
1998

Oxford University Press

Oxford New York

Athens Auckland Bangkok Bombay
Calcutta Cape Town Dar es Salaam Delhi
Florence Hong Kong Istanbul Karachi
Madras Madrid Melbourne Mexico City
Nairobi Paris Shah Alam Singapore
Taipei Tokyo Toronto

and associated companies in
Berlin Ibadan

Oxford is a trade mark of Oxford University Press

Published in the United States
by Oxford University Press, New York

© Oxford University Press 1998
First published 1998

British Library Cataloguing in Publication Data
Data available

Library of Congress Cataloging-in-Publication Data
Saunders, Graham E.
Tropical interludes: European life and society in South-east Asia
Graham Saunders; with a foreword by Victor T. King.
p. cm. — (Oxford in Asia paperbacks)
Includes bibliographical references.
ISBN 983 56 0036 8 (pbk.)
1. Europeans—Asia, Southeastern—History. 2. Europeans—Asia,
Southeastern—Social life and customs. 3. Asia, Southeastern—
Social life and customs. I. Title. II. Series.
DS523.4.E89S28 1998
959'.004034—dc21
97-23844
CIP

Typeset by Indah Photosetting Centre Sdn. Bhd., Malaysia
Printed by KHL Printing Co. Pte. Ltd., Singapore
Published by Penerbit Fajar Bakti Sdn. Bhd. (008974-T),
under licence from Oxford University Press,
4 Jalan Pemaju U1/15, Seksyen U1, 40150 Shah Alam,
Selangor Darul Ehsan, Malaysia

For Andrew, Anthony, Daniel,
and Michael

Foreword

VICTOR T. KING

IT is still fashionable in certain quarters to criticize European colonialism for its economic exploitation of the dominated populations and territories, its denial of political rights and its racist ideology and cultural imperialism. Of course, there are important elements of truth in these charges, and the selection of writings in this present anthology confirms some of them. Yet, Dr Graham Saunders's volume provides us with much more than a record of European perceptions of local peoples and cultures, and examples of European social and cultural superiority, economic control, and political dominance. It dwells in particular on the everyday lives, experiences, and states of mind of Europeans in the tropics—their reactions, thoughts, and impressions; their working, domestic, and social lives; their relations with local South-East Asians and, more particularly, with their own kind. In these respects, Dr Saunders's book provides a perfect complement to the first anthology in our series by John Gullick which focused on the adventures, travels, and encounters of Europeans in the East.

The world which is brought to life here in the travelogues, novels, memoirs, diaries, autobiographies, and personal reminiscences of European writers, has largely disappeared; one might say the *worlds* presented here, because the lives of Europeans varied depending on time, place, social status, occupation, and gender, and more broadly, national culture.

Dr Saunders has tapped this rich source of colonial experience, and presents extracts on most of the former dependant territories of South-East Asia over a period of more than one hundred years from the mid-nineteenth century to just after the Second World War. We are able to compare and contrast the conditions of life of European men and women in the remote outposts of Empire in Burma, Malaya, Indo-China, the Philippines, and the East Indies with those in the bustling colonial towns and cities of Rangoon, Batavia, Singapore, and Saigon. Many of our writers are women who kept diaries and conducted much of the correspondence with relatives and friends back in Europe. They provide us with some of the most intimate and revealing details of domestic life, pastimes and leisure activities, social gatherings at the club, and behaviour and etiquette among the various expatriate communities. Among others, we enter the different worlds of the colonial planter in East Sumatra in the early twentieth century; the wife of a teak-wallah in northern Thailand in the 1930s; the wife of a British Assistant Resident in a lonely and difficult frontier post in the Malaya of the 1870s; missionaries in Burma in the late nineteenth century; young working males in the British commercial community of Dutch Java in the early twentieth century; a subdivisional police officer in Pegu in the 1930s; and the wife of the White Rajah of Sarawak in the last quarter of the nineteenth century.

Dr Saunders arranges the material appropriately in a chronological scheme—Europeans arrived, settled in, established a daily round, and most of them sooner or later departed. As he notes, of course, not all Europeans conformed to this pattern, nor did certain of our writers. Some Europeans never really settled into, and adjusted to, a different culture and country. For those in physically isolated regions, social life could be rather attenuated. There were also those who stayed on, and for a not inconsiderable number of Europeans who succumbed to disease or some other misfortune, there was no return to the native land. However, for the majority there was the expectation that, after a sojourn in the region to govern, administer, plant, trade, produce, or simply accompany and support one's partner, there would be farewells and, hopefully, the opportunity to enjoy the fruits of one's labour with family and friends at home in Europe.

What is revealed in this anthology is that the popular view

of colonial life in the East—large bungalows, sundowners on the veranda, servants, frivolous parties, and gatherings at the club—is only part of the story. These features of expatriate life became much more common in the 1920s and 1930s with the establishment of a much larger European community in South-East Asia. Examples of this colonial privilege, associated closely with their power and status, certainly abound in this volume, but the more trying and unpleasant aspects of everyday life also appear.

We move from Joseph Conrad's powerful evocation of the East—'mysterious, resplendent, and sombre, living and unchanged, full of danger and promise'—to the mind-numbing tedium and extreme discomfort of life in frontier Malaya described by Emily Innes.

Often the first encounters with the East are the most acute and vivid for our writers. Ladislao Székely, arriving for the first time in the East Indies, refers to 'a deadening, stupefying heat' and Noel Wynyard captures the experience of tropical heat in northern Thailand: 'It got steadily hotter and hotter; there was no shade at all, and the sweat poured off me in rivers, my shirt and shorts sticking to me as if I'd been out in a rainstorm. . . .' The missionary, Henry Cochrane, in Burma, also gives us this feeling of intense heat when he comments that '[t]he drinking water is so warm that it seems to have lost much of its wetness'.

The overpowering, sometimes suffocating climate, is frequently associated with other sensations in the European mind—with the intensity of smells, the intoxication induced by the heavy scent of flowers, and the vividness and depth of natural colours. Székely is far from gracious in his description of Oriental odours—'strange-smelling abominations', the 'terrible stench', 'rancid grease-smell', and 'stinking water'. There was also a European preoccupation with the abundance of insect and animal life.

As Dr Saunders suggests, once they settled in, life for European men was usually occupied with work in office, plantation, mine, or factory. It was not so easy for female partners, although as more European women went out to

South-East Asia, especially during the inter-war years, their social life improved immeasurably. But even then residence in remote places remained difficult. The 'heartrending' loneliness and ennui is best described by Noel Wynyard. For her, when her husband was away, it was 'a dragging hell'. Of course, it was not always and everywhere unpleasant, and certainly for someone like the Ranee Margaret Brooke of Sarawak, who enjoyed an elevated status in contrast to Emily Innes, there were many happy times; some of the happiest being spent on the large veranda at the Astana in Kuching. Emily Innes resided in a 'fearful place', and tolerated a life of extreme dullness.

Even for some European males whose work took them out on long official up-country tours, there was often monotony and inconvenience. Ladislao Székely and Madelon Lulofs describe aspects of the colonial planter's life in Sumatra. It too was often lonely, compensated for by the routine of boisterous nights at the club. Lulofs links the loneliness of the planters with the coarseness of their behaviour. Isolation 'had taught them to drink, to swear and to fight'. This solitary existence, compounded by the fact that even where European communities existed, these were often small, commonly resulted in bad-temperedness and irritability—Székely's 'tropic frenzy' or 'fever'; and a closed incestuous environment bred petty jealousies, gossip, and arguments, with not a little eccentricity and boorishness.

Some of the most interesting aspects of European life were learning about new social and cultural mores—both Asian and colonial European. There were unusual things to get used to—and predictably the immediate preoccupations were with bathing arrangements and sanitary facilities, becoming accustomed to the taste and smell of spicy foods, and coming to terms with strange foreign languages. Even the Anglo-Malay patois of British Malaya had to be mastered. In addition, establishing the rules of the game in relations with local people—usually as domestic servants, cooks, drivers, house-boys, dhobis, and gardeners—and fitting into a set of expatriate interrelationships and social positions based on such principles as hierarchy and gender—kept the newly arrived European exercised for some time.

In this volume, there is an evocation of the experience of another world, of difference, of the strange and unusual. Underlying this there is a central theme, sometimes made explicit, often implicit in the various extracts. Although there were social, cultural, and other divisions and differences within the several European communities in South-East Asia, the primary distinctions were drawn between Europeans and Asians, and between European culture and civilization and the Asian 'other'. Joseph Conrad, in almost lyrical mood, asserts that, in his encounter with the East, he had 'seen its secret places and ... looked into its very soul'. Yet, there were very few Europeans who crossed the divide, and certainly most of our writers in this volume had no intention of doing so. They were mainly concerned with recreating in one form or another, familiar elements of European society and culture in Asia.

The 'question of the brown woman'—the relations between European men and Asian women—also occasioned much debate in European circles because divisions were bridged. Yet, as Lulofs shows, in one of her extracts, the relation was still based on differences of power and status.

Ladislao Székely expresses the distinction between Europe and Asia in terms of culture, civilization, and development on the one hand, and the uncontrolled, unknown, natural state of the East. Specifically for him the order imposed by Dutch plantation agriculture transformed the untamed condition of tropical forest and swamp.

The divisions between European and Asian were also sustained by social and cultural convention, based on power and prestige. Expressions of the superiority and distance are provided in this volume in the patronizing, pejorative comments made about local cultures. Emily Innes confirms the differences and status distinctions between her own and Malay culture in her reference to their dwellings as 'wigwams'. Székely refers to local people as 'slothful'.

In order to gain a perspective on the nature of European governance and conduct in South-East Asia, we have to rely mainly on the commentaries of Europeans on each other. Some of these accounts by Europeans of other Europeans do sometimes give us a sense of the ridiculous, and the fragility and impermanence of the European position. After all it was the Europeans who had to acclimatize and adjust to something different, and some of the personal difficulties occasioned by this process of accommodation are revealed in this volume. For example, many Dutch colonials settled in Java and adapted Holland to the East Indies; the French, on the other hand, were bent on transplanting France in Vietnam; and the British principally saw Malaya as a way-station on their return to their native land. Various peculiar features of these European colonialisms followed from their differences in attitude and approach. The Dutch conducted a relaxed family and domestic life in Java, almost a colonial suburbia, with the adoption of some Oriental customs, particularly in costume and cuisine. In comparing the French with the British and Americans, Harry Franck says 'the French think that they cannot live in the tropics without a pith helmet, a cholera belt, wine, and a woman. One might add ice in the place of song.' The club was mainly a British colonial institution in the East. In Rangoon, for example, men's clubs were focused on bridge and drinking; mixed clubs on golf and tennis. For me, George Orwell's description in *Burmese Days* of a small town in upper Burma in the 1920s captures the importance of the club. He says 'when one looked at the Club—a dumpy one-storey wooden building—one looked at the real centre of the town. In any town in India the European Club is the spiritual citadel, the Nirvana for which native officials and millionaires pine in vain.'

For critics of colonialism, certain narratives in this volume will confirm their views; for the expatriates who experienced this colonial world, the anthology will provide something of a nostalgic look back to ways of life which are no more. For those who have no particular convictions, it is simply a good read. It gives us insights into the lives of Europeans, who, whatever their prejudices and commitments, experienced something fascinatingly different.

Acknowledgements

FULL bibliographical details of the work from which an extract is taken are given at the end of the extract.

The compiler and the publisher gratefully acknowledge permission to reproduce the extracts from the copyright holders listed below. The numbers refer to the relevant extract, or extracts, in the body of the work.

John Murray Publishers Ltd (45)

HarperCollins Publishers (20)

Oxford University Press, Oxford (5, 12, 15, and 27)

Rhodes House Library, Oxford (25 and 33)

Dr Nicholas Tarling and the University of Auckland Centre for Asian Studies (24 and 36)

Mr Bill Tydd & BACSA (British Association for Cemeteries in South Asia, 76 1/2 Charterfield Ave, London SW15 6HQ (30)

For permission to reproduce the illustrations accompanying the extracts indicated below, the compiler and the publisher would like to thank the following:

Mr Steven Tan (Cover, 4, 15, and 21)

The compiler has made every attempt to locate the copyright holders of those extracts and illustrations still subject to copyright and to secure permission for their copying. In those cases where these efforts have been unsuccessful and an owner of copyright still exists, the compiler and the publisher apologize to the copyright holder, trusting that their good intentions will be acceptable.

Contents

Introduction

GRAHAM SAUNDERS

WHAT sort of lives did Europeans in South-East Asia enjoy or endure during the colonial period? Was it all, as the popular image would have it, epitomized by spacious bungalows, hordes of servants, tennis parties, frivolity, picnics, balls, and evenings at the club? For some people in some places for some of the time, yes; particularly in the period between the two world wars. Such a life was also more likely where there was a number of Europeans and, particularly, a number of European wives. As several of the following extracts show, for many people the reality was different, particularly for those in remote districts and for the period before the late nineteenth century.

The situation differed also for women and men. The men had their occupations, the women were more often burdened with lonely domesticity without the interest and stimulation of worthwhile activity; although much depended on the characters concerned. Some women found their role in supporting their husbands. Others found delight, interest, and reward in their own pursuits and in their observation of the strange world in which they now moved. For this reason, many of the accounts which follow are by women, who often kept diaries and were mainly responsible for maintaining family correspondence in which their days were recorded. The men were too often absorbed in their work and leisure, their writings were often of an official or semi-official nature, and only a few wrote their reminiscences with reference to how they had actually lived their years in Asia. As always, there were exceptions and some of these appear here.

This selection of readings attempts to provide examples of

European life from all the countries of South-East Asia over the period from approximately 1800 to 1940. It is concerned with how Europeans actually lived, who settled and made a home during their time in South-East Asia. Other volumes in this series describe other aspects of the European experience and provide European impressions of the region and its peoples. These extracts are not about South-East Asians, but about Europeans and their attitudes, their life-styles, their entertainments. Visiting Europeans appear only when they observe and comment on the lives of those living and working in the region. The European experience is our theme. That experience has inspired works of fiction from which extracts have also been taken when authentically based on real experience.

Inevitably, this selection is unrepresentative in that the passages are taken from writers in English or from translations. Nevertheless, they refer to all the countries of South-East Asia and to the experiences of representatives of all the colonial powers in the region. It is clear that there were similarities in the European colonial experience whether British, French, or Dutch. At the same time, national differences did exert an influence. The Dutch, for example, settled in Java more completely and comfortably than the British in Malaya, Borneo, or Burma, or the French in Indo-China. Hence there is an air of greater domesticity in descriptions of colonial Dutch society in Java. The British, for example, generally looked forward to periods of leave and eventual retirement in Britain and sent their children home to school from a young age. The Dutch, on the other hand, built their children schools in Java.

The similarities were greater in the earlier period and in remoter areas, where the conditions of life were such that basic necessities were in short supply and the number of European women was small. In these largely male societies, work dominated the European's life and leisure was often solitary, interspersed with boisterous nights at the club or the occasional extravagant visit to a town; in all of which heavy drinking often featured. In these solitary outposts, the question of the 'brown woman' arose. It was generally accepted that the solitary white male would take a woman, a 'sleeping dictionary' as she was sometimes known, for through her he would learn the language and customs of those whom he governed or commanded. Governments and commercial companies alike forbade a young man marrying until he had served a period of years. A white woman, it was believed, could not be expected to live in a remote outpost; an attitude which slowly changed as communications, material conditions, and medical knowledge improved. Even then, there was a lingering feeling that a wife distracted a man from his real duty to his firm and its interests, if an unofficial, or to his duties and the people he administered, if an official.

For many of the men, there was real satisfaction in their work which made up to a large extent for the hardships, tedium, discomfort, ill health, and separation from homeland and family. Many rose higher in colonial society than they would have done at home. Others could survey a thriving plantation where once there had been jungle, or take satisfaction in bridges built, railways laid, towns surveyed, and the provision of hospitals, schools, Christian converts, prosperity, and peace. Some identified strongly with those they administered and cared for. Others never settled and were never or rarely happy, remaining exiles in spirit.

South-East Asia claimed many of them, but most eventually departed and returned to their homeland. Some, who had achieved wealth or high station, returned to honours and comfort, and an often dignified retirement. Most of those who appear in this book left with mixed feelings. All were changed in some way. Many could not settle comfortably into their homeland. They had spent the best years of their lives in Asia; they had little in common with those who had stayed at home. In many cases they had left loved ones buried in foreign soil. In their houses the mementos of the East proclaimed their difference. They could feel at ease only with other ex-colonials: and created or joined associations and societies where they could meet their fellows. In this they shared an affinity with military families, whose lives also set them apart but whose experience of living in far off lands was tempered by the closed society of the cantonment.

This book has been divided into unequal parts entitled 'Arrival', 'Settling In', 'Daily Life', 'Social and Community Life', and 'Departure'. Some overlap, is inevitable. 'Daily Life' and 'Social and Community Life' are the largest sections. Some writers appear in more than one section and readers will thus obtain a sense of continuity. There has been little attempt to arrange items within a section in any particular order, by subject-matter, chronology, or region. The continuities, similarities, and differences are best revealed by the almost fortuitous juxtoposition of experiences. Each individual who felt it worthwhile recording his or her experience is already a person out of the ordinary, so this selection may not be completely representative. Some excellent accounts remain in copyright and interested readers may wish to peruse those listed under Further Reading. Nevertheless, the present selection provides a window into European life and society in colonial South-East Asia, a world that has largely passed away. If a tinge of nostalgia creeps in, the writer was once there too.

Further Reading

Allen, Charles (ed.), *Tales from the South China Seas: Images of the British in South-East Asia in the Twentieth Century*, London: Andre Deutsch/British Broadcasting Commission, 1983.

Barlow, Henry, 'Anna Forbes: A Naturalist's Companion in the Far East', in John Gullick (ed.), *Adventurous Women in South-East Asia: Six Lives*, Kuala Lumpur: Oxford University Press, 1995, pp. 246–70.

Butcher, John G., *The British in Malaysia 1880–1941: The Social History of a European Community in Colonial South-East Asia*, Kuala Lumpur: Oxford University Press, 1979.

Dauncey, Mrs Campbell, *An Englishwoman in the Philippines*, London: John Murray, 1906.

Gullick, John, 'Emily Innes: Keeping Up One's Standards in Malaya', in John Gullick (ed.), *Adventurous Women in South-East Asia: Six Lives*, Kuala Lumpur: Oxford University Press, 1995, pp. 147–95.

Reid, Anthony, 'Introduction' to Ladislao Székely, *Tropic Fever*, Kuala Lumpur: Oxford University Press, 1979, pp. v–xv.

Saunders, Graham, 'Harriett McDougall: First Woman Missionary to Sarawak', in John Gullick (ed.), *Adventurous Women in South-East Asia; Six Lives*, Kuala Lumpur: Oxford University Press, 1995, pp. 44–93.

Sim, Katherine, *Malayan Landscape*, London: Michael Joseph, 1946.

Stevenson, Rex, 'Cinemas and Censorship in Colonial Malaya', in *Journal of Southeast Asian Studies*, 5, September (1974): 209–24.

Waugh, Alec, *Hot Countries*, New York: The Literary Guild, 1930.

Wood, W. A. R., *Consul in Paradise: Sixty-nine Years in Siam*, London: Souvenir Press, 1965.

Young, Gavin, *In Search of Conrad*, London: Hutchinson, 1991.

General Information

OUTfiT: In regard to clothing the prospective visitor to North Borneo will do well not to purchase an expensive outfit until experience has taught him what is best suited to his needs. European clothes are too heavy for wear in a tropical climate, though they will be found of use on the voyage out and home. For day-wear drill suits are customary and these can be made quite satisfactorily locally, the present price being about $7 to $10 a suit; frequent washing will necessitate about twelve suits. They should not be bought in England where cotton clothes are nearly as expensive as tweed. Very light tweed, serge, or flannel clothes are useful in the afternoons, and these are better obtained in England. A dress suit should be brought. Underclothing is not easily obtained locally, and is very expensive in Singapore, so this should be purchased at home; socks, ties, and collars should also be bought in the United Kingdom. The canvas boots and shoes made by the Chinese bootmakers locally, costing $5 to $6 a pair, are quite satisfactory and just as useful as expensive European foot-gear, except for formal occasions. A pair of mosquito boots, purchased at home, will be found useful. A topi (sun-helmet) is absolutely essential; this may be purchased locally for about $12, but can also be obtained in Colombo or Singapore, where it will be necessary if the passenger wishes to go ashore. A felt hat or two will come in useful in the afternoons. Caps are not of much use. Steel uniform cases should be bought rather than leather bags.

Ladies are advised to buy everything in the United Kingdom: washing frocks for general wear, voile, muslin, cotton or any other washing materials. Lace and net wear very well for afternoon use or for small evening entertainments, and are cool. Silk or chiffon is hot and does not wear well. Three or four good evening dresses are necessary; a black one is always useful. A good stock of underlinen is necessary; it should not be too fine on account of the hard washing. A good raincoat and one or two sports coats are essential; one of these should be woollen. Shoes should be taken out (not heavy ones—white canvas are the best for ordinary wear), together with a good stock of cottons, needles, pins, buttons, tapes, etc. A bathing costume is useful. Hats fade quickly, and several should be taken out—light, shady ones are most useful.

Provisions: Practically anything may, of course, be obtained from Singapore and almost all requisites of European house-holds and tinned provisions may be purchased in the towns in Borneo, but the latter are seldom necessary. There is abundance of fresh meat, pork, fowls, and ducks to be obtained in the local markets, and in most places there is little difficulty in obtaining plenty of good fish. Eggs are plentiful, and the Chinese gardens, which are to be found everywhere, produce ample supplies of fruits and vegetables.

There is a cold-storage supply in Sandakan where fresh butter, cheese, etc., may be obtained: and coast stations can augment local supplies from the Singapore, Hong Kong and Australian steamers.

Cost of Living: The following table gives the market prices at Sandakan on the 1st October, 1928, of the principal articles of consumption:–

(a) IMPORTED: ....

Biscuits, 2lb. tin	$1.50–$2.20
Butter, 1lb. tin	.85
Cigarettes (Nay Cut 50 tin)	.73
Coffee, 1lb. tin	1.05
Flour, per bundle of 4 bags	12.60
Jam, 1lb. tin	.40–.60
Lard, per lb.	.33
Milk (tinned) per tin	.35
Onions, per lb	.12
Potatoes, per lb.	.11
Salmon, 1lb. tin	.25
Salt, per lb.	.03
Sugar, per lb.	.12
Tea (Ceylon) per lb.	1.10–1.20
Tea (common) per Chinese lb.	.35

Tobacco (Navy Cut) $\frac{1}{4}$ lb. tin	1.25
Whisky (J.W.) quart....................................	3.25.

(b) PRODUCED LOCALLY:

Beef, per lb..	.30
Bread, per lb...	.10
Ducks, per lb.	.56–.64
Eggs, each...	.04
Fish (fresh) per lb.	.09–.21
Fowls, per lb...	.49–.53
Milk (fresh) 1 quart bottle	.20
Pork, per lb.	.38–.60
Vegetables, per lb..	.06

(Note: 1\$=2s.   4d. $3\frac{1}{2}$ cents = 1d.)

Providing care is exercised, the average total cost of living for a person from the United Kingdom should not exceed \$200 to \$250 a month (£280 to £350 a year). It should be borne in mind that the standard of living is higher than in England; more servants are kept, more courses are served at meals, and more entertaining is done. Club life is an important feature in the bigger towns; a club entrance fee as a rule is \$25 and monthly subscriptions \$6. When tennis and golf clubs are distinct from social clubs, the same rates usually apply.

The cost of native servants is as follows: Cook, \$25 to \$30 a month; boy, \$16 to \$25 a month; water-carrier, \$18 to \$25 a month.

Handbook of the State of North Borneo; with a Supplement of Statistical and Other Useful Information, The British North Borneo (Chartered) Company, London, 1929, pp. 94–6.

Arrival

BEFORE the Second World War, Europeans usually arrived in South-East Asia by sea. In the immediate pre-war period, air travel was still in its infancy. The coast of Asia was first glimpsed from the deck of a ship; the harbour and port came gradually into view, and first impressions were of a variety of shipping and native craft, a dockside crowded with strangely clad people, of heat, humidity, bustle, noise, unintelligible languages, exotic smells both enticing and repulsive, and the relief of sighting a welcoming figure. The formalities over, there was the drive to hotel or rest-house and a period of bewilderment as the process of adjustment to a new environment and way of life began.

That adjustment was not so much to the local population and its way of life but to joining the European community, a community that was itself very different from that of the homeland. It had its own patterns of behaviour, dress, and speech, its own customs, attitudes, and prejudices, all of which were as strange to the newcomer as anything he or she witnessed among the Asian population. The passages that follow reveal the impressions and thoughts of new arrivals as they first came to terms with South-East Asia, and with European society in South-East Asia.

P. & O. Steam Navigation Co.

PASSENGER and FREIGHT SERVICES.

Carrying His Majesty's Mails.

MEDITERRA-
NEAN
EGYPT
INDIA
PERSIAN
GULF
BURMA
STRAITS
CHINA
JAPAN

AUSTRALIA
NEW
ZEALAND
CEYLON
EAST and
SOUTH
AFRICA
MAURITIUS
Etc.

Before the advent of commercial air travel, many Europeans made their passage to South-East Asia by ship.

1
Asian Landfall

JOSEPH CONRAD

Joseph Conrad needs no introduction as a novelist. This passage from his short autobiographical novel *Youth*, first published in 1902, recounts his own arrival at Muntok on the island of Bangka in March 1883. The young Conrad Korzeniowski, as he then was, was Second Officer on the barque *Palestine* (*Judea* in the novel) carrying 557 tons of coal from Newcastle-on-Tyne to Bangkok when it caught fire in the Bangka Strait between Sumatra and Bangka and, on 14 March, blew up. The crew abandoned ship and watched it sink before rowing in three boats to Muntok. Conrad was in command of one boat. In *Youth* they rowed for days. In reality it was for thirteen and a half hours. In any case, they arrived at night and exhausted, as described in *Youth*. There is no doubt that Conrad, in the guise of Marlow, is evoking the memory of his own first landfall in South-East Asia.

There is a personal reason for choosing this passage to begin this anthology. I read it as a schoolboy in South Australia and it remained with me until, eighty years after Conrad, I made my own more comfortable landfall, knew that same fascination, and recall it now from a similar perspective.

AND this is how I see the East. I have seen its secret places and have looked into its very soul; but now I see it always from a small boat, a high outline of mountains, blue and afar in the morning; like faint mist at noon; a jagged wall of purple at sunset. I have the feel of the oar in my hand, the vision of a scorching blue sea in my eyes. And I see a bay, a wide bay, smooth as glass and polished like ice, shimmering in the dark. A red light burns far off upon the gloom of the land, and the night is soft and warm. We drag at the oars with aching arms, and suddenly a puff of wind, a puff faint and tepid and laden with strange odours of blossoms, of aromatic wood, comes out of the still night—the first sigh of the East on my face. That I can never forget. It was impalpable and enslaving, like a charm, like a whispered promise of mysterious delight.

We had been pulling this finishing spell for eleven hours. Two pulled, and he whose turn it was to rest sat at the tiller. We had made out the red light in that bay and steered for it, guessing it must mark some small coasting port. We passed two vessels, outlandish and high-sterned, sleeping at anchor, and, approaching the light, now very dim, ran the boat's nose against the end of a jutting wharf. We were blind with fatigue. My men dropped the oars and fell off the thwarts as if dead. I made fast to a pile. A current rippled softly. The scented obscurity of the shore was grouped into vast masses, a density of colossal clumps of vegetation, probably—mute and fantastic shapes. And at their foot the semicircle of a beach gleamed faintly, like an illusion. There was not a light, not a stir, not a sound. The mysterious East faced me, perfumed like a flower, silent like death, dark like a grave.

And I sat weary beyond expression, exulting like a conqueror, sleepless and entranced as if before a profound, a fateful enigma.

A splashing of oars, a measured dip reverberating on the level of water, intensified by the silence of the shore into loud claps, made me jump up. A boat, a European boat, was coming in. I invoked the name of the dead; I hailed: *Judea* ahoy! A thin shout answered.

It was the captain. I had beaten the flagship by three hours, and I was glad to hear the old man's voice again, tremulous and tired. 'Is it you, Marlow?' 'Mind the end of that jetty, sir,' I cried.

He approached cautiously, and brought up with the deep-sea lead-line which we had saved—for the underwriters. I eased my painter and fell alongside. He sat, a broken figure at the stern, wet with dew, his hands clasped in his lap. His men were asleep already. 'I had a terrible time of it,' he murmured. 'Mahon is behind—not very far.' We conversed in whispers, in low whispers, as if afraid to wake up the land. Guns, thunder, earthquakes would not have awakened the men just then.

Looking round as we talked, I saw away at sea a bright light travelling in the night. 'There's a steamer passing the bay,' I said. She was not passing, she was entering, and she even came close and anchored. 'I wish,' said the old man, 'you would find out whether she is English. Perhaps they could give us a passage somewhere.' He seemed nervously anxious. So by dint of punching and kicking I started one of my men into a state of somnambulism, and giving him an oar, took another and pulled towards the lights of the steamer.

There was a murmur of voices in her, metallic hollow clangs of the engine-room, footsteps on the deck. Her ports shone, round like dilated eyes. Shapes moved about, and there was a shadowy man high up on the bridge. He heard my oars.

And then, before I could open my lips, the East spoke to me, but it was in a Western voice. A torrent of words was poured into the enigmatical, the fateful silence; outlandish, angry words, mixed with words and even whole sentences of good English, less strange but even more surprising. The voice swore and cursed violently; it riddled the solemn peace of the bay by a volley of abuse. It began by calling me Pig, and from that went crescendo into unmentionable adjectives—in English. The man up there raged aloud in two languages, and with a sincerity in his fury that almost convinced me I had, in some way, sinned against the harmony of the universe. I could hardly see him, but began to think he would work himself into a fit.

Suddenly he ceased, and I could hear him snorting and blowing like a porpoise. I said—

'What steamer is this, pray?'

'Eh? What's this? And who are you?'

'Castaway crew of an English barque burnt at sea. We came here to-night. I am the second mate. The captain is in the long-boat, and wishes to know if you would give us a passage somewhere.'

'Oh, my goodness! I say.... This is the *Celestial* from Singapore on her return trip. I'll arrange with your captain in

5

the morning … and … I say … did you hear me just now?'

'I should think the whole bay heard you.'

'I thought you were a shore-boat. Now, look here—this infernal lazy scoundrel of a caretaker has gone to sleep again—curse him. The light is out, and I nearly ran foul of the end of this damned jetty. This is the third time he plays me this trick. Now, I ask you, can anybody stand this kind of thing? It's enough to drive a man out of his mind. I'll report him…. I'll get the Assistant Resident to give him the sack, by … ! See—there's no light. It's out, isn't it? I take you to witness the light's out. There should be a light, you know. A red light on the—'

'There was a light,' I said, mildly.

'But it's out, man! What's the use of talking like this? You can see for yourself it's out—don't you? If you had to take a valuable steamer along this God-forsaken coast you would want a light, too. I'll kick him from end to end of his miserable wharf. You'll see if I don't. I will—'

'So I may tell my captain you'll take us?' I broke in.

'Yes, I'll take you. Good-night,' he said, brusquely.

I pulled back, made fast again to the jetty, and then went to sleep at last. I had faced the silence of the East. I had heard some of its language. But when I opened my eyes again the silence was as complete as though it had never been broken. I was lying in a flood of light, and the sky had never looked so far, so high, before. I opened my eyes and lay without moving.

And then I saw the men of the East—they were looking at me. The whole length of the jetty was full of people. I saw brown, bronze, yellow faces, the black eyes, the glitter, the colour of an Eastern crowd. And all these beings stared without a murmur, without a sigh, without a movement. They stared down at the boats, at the sleeping men who at night had come to them from the sea. Nothing moved. The fronds of palms stood still against the sky. Not a branch stirred along the shore, and the brown roofs of hidden houses peeped through the green foliage, through the big leaves that hung shining and still like leaves forged of heavy metal. This was the East of the ancient navigators, so old, so mysterious, resplendent and sombre, living and unchanged, full of danger and promise. And these were the men. I sat up suddenly. A wave of movement passed through the crowd from end to end, passed along the heads, swayed the bodies, ran along the jetty like a ripple on the water, like a breath of wind on a field—and all was still again. I see it now—the wide sweep of the bay, the glittering sands, the wealth of green infinite and varied, the sea blue like the sea of a dream, the crowd of attentive faces, the blaze of vivid colour—the water reflecting it all, the curve of the shore, the jetty, the high-sterned out-landish craft floating still, and the three boats with the tired men from the West sleeping, unconscious of the land and the people and of the violence of sunshine. They slept thrown across the thwarts, curled on bottom-boards, in the careless attitudes of death. The head of the old skipper, leaning back in the stern of the long-boat, had fallen on his breast, and he looked as though he would never wake. Farther out old Mahon's face was up-turned to the sky, with the long white beard spread out on his breast, as though he had been shot where he sat at the tiller; and a man, all in a heap in the bows of the boat, slept with both arms embracing the stem-head and with his cheek laid on the gunwale. The East looked at them without a sound.

Joseph Conrad, *Youth; Heart of Darkness; The End of the Tether: Three Stories*, J. M. Dent & Sons, London, 1948, pp. 37–42.

2
A First Arrival in East Sumatra

LADISLAO SZÉKELY

Ladislao Székely wrote *Tropic Fever* in the 1920s but the first Hungarian edition was little noticed and he did not find a large audience until the 1930s, this English edition appearing in 1937. Although not a personal reminiscence, the book has strong autobiographical content and draws on Székely's experience as a rubber planter in East Sumatra between about 1902 and 1918, a time of rapid economic development. His book reflects awareness of the exploitation of the local population and of the immigrant labour force, while acknowledging the pride in achievement that the Dutch planters felt. Székely returned to Sumatra at some point in the later 1920s and created a scandal by his affair with Madelon Lulofs, then married to a planter whom she left to marry Székely in 1930. Madelon Lulofs then herself took up a literary career, and extracts from her novel *Rubber*, published in 1931, appear in this selection.

Contrast Székely's account of his narrator's arrival in Sumatra with the passage from Conrad in Passage 1.

A T last we sighted the coast, and as we drew closer, we could see nothing but forest and marshland; nowhere was there a sign of human habitation. Ahead of us in the distance, we saw masts rocking, and the grimy-grey sails of a few fishing-boats. From the mainland a terrible stench was wafted over to us, the stench of putrefaction.

The bay closed in round us, the banks drew nearer. Behind a bend the harbour lay before us: a few grey hovels of sheet iron, built on piles; rickety Malay huts made of palm leaves; a shaky landing-stage, covered with small sea animals, moss and green slime. The mud steamed in the broiling sun, and a grey vapour lay over the desolate region.

On the opposite bank, built into the water on piles, was a fish-drier. Its terrible stench mingled with the pestilential breeze from the island swamp and the rancid grease-smell of the 'Hercules.'

Slowly we turned in the direction of the landing-stage. A couple of slothful Malays came crawling out from some-where and flung the cables over to us. Then the ship landed and we could get off. I took my small trunk and walked a few steps with it. Van Kuit, the man with the crooked neck, shouted at me in an irritated manner:

'Put that trunk down!'

Startled, I dropped it and looked at Van Kuit dumbfounded. 'What are you thinking of? You as a European can't lug your baggage! Nothing like that here. Please don't forget the prestige of the Whites!'

I was ashamed to have begun my life in Sumatra with so serious a slip, but I really had not considered that one's prestige depended on such things.

A zealous Malay coolie crept up to us. From afar he had been crawling along with bent back; now he seized my trunk. With his left hand he held his right wrist as a sign that he asked for forgiveness, and was holding back the right hand with his left in order to prevent its boldly touching the belongings of the *tuan*. The *adat*, that is to say, tradition, demanded it. And one must demand the adat from the natives, or one's prestige is gone. I knew that much already.

We white tuans sauntered over the bridge to the Custom House. We had no passports, nor was there need of them. The coolies placed our trunks in the scorching corrugated iron hut. From a corner, in the semi-darkness, a drowsy half-caste Customs official crawled forward. He said something in Dutch, Van Kuit answered. Then the Dutchman snarled at the coolie: '*Ajo, ankat!*' And we passed on. The white man's word is sacred: if he says that he carries no fire-arms, then he has none. With shame I thought of our rifles and revolvers, but I trotted on.

Opposite the Custom House was the railway station. The harbour was built on dredged mud. The swamp could not reach the more important buildings, the station and ware-houses. But the village, consisting of a mere handful of Malay and Chinese houses, was built in the swamp. Each house was erected on piles, and a little chicken-ladder led up to it. Every-where was slime and stinking water, with thousands of sea crabs, myriapods and water spiders exposing themselves to the sun in the thick mud and cruising about in the putrid pools.

The station was a small stone building; there were two rail-way lines, a little old locomotive with a long funnel, and a few ramshackle open carriages. Beyond the station, forest. Dark, opaque forest, growing out of blackish water, lianas, palm trees, mangrove trees, ferns. The muddy spots showed traces of crocodiles. The asthmatic little locomotive puffed and smoked. In the carriages sat half-native Chinese, Indians, Arabs, Tamuls—they sat there quietly, with the patience of Orientals waiting for the train to start.

The heat was terrible: a deadening, stupefying heat.

Leaning against the wall of the station building, the native station master chatted drowsily with the conductor. A naked train-driver sat on the step of the locomotive chewing betel-nuts. The saliva, tinted red with the betel juice, ran from the corners of his mouth down his chin. From time to time he spat out the red stuff in a wide circle.

Presently the wheezing little locomotive carried us panting and puffing into the interior of the island. On both sides of the talus forest, black-green mud, dark, threatening coves, white and grey herons. Here and there an iguana slid into the dark water. A troop of monkeys was busy in the trees. A large grey monkey with a white stomach was rocking himself on a protruding root, then with a violent swing he shot into the dark-green leaves of the mangrove trees. The troop followed him. They did not run away, they merely jumped on, for the railway did not frighten them.

Nowhere a village, or even a house. Not even a coco palm. Only forest and swamp.

Presently we saw the first *campong*: a couple of coco palms rose like huge paint brushes straight into the sky; among the large, crenated, light-green leaves of the papaya trees, their fruits glistened, yellowish-green and smelling like melons; the giant tattered leaves of the banana trees, shining as if lacquered, quivered in the noonday sun despite the lack of a breeze. Hidden in the dark shade were huts of palm leaves, a couple of skinny, mangy dogs, naked Malay children with fat bellies....

Then again forest, swamp, lianas, monkeys, jungle, thicket, stillness, dark pieces of water.

Suddenly, as if marked out with a ruler, a huge clearing. Ditches dug in a straight line, paths, two-metre high tobacco plants in endless straight rows. As far as the eye could reach, there swayed a light-green sea of leaves. Everything one saw was carefully tended, almost exaggeratedly ordered.

At a railway station. (Jabatan Penerangan Malaysia)

Among the Chinese coolies with their basket-hats was a European overseer; he waved to us with his thick, pointed stick. Van Kuit yelled a lusty reply. 'An acquaintance,' he said to us.

Now one plantation succeeded another. The campongs were no longer in the forest, but around the plantations. One could see regular streets, natives bicycling, tinkling buggies drawn by ponies. And all at once we drove into the station of the capital. Everywhere order and cleanliness. Pretty stone buildings, an iron viaduct, a glass-covered lobby above the platform. Native and Chinese coolies carried the baggage, Malay and Chinese travellers poured from the carriages, European railroad officials in white uniforms and red caps strutted up and down like peacocks among hens.

In front of the station a large square. Smooth asphalt roads with mighty palms on both sides, pretty bungalows, lovely well-tended little gardens, strange flowers in variegated colours.

And at a distance of half an hour from this paradise lay Belawan, the harbour of death, the home of swamp fever and a thousand lurking dangers; a few minutes from here the impenetrable virgin forest with its slinking beasts of prey, its prowling, treacherous crocodiles, with thousands of giant snakes and millions of malaria mosquitoes. A few decades ago this, too, was still forest, where elephants and tigers fought for supremacy, and where not infrequently the Bataks, cannibals who lived in the mountains, fell upon the inhabitants of the Malay campongs.

In the station square, neatly in rows one behind the other, stood little two-wheeled hackney carriages, on the opposite side a row of rickshas; the half-naked coolies that draw them, were impatiently tramping back and forth on their muscular legs.

We entered such a cab drawn by a native. The swift-footed, perspiring brown coolie bore us like the wind to the nearby hotel which lay in the shade of palm trees.

* * *

THE coolies were rushing in a long line one behind the other. The perspiration was pouring from their sinewy bare backs; the leather pieces tied under their soles shuffled over the melting asphalt. The light little carriages rolled smoothly, the coolies trotted, outstripping one another, like little horses playing for the sheer fun of it. In front Van Kuit, then Lohuis, then Meerens, and last of all came Peter and I.

Briskly we turned in before a curious building: it was the hotel.

For the past month nothing any longer had amazed me. If there had been seven-footed calves or nine-headed cows in this region, I should not have been astonished. I should have taken note of it just as I did of the fact that the odd grove standing here in front of the hotel was one single tree. It was a waringin tree, I was told; its crown was as large as a grove at home. And it had no trunk, or rather it had not only one trunk, but a hundred or perhaps a thousand trunks, air roots that were interlaced, knotted, entangled. Air roots hang from the branches which, when they have grown down to the soil, take root there, so that the trees can have a new trunk. . . . Yes, I should have taken note of this in the same way as that the strange block of buildings there was an hotel. In front a hall. No, not really a hall, only a roof built on wooden pillars; the hall had no walls, doors, or windows. To right and left of it were two equally incomplete halls. One was the billiard room, the other the dining room. In the centre two semi-circular counters, one of them the bar, behind which a Chinaman with the face of a Buddha, sat between countless bottles of various colours and sizes, waiting with mute seriousness for orders. Behind the other desk an absolutely identical looking Chinaman was entering the names of the new arrivals in a large book.

This group of buildings was connected by a walk covered with zinc plate, with two others, long and on level ground. In these buildings were the hotel rooms. In front of each room was a veranda and behind each room a bathroom.

The one Chinaman entered our names in the large book and then said something to a white-clad Malay waiter. Nor was I surprised that the waiter was bare-foot and wore a head-dress. He took our trunks and departed with them down the connecting passage. He placed them in one of the rooms and soundlessly withdrew.

Nervously we stood in the centre of this strange room. The furniture consisted of a table, a wardrobe and two curious, somewhat alarming objects: enormous frames, a metre wide and two long, and one and a half metres in height, of thin white netting. 'What can that be? Mass coffins?'... Cautiously, on tiptoe, we approached one of the enigmatic objects. We searched round and felt it, and at last we discovered what it was. Pulling back the flimsy material, we saw a mattress covered with a white sheet, while two hard-stuffed little pillows and a large white sausage were lying inside the frame. 'A bed,' Peter declared. 'The white covering is mosquito-netting, but whatever is that large funny sausage?' We gazed at it, perplexed, then continued on our path of exploration.

A few steps led down to the bathroom. As we opened the door, a swarm of black beetles dispersed; cockroaches. The less agile scorpions retreated more slowly into the damp corners between rotting boards. In a corner of the bathroom was a large cement basin filled to the brim with a yellow, putrid brew. 'Swimming-pool,' said Peter, 'come and have a bath,' but suspiciously he blinked at the mouldy corners where the cockroaches and scorpions had disappeared.

Shortly afterwards we were disporting ourselves, puffing and splashing, in the large basin. It is true the water was tepid, and stank, but in the great heat it was refreshing nevertheless.

Suddenly someone knocked at the door. It was the Swiss manager of the hotel, who protested indignantly against our bathing in this fashion. We learned that the pool was not meant for swimming, but represented a water reservoir which one must not enter. One was supposed to draw a little water from it with the tin pail standing beside it, and then pour it over one's heated body. That it was dangerous to cool off suddenly; besides, not so much water could be brought along as to allow the luxury of our taking a full bath three times a day.

'We should really have guessed that in this crazy country a bath tub is not meant to be bathed in,' Peter said reproachfully, and climbed grumbling out of the pool.

'Tell me, what is this sausage for?' he asked the Swiss.

The sausage turned out to be a *guling* or, as the English call it, a 'Dutch Wife.' When asleep, you were supposed to embrace it and put your legs round it.

'Well, we might have thought of that,' said Peter, shaking his head.

'Come, let's go for a walk and have a look at the town,' I proposed.

'You can't go for a walk in this heat,' Peter objected.

'But what about having to work in such heat?'

Peter made a dubious face and stared in front of him. With his handkerchief, which was wringing wet already, he wiped the sweat from his face and neck.

'I wouldn't have thought it could be so hot in this country,' he said, sighing....

The streets were swarming with all kinds of motley folk. Our walk seemed to me like a fairy tale from the Arabian Nights; this was a strange, fabulous country, a fabulous, paradisic vegetation, and a fabulous people. Along the kerbs stood a hundred odd varieties of palm, ramose, mushroom-shaped tulip trees with blood-red blossoms; in the gardens grew variegated flowers of a type I had never seen, which exhaled a heavy, fragrant scent; there were black, yellow, and brown people, naked or half-naked, in white garments; men in skirts and women in knickers....

Like sleep-walkers we strolled about, gaping; everything was dancing before our eyes, the noise condensed to a dull chaos of sounds.

Slowly we walked back to the hotel. In the lobby sat a few robust Europeans, their skin dark-red, drinking beer.

When we got to our rooms, we undressed, poured water over our bodies and lay down in the comic four-cornered frames. The bed linen was as warm to our naked skin as if it had just been ironed. The guling was a marvellous invention. You press it to you, and sleep like a dead man.

15

When we awoke the evening was dark. Our pillows and sheets were wringing wet as if they had been dipped in water. Peter lay faint and exhausted and would not get up. Someone had placed two cups of tea and two bananas on the table. Ants were crawling round the cups, and millions of insects flitting round the burning lamp. Mosquitoes buzzed as they flew against the light, then, stupefied, they dropped on the table and into the tea cups. Little yellow geckoes sat in hundreds on the walls, gazing, rigid and motionless, at the insects flitting about in their frenzy. With a sudden leap they would snap at some improvident little beetle, then stiffen again to immobility. Outside in the street, an occasional coolie ran past with his ricksha; in front of the hotel a man's voice could be heard from time to time roaring 'Boy ... beer ...!' Then all was quiet again.

Ladislao Székely, *Tropic Fever*, Harper & Brothers, New York, 1937; reprinted by Oxford University Press, Kuala Lumpur, 1979, pp. 25–36.

3
A Ranee's Welcome

MARGARET BROOKE

In April 1870, at the age of 20, Margaret Brooke arrived in Sarawak, newly married to Rajah Charles Brooke and already pregnant. Charles was twice her age, set in his ways, kindly, but distant. He had needed a wife in order to produce an heir and Margaret, bored at home and intrigued by the idea of being queen of a wild and romantic country, had accepted his strange and stilted proposal. After three days in Singapore, the couple boarded the Rajah's yacht for the 48 hours passage to Sarawak. Prone to seasickness, Margaret remained in her berth until the ship crossed the bar into the calm waters of the Sarawak river.

I sprang up and looked out of the port-holes. Towards the north I saw a large expanse of sand strewn over with great brown boulders; a few cottages roofed with what looked like straw were scattered here and there. Some men, women and children were moving about on the sand, while others were jumping in and out of canoes, paddling up and down the river. Further inland, a great mountain, forest-clad up to the peak, refreshed my eyes with its green beauty after the long monotonous days at sea. On the other side of the vessel I noticed that the land was very flat and covered with trees which appeared to have their roots in the water. The glimpse of it all made me long to see it better. I bathed and dressed at once, and, feeling wonderfully restored, went up on deck, where I found my husband and Dr. Houghton silently smoking Manila cheroots after their early tea. They rose to greet me, the doctor pulling forward a bamboo couch. 'You had better lie down,' he said, and I forthwith flopped on to it, the two men relapsing into silence.

'How lovely it is, Charlie,' I said. 'Trees everywhere! And that glorious mountain! Can we go up it some day?' 'Better try!' said my husband grimly. 'That mountain is called Santubong!'

Presently one of our sailors came along the deck, and as he was about to pass the Rajah and myself he bent double and groped himself by. 'Oh, the poor man!' said I. 'He's ill! He must have a bad stomach-ache!' 'Stomach-ache!' retorted my lord and master; 'Malays always do that when they pass us. It's their way of showing respect.' I felt somewhat squashed and again we relapsed into silence.

The next thing that met my view was a large mud flat, as yet uncovered by the incoming tide. On this I saw what I imagined to be some great trunks of trees. The next moment one of these suddenly came to life, reared aloft a huge horrible head and, with widely opened jaws, flumped into the river! 'Oh, Charlie, look!' I cried in horror. 'Can these muddy stumps be real crocodiles?' 'Of course they're crocodiles,' said 'Charlie.' 'What else could they be?' 'Of course,' said the doctor. Silence again!

On we glided through reach after reach of densely wooded land, the banks becoming higher and the vegetation more varied: leafy palms, like green diadems, crowning the forest here and there. At one point the depth of the channel compelled us to hug the shore. Wonders will never cease, I thought, for there, jumping and swinging from branch to branch, I saw crowds of little monkeys, who, by their darting beady eyes, their chattering and grimacing, plainly showed us that they resented our intrusion.

'Oh, Charlie!' I cried in delight. 'Just *look* at the darlings! Are they apes or monkeys?' 'Monkeys, of course,' said my husband. 'Monkeys, of course,' echoed the doctor. Silence once more! By this time I could not help noticing how the doctor seemed to model himself on the behaviour and manner of the Rajah, adopting his silences, echoing his remarks and even imitating his gestures. I discovered later that all my husband's officials did the same.

Now and then in a clearing we would see a few thatched cottages. On the river we met several covered canoes being paddled along by solitary males. They paid no attention whatever to the 'Heartsease' as she steamed by. 'They don't seem to take much notice of your return,' I remarked to the Rajah. 'Oh no,' he replied. 'Malays are not demonstrative in that way.'

I thought of my childhood home in France and of how the dear French people would manifest their joy on my parents' return home to Epinay after even a short absence. I had, indeed, I felt, come into a different world.

Finally we arrived at a bend of the river, on the right bank of which, on the top of a hill, stood the Fort. A puff of smoke was seen; this was followed by a loud report. They were firing a salute! Then I saw the Sarawak flag flying from the top of a mast on a building near by. On a low hill on the opposite bank stood a good-sized white-washed bungalow, below which, by the water's edge, ran a street of picturesque shops which composed the Chinese bazaar. This was the principal thoroughfare of the town. Moored close to the shore were all sorts of odd craft—Chinese junks, Malay schooners, barges and canoes. Looking back again, across the river, I made out a small landing-stage on which were groups of Europeans and Malays, while on the top of the road leading from it stood the Residency, which was occupied at that time by Mr. and Mrs. Crookshank.

Mr. Crookshank was first cousin to my mother and my husband. He had been many years in Sarawak in the time of Sir James Brooke, and thoroughly understood the people. For this reason he had been left in charge of the principality during my husband's absence in England.

We anchored in mid-stream, whereupon the large and sumptuous state barge came alongside to take us ashore. It was manned by some twenty Malays with paddles. These men looked quite imposing in their white uniforms and embroidered caps. We descended into the barge and a few well-directed strokes of the paddles brought us to the landing-stage.

The Resident, Mr. Crookshank, and his wife were there to receive us together with Mr. and Mrs. Helms. Mr. Helms was the Sarawak agent of the Borneo Company. With them were Mr. St. John, Treasurer of Sarawak, and several gentlemen belonging to the Rajah's staff. By far the most impressive were four Malay chiefs, members of the Rajah's government, in their long flowing silken robes and beautiful turbans. It was a scene of brightness and gaiety, the people having gone to some trouble to give a good welcome to their Rajah and their Ranee. Bunting and paper streamers were to be seen everywhere and fire-crackers were being let off in all directions. Suddenly, from out of the others stepped a thin, somewhat elderly Malay holding a huge umbrella of yellow satin which he unfurled and held over my husband's head. The Rajah then led the way, the Resident offered me his arm, the rest of the company formed themselves into a sort of procession and we proceeded on foot up the narrow path that led to the Residency. At this point I ought to explain that we were to stay for a few days with Mr. and Mrs. Crookshank until the newly-built Astana (or palace) on the same side of the river was made ready for our reception. Although the building was completed the furniture had not yet arrived from England.

On reaching the Residency and before proceeding to luncheon, the attendant company were presented to me. How I

Margaret Brooke, From The Ranee of Sarawak, *My Life in Sarawak*, Methuen, London, 1913.

loved the Hadjis, who touched their heads and their hearts in turn as they bowed beautifully and courteously before me. The Europeans left me somewhat cold. They were all very deferential to the Rajah but seemed inclined to ignore me. I had met Mr. and Mrs. Crookshank on a visit they had paid to my mother in Wiltshire a few years previously, when they were home on leave from Sarawak. I admired her intensely, both for her beauty and for her brave steadfast character. Not very tall, she had a slim and graceful figure, an exceedingly pretty face with small delicate features and large lovely brown eyes, while her dark hair, smooth and abundant, when unbound fell nearly to her feet. She and her husband had met and fallen in love in England and she had followed him out to Sarawak on his return there. Early in their marriage, when she was only seventeen, she had nearly met her death during the time of the Chinese insurrection, which was such a menace to Sarawak. Refusing to leave her husband's side, she had been exceedingly courageous and was greatly respected. She was also much liked for her kindness and hospitality to all the Rajah's English officials. Up to the time of my arrival Mrs. Crookshank had been the first lady in Sarawak. Can one be surprised, therefore, if at the back of her gentle mind she, a woman of thirty-three, should feel just a tiny bit annoyed that I, a young girl, 'just out of the school-room' as she rather inaccurately phrased it, should take the place she had come to regard as hers?

Never shall I forget that first official luncheon. How strange and forlorn I felt and how I longed for someone who would stick up for me!

When luncheon was over we three ladies left the men downstairs and established ourselves upstairs in the drawing-room. Mrs. Crookshank and Mrs. Helms then proceeded to discuss the new Bishop Chambers and his wife. 'Horrid woman!' said Mrs. Crookshank. 'She will want to go in to dinner before me. However,' she continued in a serene but very decided voice, 'my husband is the Rajah's prime minister, and prime ministers' wives always take precedence over bishops' wives.' Then, turning to me, she said with rather a forced smile, 'And what are *you* to be called? I hear that Mrs. Chambers has put it about that it would be wrong to call you 'Ranee.' 'Why?' I said, meekly enough, but remembering the poem at Innsbrück in which the Rajah had asked me to become his queen. 'Because, dear, you would not like people to imagine that you were a *black* woman!' 'But Sarawak people are *not* black,' said I, remembering the four dear Datus, their courtesy and politeness on being presented to me. 'I should rather *like* being taken for a Malay.' 'Well!!!' exclaimed both the ladies. And there, for the time, the matter rested.

Margaret Brooke, *Good Morning and Good Night*, Constable, London, 1934, pp. 39–46.

4

A Home in a Swamp

EMILY INNES

Emily Innes had lived a few months in Kuching, Sarawak, before her husband, James, was dismissed for financial irregularities, brought about by incompetence rather than criminal intent. During a brief sojourn in Singapore, she apparently used an early family acquaintance with Sir William Jervois, Governor of the Straits Settlements, to obtain her husband's appointment as Assistant Resident at Bandar Langat, the village in which resided the Sultan of Selangor, recently brought under British influence. James Innes took up his appointment in May 1876 and Emily followed him to Bandar Langat shortly afterwards.

She arrived after a cramped and uncomfortable journey of twenty-four hours in a Malay boat. Although she had been warned of conditions at Bandar Langat, what she found exceeded even the worst reports.

T HE house was worse than I had expected. It was an ordinary Malay wigwam, made partly of dried palm-leaves, and partly of wooden boards, and raised about four feet from the ground on wooden piles. It had no verandas, but consisted merely of a biggish loft—called the Court-room, where Mr. Innes was to hear cases brought before him by the natives—and of two or three little compartments at the back. We turned the latter into bedrooms and a store-room, while the passage between them served as a dining-room. The palm-leaf roof was tolerably watertight; but owing to there being no verandas, the only way of keeping out the rain was by shutting the small wooden shutters, which shut out the light as well, so that when there was a storm we had to choose between sitting in darkness till it was over, and abandoning our belongings to the mercy of the elements. Mr. Innes generally preferred the latter course, but the consequence was that during a storm the Court-room was often swept completely bare of furniture by the wind, and we had to go out afterwards and pick up everything it

A cluster of Malay houses typical of those found in Bandar Langat where Emily Innes and her husband took up residence. (Steven Tan)

had contained, for it had no walls on two sides. Papers, ledgers, pens, inkstands, rulers, and even the cane chairs and tables were blown out on to the mud below; fortunately the mud was so sticky, and the rain so heavy, that the papers never flew far, though sometimes they were reduced to a pulp by the shower.

As soon as the sun had gone down, we went out to look at the village, I being anxious to know the worst at once and get it over. The first bit of the mud-path took us between Malay wigwams, called by courtesy the bazaar, where squalid wares were displayed hanging from strings, or shut up in glass bottles on account of the ants. The population turned out to look at us; some glowered sulkily, others called out 'Tabek, Tuan!' ('Salaam, sir!') in shrill cracked voices. They were all Malays of the poorest class, except a few Chinese shopkeepers and carpenters.

Having passed the bazaar and the Sultan's palace—a dilapidated wooden building—we continued our walk. Here the path became narrower, and it was necessary to walk in single file, as the surrounding ground consisted of seething black mud. Land–crabs darted into their holes as we appeared, and the ikan biludu (velvet fish), an amphibious creature, hopped on and off the slimy logs that lay rotting in the sun. The only vegetation was a kind of bog-myrtle, and the only rising-ground to be seen in the country was a hill about four miles off, called Jugra.

At about two hundred yards from the last wigwam the path came to an abrupt end, and lost itself in the swamp. We stopped a minute or two to look at the hill of Jugra, and agreed aloud that if we had to remain six months in this fearful place we must either leave the service or commit suicide.

Emily Innes, *The Chersonese with the Gilding Off*, 2 vols., Richard Bentley & Sons, London, 1885; reprinted in 1 vol., Oxford University Press, Kuala Lumpur, 1974 and 1993, Vol. 1, pp. 15–19.

5
Into Northern Thailand

NOEL WYNYARD

Noel Wynyard's husband was a 'teak-wallah' in northern Thailand. When she arrived in the mid-1930s, motor vehicles and the railway had improved communications with Bangkok, but she soon learned that road and railway stopped well short of her final destination. Although she entitled the chapter from which this extract is taken 'The Jungle at Last', reaching her new home was hazardous, tedious, and tiring and its remoteness reinforced as a result. We do not, in this passage, accompany her all the way, but her sense of relief when arriving at a European bungalow foreshadows that with which she greeted the end of her journey and her new home. In their piano playing host, we also catch a glimpse of the eccentricities which isolated Europeans in remote areas sometimes exhibited.

AFTER what seemed an impossibly short time in station, we collected gear together for the jungle. I have never seen so many things: tents, beds, mosquito nets, chairs, boxes of office materials, money, an enormous amount of stores, all the cook's pots and pans, and, finally, our two baskets of clothes. I was horrified to learn that I had a small wicker receptacle measuring some 3 ft. by 2 ft. in which to pack everything that I should need for the next six weeks: clothes, books, amusements, sewing, and cosmetics. However, there was no getting out of it and, when I timidly suggested the addition of another small case, I met with a very definite refusal which I realized was fully justified when I saw that everything had to be packed on to three elephants and that a surplus stone or so made a lot of difference. I had been camping several times at home, but never longer than a week, and we were always within range of, at any rate, a village shop where we could replace forgotten trifles such as toothbrushes or mending materials, but the thought of six weeks completely out of touch with civilization filled me with horror, as I debated amongst frocks and underclothes, Cutex and cold cream, handkerchiefs and boots, knitting and writing materials.

At last everything was packed, and we set off by the afternoon train, taking five hours to arrive at our destination. We had a 25-km. drive afterwards and the bus that was to convey us there was waiting to meet the train. I have never seen anything quite like it anywhere. The whole contraption was painted a vivid orange and rather resembled a fair cart with a roof mounted on a Ford chassis; the entire body was of wood, and in the place of windows were slats through which the dust poured in such a cloud that the unfortunates sitting in the rear, or on the steps, were choked and blinded, and when they arrived resembled men who had been in the trenches for several weeks without a bath. I had the place of honour on the front seat next to the driver, and I can safely say that I was too paralysed even to attempt a remark, although he kept up a flowing stream of expletives and wisecracks the whole way, of which I understood nothing. The bus was packed with baggage and humans; only two were allowed in front by strict regulations, but that did not deter a gentleman of most evil countenance from hanging on to what was left of the running board on my side, and every

Although motor vehicles had improved travel to the interior, comfort was another matter as Noel Wynyard discovered.

now and then leaning across me to whisper profanities to the driver as we passed a pretty girl, and the driver in his turn responded by further details, at which they roared and screamed with mirth, entirely oblivious of the fact that we were proceeding at about 40 m.p.h. on an appalling road. Two others were happily ensconced between the wings and the radiator, and when we stopped every twenty minutes or so one or the other leapt off and proceeded to pour gallons of water into the boiling radiator. Every now and then we would pass landmarks and places of interest, and the outrider would call the driver's attention; he immediately took both hands off the wheel and pointed them out to me. In the meanwhile the vehicle bounced, ricochetted into the ditch, and over anything that was in the way. We killed several ducks and hens, a goose, a goat, three dogs; bumped into a small bullock and sent it spinning; and drove right through a flock of small pigs that scattered screaming but miraculously unhurt to the nearest house. At one time we narrowly missed a small child, which was lucky, as we might have had to stop and pay for it. We progressed in this careless fashion, leaving a trail of corpses in our wake, quite unperturbed, as this was the regular procedure. The worst thing of all was the noise; there were two horns on the car, one on the driver's side, the old-fashioned bulb type, and one by my side of a strident klaxon variety, and for the whole 25 km. never once did they stop blowing them. I have seldom heard such a deafening row. When we finally came to a standstill I crawled down from my seat, my posterior aching from the bumps and jolts sustained by the ceaseless, rapid levitations and sudden descents on to the boards that had been my seat, my head rather tender in more than one place where it had met the roof on several occasions, my hands stiff from clinging on like grim death to the wind-screen to avoid being bumped out altogether, as there was no door, and my nose, ears, mouth, and throat full of a rich, brown dust. When I took off my dark glasses I had a surprised look like a loris, owing to the completely white skin around my eyes, the only part of my face that had been protected.

The bungalow in which we were to spend the night was the old Consulate rest-house, but it was many years since it had been inhabited permanently—in fact, the town now only boasted one European to the ten of a few years ago. It was very dark, very gloomy and very decrepit, built of teak on the inevitable high, wooden posts about 8 ft. from the ground, the top ends of which supported the roof, giving the whole a veranda-like appearance. It was quite dark when we arrived and the whole place looked incredibly gloomy, the only light a small lamp and intermittent flashes of lightning. We had just had a bath—a strange affair with only a round enamel basin, and large Ali Baba jars of water that ran through the floor-boards on to the ground beneath—when the only other occupant of the town turned up and invited us to dinner. After changing into a clean shirt, a pair of cotton Chinese trousers, and mosquito boots, we set off; I feeling particularly strange in my unorthodox garments, but unable to do anything about it, as my only frock was filthy after the train and bus journey. Our host had a most delightful bungalow on the

27

top of the old city wall. Ancient brick steps led up to it, and from the veranda of the second story one was surrounded by flowers, as it was on a level with the tops of the trees, all of which were covered with sweetly smelling blossoms. The moon shining down on them and the heavy scent hanging in the warm air made us feel almost intoxicated, especially when the strains of Chopin and Beethoven came floating up through the silent night. Our host possessed a piano, an unusual luxury in this material land—in fact, I never heard of another up-country—and many were the hours that he beguiled us. A gramophone is more or less inevitable in any house, but we seldom had the chance of hearing any instrument played firsthand, and never so beautifully.

The next morning we set off again by bus and drove for about an hour. On stopping, all the gear was transferred into three bullock carts, and we started off on my first march, with just the cook and a coolie, the one to carry water and the other to cook our lunch when we wanted it. I was thrilled to the core. The hills we were aiming for looked so near and so blue; the sun was hot, but there was a fresh breeze; and the immediate prospect was one I had been imagining and longing for for many years. The jungle! Just a few fields with a little scrub here and there was the immediate prospect—not particularly arduous. But I was soon to find my mistake. We came to a river after about half an hour and I wondered how we were to get across it, as there was no bridge. We had to wade! There was a certain amount of mud which I took great pains to avoid; this seemed to amuse my husband, and it was not many days afterwards that I found out why.

It got steadily hotter and hotter; there was no shade at all, and the sweat poured off me in rivers, my shirt and shorts sticking to me as if I'd been out in a rainstorm.

We were walking through *padi*-fields, a great flat plain, with each tiny field surrounded by mud banks, so we were perpetually jumping up or climbing down them, our feet heavily caked with mud, whilst I, unaccustomed to this kind of thing, had to get used to walking in heavy boots as well. I was also wearing shorts and the sun burned the backs of my knees until they were scarlet and very painful. My topee felt heavy to one unused to it, and the paper parasol I was carrying to try to divert the direct rays of the sun felt like lead. The temperature was over 110° in the shade, and must have been considerably more in the sun.

I got crosser and crosser. I had no idea where we were aiming for and I did not care. We had only eight miles to march but it seemed more like twenty, and I was glad to see the bungalow looming up through the trees at last. We arrived about 2.30 and the first thing we did was to order up innumerable buckets of water from a well near by, take off all our clothes and hang them in the sun to dry, while we threw the water over one another. It was glorious, but I'm sure most unwise. I was so tired that I lay on the only available couch—a very hard deal table—and slept for about four hours. By this time the gear had arrived and we were able to change and also to rest our weary bones in long, canvas chairs. During tea two ugly, elderly females crept up the steps and squatted, salaaming, in front of us. They both had enormous goitres, a very common complaint in the country. They had brought up some coconuts to sell, of which we bought six for 3d. The milk tasted filthy, but the cook made quite a good pudding for dinner out of the flesh. They also brought up a small boy aged about four or so, whom they offered to sell to us for about 1s., but of course it was impossible to take him with us on such a journey as ours. A little later six men came up to talk to my husband about work. They were very polite, bowing and saluting me as they passed, and dropping silently into a crouching position on the floor, where they remained for hours. At first this seemed rather strange, but I soon got used to them, as the same thing happened everywhere we went. By this time the air was thick with every kind of insect and flying beetle. They fell down my neck and got into my eyes and, worse still, into the soup. There was not time to lift a spoonful from plate to mouth without something flopping into it. We got so fed up that we improvised a trap for them, hanging a sheet in front of the lamp and putting a large bath of water on the other side. This rapidly became full of corpses and had to be emptied several times, but it served its purpose, as the swarms were considerably diminished.

Noel Wynyard, *Durian; A Siamese Interlude*, Oxford University Press, London, 1939, pp. 40–6.

6
A Missionary Arrives in Burma

HENRY PARK COCHRANE

One might expect a missionary to perceive his or her experience through the glass of faith. Certainly Henry Park Cochrane did so. Writing in 1904 of his experiences some fifteen years before, he expressed them in the language and sentiment appropriate to his calling: and no doubt he and his wife were filled with zeal to convey the Christian message. Nevertheless, their first experiences are strikingly similar to those of other arrivals as they come to terms with a strange country, its people and its ways. Cochrane acknowledges that British Indian bureaucracy may be 'trying to spirituality' and that the newcomer indeed may learn from the advice of the old hands he or she first scorns. In this passage he acknowledges the naïvity of the new arrival come to set the East to rights.

T HE *Chanda* was slowly making her way with the tide up the Rangoon River. Two young missionaries, myself and wife, were leaning on the rail, deeply interested in the scene before us. The rising sun, sending its rays over the land, seemed to us a pledge of the Master's presence in the work to which we had consecrated our lives. On every hand were strange sights and sounds, strange scenery, strange craft, strange people; everything far and near so unlike the old life that we had left behind. But it was something more than new sights and sounds that stirred in us the deep emotion expressed in moistened eye and trembling lip. Thoughts were going back to the time when we heard the call, 'Whom shall I send, and who will go for us?' And now that we were about to enter upon the realization of that to which we had so long looked forward, hearts too full for utterance, were stirred with gratitude and praise. But not long were we permitted to indulge in either retrospect or prospect. As the steamer drew near the dock all was turmoil and excitement,— officers shouting their orders; sailors dragging the great ropes into place; passengers getting their luggage ready for quick removal; friends on ship and shore eagerly seeking to recognize a familiar face; waving of handkerchiefs; sudden exclamations when an acquaitance or loved one was recognized.

At last the gangplank is in place, and on they come,— officials, coolies, business men, hotel-runners, representatives of many races, and conditions, energy for once superseding rank; missionaries well to the front to extend a welcome to the newcomers.

What a power there is in the hearty hand-shake and cordial greeting! To the newcomer, who has everything to learn and much to unlearn,—this warm reception by the veterans is a link to reconnect him with the world from which he seemed to have been separated during the long voyage; a bridge to span the gulf of his own inexperience; a magic-rite of adoption into the great missionary family; a pledge of fellowship and cooperation for all the years to come.

It was Sunday morning,—though few in that motley crowd either knew or cared. Mohammedan, Hindu, Parsee, Buddhist, and 'Christian' jostled one another, each intent on his own affairs, and all combining to make this the farthest possible extreme from a 'day of holy rest.' Little wonder that this first Oriental Sunday was a distinct shock to the new missionaries. They had yet to learn that on many such Sundays they would long for the 'Sabbath and Sanctuary-privileges' of the home-land. But soon it became evident that the missionaries at least, were about the 'Father's business,' each hurrying away to be in time for the morning service in his own department of mission-work among many races. To the eye of one who has just landed in Rangoon each individual in the throng of natives on the street seems to have arrayed himself as fantastically as possible, or to have gone to the other extreme and failed to array himself at all. But at these Christian services one sees the natives classified according to race, and learns to distinguish certain racial characteristics,—of feature, costume, and custom. A congregation of Burmese is a beautiful sight, their showy skirts, turbans, and scarfs presenting the appearance of a flower garden in full bloom, but especially beautiful as a company of precious souls turned from their idols to the 'True and living God.'

Among our first experiences was a warm appreciation of the kind attempts on the part of the missionaries to initiate us, by means of good advice, into life in the tropics. 'Now *do* be careful about exposing yourself to this tropical sun. Remember, you are not in America now.'

'That solar tope of yours is not thick enough for one who is not used to this climate.' 'Flannel next to the skin is absolutely necessary, as a safeguard against malaria, dysentery, and other complaints so common here.' 'Now dear brother and sister, you must look out and not let your zeal run away with your judgment. Yankee hustle won't do in Burma.'

Dear souls, we thought, you mean well, but we are not subject to these troubles of which you speak. Their warnings sink about as deep as the remark of one of our party who ran down the gangplank just ahead of us: 'When you have been in the country as long as I have, etc.,'—an old expression, now under the ban. A few months later we began to take their advice. Experiences leading to such action will be described further on. Two days afterwards we reached our mission station, just as the sun was going down. While picking out our 'luggage' (it was baggage when it left America) we received our first impressions as to the British Indian system of checking, or 'booking,' as it is called.

A luggage receipt given at the starting point, called for so many pieces. Then we found that to each article was glued a patch of paper on which its destination was marked, and also a number corresponding to the number on the receipt. All well so far. The luggage clerk seemed neither to know nor care, but left each passenger to claim his own.

We noticed too that everything imaginable was allowed to be booked, a certain number of *viss* in weight being allowed free on each ticket.

To our observing eyes, each passenger's luggage indicated about how long he had been in the country, or how much he had travelled.

Some evil spirit seems to possess the luggage clerk's assistant to glue the label in a new place each time, cancelling other bookings by tearing off loose corners of old labels. This custom is specially trying to spirituality when applied to bicycles, the railroad glue having such affinity for enamel that they stay or come off together. Another thing that impressed us was the suddenness with which the darkness of night came on, as if 'darkness rather than light' reigned over this heathen land, and could hardly wait for the usurping sun to disappear behind the horizon. First impressions of our new home we gained late that night, by the dim light of a lantern. Home, did I say? As we peered through the shadows it did not strike us as being a place that could ever, by any stretch of imagination, seem like home. Bare, unpainted walls dingy with age; huge round posts, some of them running up through the rooms; no furniture except a teak bedstead, and a large round table so rickety that it actually bowed to us when we stepped into the room; lizards crawling on walls and ceiling,—interesting and harmless things, as we afterwards found, but not specially attractive to a newcomer. Oh, no,—it was not homesickness, only just lack of power to appreciate a good thing after the weary experiences of our long journey. In the night I was roused from sleep by hearing some one calling. Half awake, I was getting out from under the mosquito net, when my wife remarked, 'Better get back into bed. It is only that *taukteh*, that Mrs.—told us about.' The taukteh is the 'crowing,' or 'trout-spotted lizard.' The English call it the tuctoo, from the sound it makes. The Burmans call it tauk-teh, for the same reason. Some declare that it says 'doctor, doctor,' as plain as day. Alarming stories are told of this terrible creature; how it loses its hold on the ceiling to alight in a lady's hair, and that nothing short of removing scalp and all will dislodge it. The worst thing we have known it to do was to wake the baby in the dead of the night, when we had got fairly settled to sleep after hours of sweltering. I have shot several for this unpardonable offense. The taukteh's sudden call in the night causes some children to suffer much from fright, though no harm is intended.

Our house was situated on a narrow strip of land with streets on three sides, and school dormitory in the rear. Just across one street was a native Police Guard, but we did not know what it was until next morning. We had come into our possessions after dark, so knew nothing of our environment. These were dacoit times. Disturbances were frequent. Of course our ears had been filled with exciting stories of dacoit atrocities. The incessant and unintelligible jabbering of the Paunjabby policemen, sometimes sounding as though they were on the verge of a fight, and the sharp call of the sentry as he challenged passers-by were anything but conducive to sleep through that first night in our mission bungalow.

Henry Park Cochrane, *Among the Burmans: A Record of Fifteen Years of Work and Its Fruitage*, Fleming H. Revell Company, New York, 1904, pp. 9–14.

7
A Bride-to-Be in Batavia

ANNA FORBES

Anna Forbes arrived in Batavia as Anna Keith at the end of March 1882 to marry Henry Ogg Forbes, a naturalist to whom she had become engaged some four years before, prior to his departure for South-East Asia. Their courtship had been maintained by letter and they were married on 5 April, a week after her arrival. Surprisingly, Anna makes no reference to the marriage in this account although the letter from which it is taken was written on 8 April 1882 from

Buitenzorg (Bogor) while, presumably, on her honeymoon. No doubt there was self-censoring for publication and perhaps her voyaging alone as a young unmarried lady was regarded as indiscreet. Anna travelled widely with her husband through the archipelago and nearly died from fever in Timor before the couple departed for Europe in July 1883. Like all new arrivals, Anna was surprised by much of what she saw. In this account of her first days in Batavia she recognizes that her initial embarrassment on first exposure to the more relaxed manners and dress of colonial Dutch society was prudishness and that the Dutch adoption of elements of native costume had much to recommend it.

AFTER another fortnight at sea, it was pleasant again to look on land; and all that last day of the voyage we never wearied of standing, glass in hand, watching on the right the amphitheatre-like slopes of the Java coast, laid out in coffee-gardens and rice-terraces, and on the left the more distant, deeply indented coast of Sumatra. The lovely islets which stud the ocean recalled at once Max Havelaar's exquisite simile, where he speaks of 'Holland's magnificent empire of Insulinde, which winds about the equator like a garland of emeralds.' These islets we passed now so close as to see distinctly the forms of tropical vegetation, the huts, and even the dusky inhabitants; again at such a distance that we could only contrast the rich hues of their verdure with the deep blue of the sea. The coast of Java, nearer Batavia, presents a singular appearance: for miles into the interior it seems elevated above the sea-level scarcely more than the height of the trees that cover it, and nothing can be seen save the sea-fringe of vegetation in front of a green plain, behind which rise the hills of Bantam and the Blue Mountains, as the old mariners call the peaks of Buitenzorg.

It was already dark when we moored in the roads of Batavia, one of the greatest centres of commerce in all these seas, where rides a fleet flying the flags of all nations. H., who had returned to Batavia from a prolonged tour in Sumatra to meet me, now joined me, and took at once all responsibility.

Transferred into a steam-tender, we approached the mouth of the long canal by which the town of Batavia is reached; and having passed on shore at the Custom House, where we had moored, we entered a carriage drawn by two fleet ponies of the famous Sumbawa breed. We sped on for some miles through what seemed an endless row of Chinese shops and dwellings, before which the occupants, visible in the lamp-light as we flashed past, sat smoking at their ease. Thence we emerged into a more genial atmosphere, where trees margined the street, and brilliantly lighted residences and hotels with pillared marble fronts gleamed through the delicate curtains of foliage which intervened between them and the roadway.

Apartments were ready for me in the Hotel der Nederlanden, and there I remained some days; but as I found the heat very oppressive, we have come here to Buitenzorg, some thirty miles inland, and considerably above the sea-level, where the climate is much pleasanter.

But I must try to give you some idea of my first impressions of life in the East,—how different from Western life and ways you must come here fully to learn.

About 5.30 of the morning after my arrival, I was awakened by the rattle of cups in my verandah. Coffee was already there, but, except to notice that it was neatly served, I did not heed that refreshment, for curiosity and wonder at the scene before me. Hotels here are all rather similar in plan. Imagine a quadrangle, the front of which is isolated from the three other sides of the square by the carriage-ways which lead into the centre. In this front block is the reception-hall, fronted by a verandah. The verandah is paved with marble, and disposed in it are numerous small tables, chairs, and lounges. Towards evening it is brilliantly lighted, and is the resort of the occupants of the hotel before and after dinner. Passing from the verandah through the reception-hall, you find the dining room extending back into the square. It is simply roofed, and flowers in pots and pendent creepers fill the open sides. A few bedrooms have place in this front block: they are perhaps cooler, and are generally occupied by bachelor gentlemen who permanently reside in the house. For my part, I prefer one of those out in the courtyard formed by the remaining three sides of the square, for these have each a verandah, furnished with a table and a lounging-chair, making as it were a parlour for the occupant of the bedroom behind. I could best picture these rooms by comparing them to a row of cottages; but instead of a porch to each, imagine a continuous verandah the length of the row. They are of one storey; the floors are of flags, for coolness, with mats thrown here and there, and very simple furniture. The beds, however, are the largest I have ever seen, and are curtained top and sides with mosquito-screens: they are not furnished with any upper sheet or covering.

My room was quite at the end of the row, and had a verandah at the end, as well as in front, with blinds drawing to the ground, which screened me from the gaze of passers-by, but through which I could easily see them. When I looked out that first morning, the occupants of the various 'cottages' were just emerging, and, seating themselves in their sleeping attire; sipped their morning coffee. I had been told that the bath-house was at the farther end of the square, and, summoning all my courage, I set off, armed with towel and sponge, to find it. Far down, I espied a lady companion of the voyage, who had been in Batavia before, and was therefore not so bewildered as I. She explained to me the Eastern mode of bathing, by having pails of water poured over the head, otherwise I should have been puzzled on entering the bath-room to know whether I was expected to climb into the large vat which stood there. The bath-rooms are arranged so as to be unspoilable from splashing: a wooden net-work, on which one stands, covers a floor of flags, and the water flows quickly out by a wide drain. The manner of bathing is exceedingly refreshing, and is less fatiguing than a plunge-bath. As I returned to my room, at every 'cottage' door sat the occupants, the gentlemen lying back in their chairs, with their bare feet extended over the long ledges which are there for the purpose. Ladies sat by them, and *baboos* and 'boys' (male servants, waiters and valets, men of all ages, are 'boys' here) hurried hither and thither; the bustle of day had already commenced. Did you ever have a nightmare, the misery of which was that you imagined you were walking out in your night-dress? That was exactly my feeling; and the fact that I wore a dressing-grown made me an object of greater curiosity and regard, so that it was with the utmost thankfulness that I gained the shelter of my own room.

All this publicity of private life is the effect of climatic influence. The easy attitudes and *negligé* costumes I describe appear fitted for a high-walled garden, or a country retreat, not for a public hotel; but gradually one comes to feel that these habits are natural in the climate....

The *sarong* and *kabia* form the native dress, adopted by European ladies for comfort and convenience in the climate, and worn by them as sleeping attire, as also during the day in a richer form, in which the skirt is of costly stuff, and the jacket of fine lawn muslin or linen, daintily trimmed with lace or embroidery. It is not worn when receiving formal visitors, and young unmarried ladies are not expected to be seen in it beyond their private apartments; but, with an apology for the liberty, it is worn almost constantly, except in the evening, when every one wears European costume for a few hours. In this country part, I see some ladies take the morning stroll in *sarong* and *kabia*, and I must confess I envy them, they look so lightly clothed and comfortable; and when the eye is accustomed to the costume, it is really becoming. I am actually, despite the amazement I experienced on first seeing it, now inclined to say it is pretty.... And how cleanly is the *kabia*. A lady puts on a fresh one twice or thrice a-day,—a frequency with which one could scarcely put a dress aside as soiled; and the wearer always looks cool and at ease.

Gentlemen wear a very loose and untrimmed form of the *kabia*, and wide, gay-patterned *pyjamas* as sleeping-dress, which they do not put off until it is time to dress for the day. They walk about the courtyard and even beyond for a short stroll, with the addition only of a short tweed shooting-jacket, and are very ludicrous figures as the wind blows out the loose garments like sails in a breeze. This dress does *not* become them!

Between 7 and 9 breakfast is laid out in the dining-room, and when it suits you, you enter: one of the many waiters brings coffee and eggs, and draws within reach a few of the numerous plates of sliced cold meat and sausage which are spread over the table. To one accustomed to an English breakfast, that offered here is very unappetising, but it is simply a go-between, and a good appetite awaits breakfast or tiffin at 12 or 12.30, when no one could complain of want of substantials or variety. It is called by the Dutch the 'rice table.' On a large soup-plate you help yourself to rice offered on an immense platter, and over this you put a few spoonfuls of Malay curry, which has the appearance of a pale yellow soup. Then in close succession are offered fish, cooked in various ways, fried, stewed, curried; fowl, likewise in different forms; stewed beef, rissoles of pork, mince patties, fritters of maize, omelette, fried eggs, various vegetables, with many Eastern delicacies and piquant side-dishes. To these, a small portion of each having been taken, are added various condiments—pickles, sliced cucumber, chili, chutnee—which are offered prettily arranged on a large china tray. Then the whole is mixed with spoon and fork, the mixture having, I am told, a delicious flavour not otherwise obtainable. I have not yet tried it. I form a wall of rice between the fish and the fowl, and allow most of the dishes to pass. H. says I shall learn, however, to enjoy the rice table soon.

Beefsteaks with fried potatoes follow this course, fritters of pine-apple and other sweets succeed, and the meal ends with coffee and fruits. How very rapidly it is got through! ...

After this mid-day meal, all who are not forced by business engagements to return to town retire to rest, and silence like night falls on the house. No one is seen stirring: even the servants fall asleep in corners until about 4 o'clock. Then tea is brought, and along the 'cottage' row the scene of early morning is repeated. One after another appears with towel on arm proceeding to the bath-houses, and about half-past 5 all are ready in European toilet for an evening stroll or drive, previous to dinner at 7.30. It seems that the fashioin so long prevalent of ladies going out at this hour in demi-toilet is passing away, bonnets and close dresses being now in vogue; but many still hold to the old fashion, and the effect is rather pretty as they promenade under the great avenues or flash past in carriages in the gathering dusk. Gentlemen, however, still go with uncovered heads.

* * *

Not far from the Hotel der Nederlanden is the Harmonie, a fine club-house, the grounds of which presented a charming scene when I first entered. Brilliant moonshine made fairyland of the rich foliage, sweet heavy scents of tropical plants pervaded the air, a band discoursed faultless music, and hundreds of gaily dressed people moved to and fro between the lamp-glare and the dimmer moonlight, or sat playing or talking at small tables in Continental fashion.

Every morning we drove to the hospital, a large and splen-didly conducted institution in a beautiful situation, to see an English friend of H.'s, who was lying there. Coming back we generally met the children going to school,—little bands of them, with faces about as white as their garments. Girls wear simply a pinafore, or chemise if you will, of white starched muslin, over rather long drawers, white stockings, and long black boots. The effect is rather odd, and my impression on first seeing them was that a number were setting off to bathe still half-dressed.

Anna Forbes, *Insulinde*, William Blackwood & Sons, Edinburgh, 1887; reprinted as *Unbeaten Tracks in Islands of the Far East: Experiences of a Naturalist's Wife in the 1880s*, Oxford University Press, Singapore, 1987, pp. 2–15.

Settling In

SETTLING in was an extension of arriving. Newcomers were still arriving mentally and spiritually even as they physically unpacked their belongings, furnished a house, engaged servants, made their first excursions into the market, learned the routine of their job, the pattern of their working day, the pecking order in society, the customs, quirks, and mannerisms of colonial society. At some point, later rather than sooner for some, the transition was made from novice to old hand. As we have seen, the process began for Székely when he was reprimanded for attempting to carry his own luggage (Passage 2). But people had not only physical luggage: all arrivals carried the mental and spiritual baggage of Europe, ideas and beliefs often in contradiction to those they encountered in Asia. In particular they had, for the most part, come from a Europe in which democratic notions of equality were increasingly accepted to find that in Asia they were members of a master race. To some, European superiority in terms of technology, economic development, material progress, and military power was only too obviously evidence of superior moral and intellectual qualities. On the other hand, some were attracted to qualities of spirituality, simplicity, dignity, courtesy, patience, and endurance which they either discovered in, or attributed to, Asians.

One part of settling in was establishing a pattern of relationships with Asians. For most Europeans this meant establishing a working relationship with subordinates—employees or servants. Social contact with Asians was slight. There is much racial comment in the extracts which follow in this and other sections, much of it patronising or distasteful, much of it based on ignorance. There is also evidence of liking, respect, mutual acceptance, and enjoyment of the other's company; and evidence also of affection. A note of warning: in reading these passages one must remember that until well into this century, middle-class households in Britain and Europe had servants and that class lines were still clearly drawn. What may appear to the modern reader to reflect racism may be as much an expression of class prejudice and reflect class distinctions. One can find plenty of contemporary reference to the 'lower orders' of society and the need to maintain a social distance from them (see, for example, Harriette McDougall's comment in Passage 33).

That aside, new arrivals had to learn how to live within a European community which was a ruling minority greatly outnumbered by the Asian population, whose language was unknown and had to be learned before effective communication was possible. Officials usually acquired a local language. Wives in remote areas and earlier times did so more usually than those who arrived in the twentieth century, when more Europeans were resident and more Asians knew the language of the colonial power. For most Europeans, however, the European community was where they felt at home and where they relaxed. Settling in, therefore, was basically a matter of of settling into an overseas European community and finding one's place within it.

8

A Ranee Acknowledged

MARGARET BROOKE

Although the wife of the Rajah, Margaret Brooke was not spared a sojourn in temporary accomodation, she and her husband staying with the Resident, the Rajah's senior officer, until the Astana, the Rajah's residence, was ready to receive them. Like all newcomers, she had to assert her place in the pecking order. Mrs Crookshank, the Resident's wife, had been 'First Lady' before Rajah Charles married, and was understandably put out by the arrival of a younger woman as the Rajah's wife. As noted in Passage 3, the European ladies of Sarawak were also shocked by Margaret's attraction to the Malays and by her ready assumption of the Malay title of Ranee. In this reading, Margaret Brooke settles into the Astana and her title is confirmed in a somewhat unorthodox but effective way. One point should be noted: she refers to English society as being composed of a small number of people. In this she is referring to 'society' as representing a particular social class. There were other Europeans in Kuching, but they were servants, skilled artisans, lay missionaries, employees of the Borneo Company or of the Government in capacities other than administration. They did not rank as 'society'.

WHEN our furniture had arrived from England and had been arranged in the Astana we concluded our stay at the Residency, and after taking leave of Mr. and Mrs. Crookshank took up our abode at the Palace. I was naturally glad to feel that at last we were settled in our own home. And a very lovely home I thought it. The Astana was built on a low green hill that overlooked the river and formed a promontory between two streamlets that emptied themselves into the main channel. It was built in the form of three bungalows, supported by square brick pillars some twenty feet above the ground. The low-spreading roof gave

43

Margaret Brooke's residence—the Astana, Kuching. (Tourist Development Corporation)

shade to the interior. The largest bungalow stood in the centre and contained the reception-rooms and dining- and drawing-rooms, which were large, lofty and cool. The smaller bungalows each contained two large bedrooms with bath-rooms attached. We occupied the western bungalow, the eastern one being reserved for the use of visitors. A large verandah was one of the pleasantest features of this delightful abode, and on it were passed some of the happiest hours I spent in Sarawak.

A beautiful garden led down to the landing-stage amid green lawns and grassy walks, bordered and shaded by bam-boos and betel-nut palms under which grew great clumps of red and white lilies. Exotic flowers bloomed everywhere, gardenias, tuberoses, cape jessamine, filling the air with their perfume, and at the side and back of the Astana many tree-bordered paths led to the mysterious depths of luxuriant for-est which stretched for miles around.

I found our bathrooms the most original and surprising apartments. A short flight of wooden steps led down to them from the bedrooms. They were very dark, having no windows, but being lit only by rays of light through narrow chinks close to the ceiling. The floors were tiled and had little runways to carry off the water. This was all very well, but where were the *baths*? There were none, at least not the baths to which Europeans are accustomed. Sarawak was (and is) decidedly primitive in its methods of bathing. A large stone tank, or cis-tern, is to be found in the corner of these vault-like rooms. This is kept filled with water by the Chinese, who carry it up from the river. Above the tank hangs a basket made of Nipa palm leaves, and this is the procedure. You stand on a stone slab, dip the basket into the cistern and, having filled it, dash the water over yourself, soaping yourself at intervals. Quite strenuous but very refreshing, I found, after I had become expert at wielding the waterbasket or dipper. I used to resort to these baths as a restorative many times a day, much as Englishwomen at home resort to their never-failing cup of tea.

The Malays are a people who are always popping in and out of water, bathing five or six times daily in the rivers, and teaching their children to swim almost as soon as they are old enough to walk.

* * *

The English society in Kuching that year (June 1870) was composed of Bishop and Mrs. Chambers, the Resident and his wife—Mr. and Mrs. Crookshank—Mr. and Mrs. Helms (Mr. Helms besides being Agent to the Borneo Company Limited also acted as British Consul at Sarawak). The unmarried men were Mr. Oliver St. John, Treasurer, Major Rodway, who commanded the small contingent of Native troops in Kuching, and two or three young men who occupied less important posts on the Rajah's staff. The population of the small capital then numbered about 30,000, including Malays, Hindus, Chinese, etc.

The name by which I was to be known gave the English ladies at Sarawak no small concern. For my part, it gave me little thought. I was the Rajah's wife, therefore it was quite clear to me that I was the Ranee (such a pretty-sounding name, I thought!). His people were my people, and indeed I loved them from the first. That was all that mattered to me. As for my husband, he was immersed in governmental affairs and had little time to spare for the bickerings of ladies to whom he hated to have to lay down the law, disliking intensely any behaviour that savoured of pomposity or self-aggrandisement. Was I not his wife, part of himself, belonging entirely to him? That was enough, surely—anything else could wait!

At last one day, quite suddenly, my title was bestowed on me, and by a very humble bestower—a medicine bottle! A short time after our arrival at the Astana, a slight ailment necessitated the attendance of Dr. Houghton, who promised to send me a tonic that evening. The package containing the medicine bottle fell into my husband's hands. The label bore the name 'Mrs. Brooke' in the doctor's own handwriting. The Rajah glared at the poor little bottle and wrathfully sent for Dr. Houghton. The time had come, he thought, to settle this matter once and for all and let his wishes be broadcast throughout his country. On the arrival of the doctor my husband pointed sternly to the label and said, 'You must be singularly bereft of your senses if you think my wife can be addressed otherwise than as the *Ranee*. Take the thing away and address it properly.' Without my having partaken of one dose, the bottle was speedily removed, the doctor returning later to present it to me with many apologies and its amended label. One must find one's way to lands far removed from Europe to discover a medicine bottle invested with all the dignity of a Lord Chamberlain. Henceforth I became 'The Ranee' to all the English residents, while the darling Malays went one better and insisted on calling me 'Rajah Ranee.'

However, the sayings and doings of the English society did not interfere with my healthy appetite or cause me sleepless nights. I grew to understand and agree with the Rajah's wish that I should not become too intimate with the English ladies at Kuching. 'Let them say what they like,' he said, 'and don't talk too much,' and, following his advice, we all got on very well.

Margaret Brooke, *Good Morning and Good Night*, Constable, London, 1934, pp. 47–51.

9
Missionary Trials

HENRY PARK COCHRANE

For Henry Cochrane, settling in meant reconciling his Christian principles and missionary zeal to the realities of life in a tropical climate, to the missionary's position as a 'poor white' in colonial society even while a member of the 'master race' in Burmese eyes, and to the impossibility of conveying the message he burned to deliver when he had no knowledge of the Burmese language. Reluctantly, he came to realize that he had to adapt.

T HE new missionary has many trying experiences while becoming accustomed to the changed conditions of life in the tropics. Judging from our own experience and observation, covering many years, it seems utterly impossible for the returned missionary to transmit to the new missionary, while yet in the home-land, anything like true conceptions of the life upon which he is about to enter, and how to prepare for it. Either the new missionary has theories of his own which he fondly imagines never have been tried, or he considers himself so unlike other mortals that rules of living, developed by long experience, do not apply to one of his own peculiar physical make-up. But whatever his attitude of mind towards the new life and work, the fact remains that he has dropped down in the midst of conditions so unlike anything in his past experience that he must learn to adapt himself to life as he finds it. The first place to apply his gift of adaptation is in the household. First experiences with native servants are decidedly interesting, to say the least. Our cook 'Naraswamy,' 'Sammy' for short,—came to us highly recommended, and neatly clothed. We had not yet learned that the poorer the cook, the better his recommendations (often borrowed from some other cook), and the neater his clothing,— also borrowed for the purpose of securing a place, but never seen after the first day or two.

One day when 'Missis' was giving directions about the dinner she called Sammy and said, 'Sammy, how many eggs have you?' 'Two egg, missis.' 'Very well, you make a pudding the best you can, with the two eggs.' At dinner no pudding appeared. 'Sammy, where is the pudding?' Putting on a sorrowful look Sammy replied, 'I done break egg' (spreading out his hands to indicate the two eggs), 'one got child, one got child.' When Sammy felt fairly sure of keeping his place, his two little boys began to spend much of their time in and around the cook house. One of our first rules was that no child should be allowed to go naked on the mission compound. These two dusky youngsters had not a thread of clothing. Sammy was called up and instructed that if his children were coming to the mission premises, they must be properly clothed, at the same time presenting him with a suit for one child. The next day they came again, with smiles of satisfaction, one wearing the trousers, the other the jacket. Many of these Madrassi cooks are professing Christians, merely to secure a place in a missionary family. A small minority are Christians in fact. But whether a heathen cook sneaks off with a stuffed turban, or a professed Christian appropriates our food quietly humming 'I love to steal,—' the resulting loss to commissariat and spirituality is the same....

The dhoby (washerman) is always a source of much distraction. He takes away the soiled linen on Monday, *promising* to bring it back on Saturday; carries it to the riverside, stands in the water facing the shore, pounds it out on a flat stone with swinging blows, and,—brings back what is left. Garments worn perhaps but once, are found on spreading out, to be spoiled by long rents or mildew. Socks that have been filled with sand in order to strike a harder blow, still retain enough sand to cause much discomfort. One or two pieces are missing altogether. He promises to bring them the next time. In the meantime he has probably hired them out to some person of mixed blood and principles, or native aping European habits. The sweeper, waterman, and other native helpers slight their work, or perchance, with the poorest excuse, and that not made known until afterwards,—absent themselves altogether. 'But why'—some will ask 'is it necessary to employ these native cooks, washermen, etc.?

'Many of these women who go to the foreign field as missionaries' wives were accustomed to do much of their own work here at home,—why not do the same over there, and so avoid the expense,—as many of us who support them have to do?' In the first place, many of the missionaries have only one servant who is paid for full time, that is the cook. All others do a little work night and morning, their wages being made up by serving several different families. Again, it would be a physical impossibility for the missionary's wife to do the cooking and washing, adding the heat and smoke of an open fire to the tropical heat of the atmosphere. Some have tried it; only to give it up as utterly impracticable. Others have persisted in it, only to be laid away in a cemetery in a foreign land, or to return hopelessly broken in health, to the home-land.

It cannot be done. Moreover, it would be the height of folly for the wife to spend her time and strength over cooking utensils, dishpans and wash-tubs. The wife, as truly as the husband, has consecrated her life to the Master's service. There is work for her to do, among the women and children, that he cannot touch. The missionary's wife whether touring with him among jungle-villages; visiting from house to house in the town; working in the school; making her influence felt in the church; or even when prevented by family cares or failing health—from engaging in active service,—she furnishes the object lesson of a well-ordered Christian home, her life is of just as much worth to the cause of Christ as is that of the missionary whose helpmate she is.

We had not long been in our new home before Burmans,

Teachers and students of a mission school, *c.*1900. Mission schools such as this were set up throughout the region.

both Christian and heathen, began to call to see the new teachers. They evidently wanted to welcome us as their missionaries; and we, in turn, wanted them to know that love for them, for whom Christ died, had brought us among them. But how helpless we felt! An exchange of smiles, a handshake, a few words that neither party could understand,— that was all....

We found ourselves utterly powerless to communicate to them one word of all that was burning,—had been burning for years, in our hearts. Then it was that the fact fully dawned upon us that before we could hope to do effectively the work to which we had consecrated our lives, a difficult foreign language must be mastered....

By this time the newcomer has seen enough of the climate, and of the side of society in which he will move, to convince him that his Prince Albert coat, in which he has been accustomed to array himself 'every day in the week, and twice on Sunday' must be folded away in his trunk until such a time as he takes a furlough in the home-land. A fellow-missionary consoles him with the remark that he once wore back to America the same coat that he wore to Burma eight years before. Missionaries usually arrive in November, the beginning of the 'cold season.' After that comes the 'hot season,'—but it is difficult to tell just where the one leaves off and the other begins.

In any event, the newcomer soon 'warms to his work.' First the waistcoat is discarded, then the long thick coat gives place to a short thin one. For underwear, gauze flannel and singlets are in demand. Starched shirts and linen collars are reserved for special occasions. High-top shoes are relegated to the corner-closet. Even his watch hangs as an uncomfortable weight in his light clothing. In the old life he hardly perspired once in the year. Now there is hardly once in the year when he is not perspiring. The drinking-water is so warm that it seems to have lost much of its wetness. What would he not give to feel cool again. But he has not long to wait for his wish to be more than realized. Some night, after fanning himself into a restless sleep, he will wake up in a chill,

51

to find himself in the throes of the Burma fever, to which he was 'not subject.' Then he will recall the lightly-regarded advice, repeatedly violated in every particular, and now—. As this is the first attack he will get his wife to treat him the first day with the homeopathic remedies in his morocco medicine case,—his last misguided purchase before sailing.

There is nothing better to perpetuate a fever. On the second day, having recalled some more advice, his head will be buzzing with quinine, the only thing that will really help him,—as every man in the tropics knows.

Henry Park Cochrane, *Among the Burmans: A Record of Fifteen Years of Work and Its Fruitage*, Fleming H. Revell Company, New York, 1904, pp. 14–26.

10
'Hari Besar' in East Sumatra

LADISLAO SZÉKELY

Ladislao Székely could not settle in until he was employed. He had arrived hoping to find employment on a rubber plantation in East Sumatra, but had no contacts. As this extract begins, he is sitting alone in the hotel as the planters arrive for their 'Hari Besar', literally 'big day', when they are free and on the town. By the end, he is one of them. Incidentally, this and the extract from Madelon Lulofs which follows, are celebrated descriptions of European planter society at its least attractive.

THE guests were assembling on the large hotel terrace with its laid tables. With a sharp turn, a tiny carriage with gigantic wheels came rolling up. On its single seat, in a white suit, sat a man of huge stature, red-brown complexion and a grim moustache; behind him on the step stood a white-clad coachman. The copper studs glittered on the head-harness of the fiery little steed, and at every step of his swift, slender feet sparks flew from his shoes. With a jerk the animal stopped at the entrance; like lightning the coachman jumped from the step, stood at the horse's head and grasped the bridle. With slow and ponderous steps the tuan walked up to the terrace.

'Boy, beer!' rang through the hotel.

Presently came others. One buggy after another drove up, with each steed more frisky than the last. The tuans from the plantations looked radiant in their crackling, dazzling-white suits; all their faces were dark red, and all had shaggy moustaches and close-cropped heads.

The hotel boomed. Acquaintances greeted one another with loud cries, there were shouts for the boy, for drinks; Dutch, German, English and Malay words mingled in a chaotic buzz; glasses clinked, corks popped; somewhere a gramophone was howling: 'Dolly, you're the apple of my eye...' and powerful men's voices tried to make themselves heard above the hoarse instrument. The whole room quivered and buzzed, boys flitted about with alarming quantities of drinks, and the manager agitatedly threaded his way from one table to another.

Solitary, I sat at my table, gathering impressions.

There was nothing but men, not a single woman could be seen in the whole room. They were all between twenty and forty. Only now and again did one see an older man. This was the land of the young, the land of the healthy, of those who could work hard. You did not come here to grow old, but to get rich quickly and, after working for fifteen to twenty years, to go back to Europe and live well there. Women, planters' wives, were still rather rare at that time, and those there were, avoided the neighbourhood of the hotel on Hari Besar day. The planters are coarse people, their mirth and their jokes were not intended for women's ears. The townspeople, too—the officials and merchants—preferred to stay at home on such days. Hari Besar was the planters' day. After two weeks of hard work and a solitary life, these rich men enjoyed their day of freedom and tried not to think of tomorrow when the drudgery would begin all over again, exactly to the minute, from break of day to evening dusk, the continuous struggle with hundreds of coolies, the dangers that constantly threatened one's life. But today was Hari Besar, the holiday, today there was no boss, no duty. Today they could drink and enjoy themselves.

I sat at my table and grew sad. How was I to tackle this business? I had no friend here, not even an acquaintance.

All at once a red-haired fellow, as tall as a lamp-post, stopped at my table and made a long speech to me in an unknown language. He gesticulated violently as he spoke, and at intervals he laughed aloud. I sat there looking at him. When he had finished his speech, I told him in my broken German that I had not understood a word of it.

'Doesn't matter,' he then said in German, 'I was merely asking what you were doing here sitting all alone and moping. After all, this is Hari Besar, and it doesn't seem right for anyone to be sitting all alone and drawing such a long face.' He sat down, stretched his long legs, and shouted so that the glasses on the table began to clatter: 'Boy! Beer!'

'I have to sit alone,' I answered, 'because I don't know a soul. And I've certainly every reason to mope. For I've been here a week already and haven't any work,' I confessed, reddening.

'But why not?' he asked with surprise.

'I don't know. Where should I get work?'

'Where? Well, there,' and he pointed with a broad move-ment of his hand to the crowded house. 'All these here are planters, some of them, even big bugs, who all need hands. To whom have you introduced yourself?'

'To no one,' I confessed in a low voice, 'I didn't dare. Or I felt awkward about it.'

'Oh well, of course, you can't get work that way if you don't dare to open your mouth. Where do you come from anyway? From what country?'

'I am a Hungarian.'

'Oh, a Count. Doesn't matter, I'll look after you. Boy!'

The boy swept through the room as if shot from a gun. 'Chit! *Kaju tulis!*'

Immediately the boy handed him book and pencil. He took them and flung them in front of me.

54

'Write!' he said curtly.

'What shall I write?' I asked with surprise.

'What I dictate,' he answered and began: '"Dear Sir, I should like to speak with you at once, please be so kind as to come to the billiard room for a moment." Now, sign your name.'

I signed my name, he took the book from my hand, tore out the chit, gave it to the boy who was standing waiting, said something to him in Malay, and the boy hurried off.

'Where is he going with that?' I enquired, unable to over-come my astonishment.

'To the big fat man over there. That's Willem Bonk, a big man here. Director-General. I, too, am with his company. They're always needing people. Their concern is good. Dutch and English capital. A decent concern that pays well.'

'And you would send such a smeary, pencilled bit of paper to a director?' I asked and looked at the man, opening my eyes wide; and I tried to imagine what the Director-General of the Hungarian Cotton Factory Company Inc. would say to such an application for a job.

'Here we don't make as much fuss as over there in Europe. He can read the chit. Look, the boy is just giving it to him.'

At the other end of the terrace, in a large party, I saw a corpulent, sun-burned man with a bald head and a large moustache. He read the slip, asked the boy something, and the latter tossed his head in my direction. The fat man looked at me, nodded toward the billiard room, and got up.

'Now you go, too,' said my table companion, 'talk simply and calmly with him.... And don't get alarmed if he shouts. That's a habit with him. He has a terrible tongue, but a heart of gold....'

When I reached the billiard room, the corpulent man was already there.

'Well, what d'you want?' he hissed at me.

'I'd like a job on the plantation,' I started timidly.

'Precisely at this moment? You can't come back some other time?'

'Please excuse me if I am disturbing you ... if I had known

that you would take it amiss ...' I stuttered and was in the act
of leaving again.

'Now, wait a moment. Now we're here, we might as well
discuss the matter. How old are you?'

'Twenty.'

'How long have you been here?'

'A week.'

He surveyed me from head to toe for some minutes.

'All right,' he said presently, 'this is the sixteenth. Report
on the plantation on the twentieth at the head office. Two
hundred guilders a month, free lodging, a servant, free doctor
and drugs, well, and the usual ... Boy! Chit, kaju tulis!'

The boy came running up, handed him pad and pencil,
and the old fellow scribbled something on the slip.

'A month's salary in advance. There you are,' and he
pressed the chit into my hand.

I looked at the slip of paper.

'Where can I cash that?' I asked in surprise.

'Wherever you like. Anywhere. What have I to do with
that ... ?' said the old fellow, somewhat piqued. 'Report on
the twentieth on the plantation. Good-bye.' And already
he was off, walking out with large, ponderous, somewhat
reeling steps.

I stood with the chit in my hand, staring after the old man.
Then I looked down at the slip. A chit for two hundred
guilders. Under it a scrawl. What did it mean? Was it a joke?
He did not even ask my name or where I had come from....
Slowly I walked back to my new friend whose name was
equally unknown to me.

I showed him the chit.

'Well, that went off all right, comrade,' he said. 'Now
we're colleagues. That was simpler than you thought it would
be, wasn't it?'

'Yes, but can I take it seriously?' I asked, still in doubt.

What a strange world, I thought to myself, what strange
people. He didn't know my name, nor I his. I drank his beer,
grew friendly with him, got a job through him and
an advance of two hundred guilders ... everything from a

perfectly strange fellow ... and I didn't even know the name of the firm or the plantation at whose head office I was to report on the twentieth.

Later I discovered that his name was Dwars; not that he introduced himself to me, but I heard his friends addressing him by that name.

Gradually quite a party assembled round our table. I did not know a single name, but they all patted me on the shoulder, and were very friendly. The boys incessantly brought beer and whiskey. The men's white suits were soon wet with perspiration, and sweat streamed from their shining red faces. The men talked very fast and put away incredible quantities of beer at an incredible pace.

For dinner the whole party moved to the dining room. The heat in the overcrowded room was unbearable. White shirts were open to the waist, and as the wearing of underclothing here was a superfluous luxury, one could see plenty of perspiring, reddish-brown, hairy chests. A whole crowd of boys were serving without moving a muscle....

Like everything else, the dinner, too, was peculiar and strange. A dish of rice, a greenish chicken soup prepared with curry and other unfamiliar spices, and countless supplementary dishes. You put the rice in the centre of your plate, poured the soup over it, and then the vegetables—as much of them as there was room for on the plate—were piled round it. And what you could not put on this plate was placed on another. There were all sorts of queer things: sea crabs baked in oil; unfamiliar vegetables boiled with strange spices; goat's meat sprinkled with grated coconut; little round cakes of finely crushed sea crabs, baked in oil; ginger gherkins; paprika siliquae filled with meat; bananas fried in butter; small, strongly-peppered fish, done on the grill; peas that had shoots of from five to six centimetres long; grated and roasted American hazel-nuts, covered with a horribly smelling liquid, dried fish, baked in coconut oil; ground paprika siliquae mixed with putrid meat: all this served in incredible quantities and on innumerable platters. There were dishes among them that tasted of brilliantine, and some whose putrid fish smell made the eyes of an unsuspecting novice water. But in one respect all these dishes were alike: they were all unbearably peppered. Even I, accustomed as I was to paprika in Hungary, felt my throat burn as if I had drunk vitriol. The tears came to my eyes, and I started to hiccup.

Twenty-two boys were serving at our table. Deep dishes and platters were handed round.... 'Boy! *Krupuk!* ... Boy! *Aajor lodel!* ...' and the strange-smelling and strange-tasting abominations were brought along. Tears and sweat ran down my face and my intestines were burning.

Beer was flowing freely, and the party grew more and more hilarious. On the table next to us a merry planter was dancing a terrible war dance. Plates crashed under his heels, glasses broke with a clatter, those seated round the table joined in the din and beat time with their fists.

Dwars seized a half-ripe papaya fruit and stuck it on his neighbour's head. The green half-globe slid over its victim's head down to the eyes, orange-yellow pulp squirted out, poured down his white suit and ran into his neck, eyes and moustache.

'Hurrah, Jan!... You *have* got a grand hat, Jan!...' The diners yelled at the successful joke. Jan, the victim, sneezed and shaking himself flung the remains of the overripe fruit on the floor. But one prank had to be answered by another. Jan did not keep them waiting long: with a jerk he lifted up the large table by one side. With a clatter the glasses flew, the plates fell crashing to the floor, the beer flowed in streams, as the many varieties of peppered dishes and sauces flowed into the laps of those sitting opposite who, trying to save themselves, had by this sudden movement been flung with their chairs right into the débris, and now lay under the table amid the stinking fish dishes, desperately kicking and screaming. Dwars, too, fell into the broken glass, blood streaming from a deep cut on his cheek.

The party roared with laughter at this successful act of revenge, the strangers at the neighbouring tables jumped up and poured beer over those lying on the floor, who beat about them with hands and feet.

'Boy!' cried Jan like a victorious field marshal, 'chit!' And he wrote a chit for fifty-four plates, eight glasses, one chair....

The boys went on serving with rigid, motionless faces. There was no sign of consternation, amazement, or indignation.... One could not tell anything by looking at them. Their brown faces remained serious, dignified, indifferent.... The white tuan was enjoying himself as he pleased, and the coloured boy was there to sweep up the broken glass and spilled dishes, and to see that the tuans were satisfied.

They tied a napkin round Dwars' face, in a few minutes a new table stood on the site of the débris, and the Rijsttafel went on as if nothing had happened.

The white suits, bespattered with red, yellow and green juice, tattered, drenched with beer and whiskey, and giving off a smell of fish, genever and sour drinks, bore witness to a magnificently celebrated Hari Besar feast.

But I had had enough of it. The first hours that I had spent as a new-baked planter, had been fairly stormy ones. I had a burning sensation in my stomach, and my head felt dizzy.... Silently, I retired to my room.

Ladislao Székely, *Tropic Fever*, Harper & Brothers, New York, 1937; reprinted by Oxford University Press, Kuala Lumpur, 1979, pp. 49–58.

11
Planters at Play

MADELON H. LULOFS

It is not surprising that Madelon Lulofs's novel *Rubber* should contain episodes similar to those described by Ladislao Székely. After all, they married after a scandalous affair, conducted in the rubber planting world of East Sumatra which is the setting for her novel. Published in Dutch in 1931, *Rubber* shocked its readers by its revelations of planting society in the 1920s. This extract bears resemblance to that above by Székely, but, twenty years on, wives are present, although this does not restrain the young assistants.

Lulofs rather self-consciously provides a justification for their behaviour, but is also aware of the Indonesians in the background, observing it all.

Events are seen from the perspective of Marian Versteegh, whose husband, Frank, had found employment with a large American rubber planting company. The young couple had arrived in Medan only that morning.

'**O**H, you know …' Kostman suddenly resumed the conversation in an altogether different voice. 'Novices always come out filled with that idea of saving. Good God! I arrived with it too. You can do it the first year, but afterwards you simply can't hold out. You have to work so hard here. And always this heat, this monotony. You miss all you've had before—the seasons, the weather, relatives, school friends. Oh yes, I know you have friends here too, but it's not the same thing. We're all from different towns, from different social levels. We're friends just because we're all the same thing—planters, assistants. It's like prisoners or exiles. We drink together, we have fun, and that's all. All we do really is to dream of our next furlough. Oh, to see snow again! To walk in a nice March shower! To eat real beef steak, and butter that does not taste of the tin, or an apple that hasn't been kept in ice for a month! All those things eat into your nerves. You end by letting things slide. It'll all get right in the end, that's what you keep repeating to yourself. Then, if you have a bit of luck, if you become a boss, or some year get such a bonus that you can go home on it, you just slip away: But otherwise … Don't forget that the only thing that consoles you for sweating your soul out of your body is ease, comfort, and you've got to take your comfort while you're healthy enough to enjoy it. When we go back, we don't live long. Our bodies aren't healthy enough to last. We've got malaria and dysentery in our blood, and our nerves are rotten. Oh well, here's your health. Look, here comes the crowd.'

Hoogstraten, Molenaar, and De Vynt walked up through the still empty hall. There was an immediate murmur of voices.

'Hallo, you people there already? We've just slept on. Can we fit in? Boy! Boy!'

* * *

A moment later eight buggies entered the garden one after the other. The assistants drove themselves, and their drivers stood behind. There was a noise of bells and shouts as they entered. The great silence of the hotel was broken. The horses were taken out of the shafts and allowed to roam. The drivers formed a circle, chatting and smoking. If their Tuans made a night of it, they slept in the open against a post or on a bit of matting under their buggy. Sometimes the horses fought, and their neighing drowned all other sounds. And occasionally one of them broke loose and ran away, galloping through the streets of Medan followed by its driver trying to catch it.

The planters climbed on to the terrace with big strides, and dropped into chairs. They swore and called for beer. They cracked jokes and told stories. Some of them recognized Kostman and shouted: 'Hallo, Kost, back again? Had a good time?' and Kostman shouted back: 'Grand! Been tipsy every day and kissed all the girls.' 'Married?' Kostman made a deprecatory wave of the hand.

More and more buggies followed. Several managers arrived in cars with their wives. The terrace was filling. Everybody wore white. Most of the men's faces were swollen and tanned by the sun. The women were pale, anæmic, faded. There was a friendly atmosphere, and everybody seemed to know everybody else. An orchestra composed of Indos—white men born in the Indies—played antiquated airs, just a little out of tune and out of time. Nobody listened. The assistants were singing, and shouting for beer. They were at home in this hotel. It was their hotel. Then the uproar grew louder. A group of planters introduced a novice who had arrived on the previous day by a German steamer. He was slightly intoxicated, and dressed in a dark blue lounge suit that contrasted oddly with the white clothes of all the others. A thrill went through the assembly. Everybody looked at the blushing, blond newcomer.

61

'You shouldn't have done that to us,' somebody shouted. 'No, you should have spared our feelings. It's a shame to make yourself so dandified when we're all just dressed in plain white.'

'I haven't any white clothes yet,' stammered the novice. These words provoked exuberant mirth.

'We'll get you a white suit, we'll help you to one,' they shouted. 'A prettier one than you've ever seen in your life.'

'Boy! Boy!! Boy!!! Boy!!!!'

Chinese servants rushed forward. 'A pail of white-wash.'

'Right, Tuan!' The servant did not hesitate. He did not wonder what might be the meaning of this order. He merely went away and re-appeared in a moment with a pail of whitewash and a brush. One of the assistants lifted his arms to the orchestra.

'Silence!' he shouted. The music ceased at once. There was dead silence.

Then, to an accompaniment of loud cheers and howls of joy, the novice was whitewashed, his clothes, his shoes, his hair. The servants looked on from the doorways. There was a slight smile on their faces, but no amazement. It was the planters' pay-day, always a fruitful occasion for the maddest pranks.

'There's your suit, young man.'

'One moment. Music!'

'Music! The National Anthem! The Wilhelmus!' shouted voices. Obediently the musicians obliged. Everybody stood and sang the words. Then someone called for three cheers, heartily given, though no one knew precisely whether he was cheering the novice or the anthem.

'Isn't he dandy?'

'Better than a suit from Paris.'

'Let's have a look at you, young man.'

'Put him on the table. We all want to have a look at him.'

With loud huzzas, they lifted up the astonished novice and placed him on a table. He looked a sight for the gods, perspiring, crumpled, smothered with whitewash which was now running in streaks down his face.

'And now, we'll have to order his trousseau!'

There were loud cries of approval. The novice looked positively frightened. But the rag was over. They called a Chinese tailor, and made him take the novice's measurements. They ordered twelve complete suits, and one of them signed the chits on behalf of them all.

'And now you must drink our health, and thank us for our nice present.'

A glass of beer was put into the novice's hand. Suddenly taking courage, he made a little speech of thanks and emptied the glass in one gulp. This gesture won all hearts. When a little later he dropped unconscious in his chair, he was taken up and carried almost tenderly to his room.

Frank and Marian had looked on in wonder.

'You've got to get used to it,' said Kostman. 'We're a bit on the rough side, but we're not a bad lot.'

Dinner was decidedly noisy. Songs and shouts went on all the while. The *hors d'oeuvres* was thrown across the room. Plates and glasses were broken. The floor was covered with remnants of food, the tablecloths were sodden with beer. One of the assistants was baptized with the contents of three mustard pots and one butter dish. Dripping with mustard and butter, he was carried shoulder high round the room. He shouted that he wanted a better seat.

'I want an ox! I want an ox! I want to ride on an ox!'

They howled approval. Three or four ran out of the hotel. A row of ox-carts was passing. The last of them was stopped, and the driver was told to unharness his beast. He protested.

'The ox will get wild, Tuan! It's impossible, Tuan! I must be at the estate early, Tuan!'

'Shut up, you ugly black mongrel!'

'Thrash him!'

'No, give him a drink!'

'Boy! Boy! Gin! Half a bottle of Bols!'

The native looked anxiously round him. He shouted to attract the attention of the native policeman who was standing near by. The policeman glanced at the planters, and thought it wiser not to interfere. Then the man was handed the gin, smelt at the jug, and put it to his mouth. He emptied it in one gulp. Then he muttered something in his native tongue, swayed, and dropped senseless to the ground. He slept till the following morning.

The ox was led into the hall. The anointed assistant climbed on its back, but it took fright at the noise and the lights. It ran through the room upsetting the tables and chairs. The ladies fled shrieking. The men shook the ceiling with their laughter. Then the assistant dropped from the beast's back and remained lying in a heap of broken crocks.

'Gentlemen ... a little order please!' The manager, a squat Hollander, appeared in the open door. But his voice was lost in the infernal row. The ox had been cornered and was lowing. The band played on as though nothing out of the ordinary were happening. The planters again drove the beast on, imitating the driver's cry: 'Hrrt! Brr! Crrrde!'

'Gentlemen,' shouted the manager. When he saw that no one paid the slightest heed, he took one of the Chinese servants by the arm and said: 'Catch the ox and take it away.' The servants drove the ox out of the hall. It ran into the street, and roamed about the town throughout the night. In the early morning it was taken to the police station. There its native master was already waiting for it, trying in vain to remember how and where he had lost it. He was summoned and then allowed to leave with his ox, the one living creature that listened to his flood of complaints at the injustice of the world.

Madelon H. Lulofs, *Rubber*, Cassell, London, 1933; reprinted by Oxford University Press, Singapore, 1987, pp. 46–52.

12
Entering 'Society'

NOEL WYNYARD

Settling in involved meeting other Europeans and the venue for this was very often the Club. More will be said about this institution in Section IV. Suffice to say that wherever a few Europeans were stationed they would establish a club, usually exclusively European in membership, however small. Meeting the 'old hands' was often a daunting experience, as it was for Noel Wynyard in northern Thailand. In this extract, also, she first encounters the loneliness of the woman left in alien surroundings while her husband attends duties which take him away from home.

W E decided not to go down to the Club that evening until after dark, at about eight o'clock. There was a dinner at the Manager's house in our honour and it would have meant returning home to change if we had arrived dressed for games; also I had an idea that it would be infinitely easier to meet all the inhabitants of the place for the first time by the rather poor, artificial light, than by broad and merciless daylight. So, after looking over the house time and time again, having a proper bath in the luxury of a long bath as good as any home one, and the only specimen of its kind up-country, deciding on, rejecting, and finally selecting an evening frock that I thought suitable for the occasion, we set off after having taken at least two hours to dress. Women always appeared in full evening dress for dinner parties, and I was surprised to find that the men merely adopted a very informal outfit, consisting of a clean short-sleeved shirt open at the neck, a pair of black silk Shan trousers a little longer than shorts, evening pumps, and woollen stockings. This was a very excellent idea from the coolness point of view, but it was also a lazy one, for on retiring home to bed after the party they merely removed the shoes and stockings. I once said that I did not see why I should not come in my night-dress, and on being dared to, did so, only to be complimented on my attractive new frock, so the joke fell rather flat; but no one ever guessed the frock's true status!

I don't think that I have ever been so hideously apprehensive in my life as I was during that drive down to the Club; it was rather like waiting to be tried for murder and knowing that there was very little hope of acquittal. I had vaguely tried to get out of it by saying that I did not feel well and that I was very tired, but no argument was the least use. My husband was most Spartan about it all. In reality he was probably as nervous as I was, although he maintained a stoic calm throughout the whole proceedings. As the lights of the place drew nearer and nearer I felt worse and worse, and as the car swept round the corner I saw a circle of men seated in the open in front of the wooden Club house; there was no sign at all of another woman. Putting as good a face on it as possible, I descended nonchalantly from the car, endeavouring to control my clashing knees with at least an outward semblance of quiescence. As we advanced, every one sprang to their feet and there was a certain amount of coughing and chair-scraping as the introductions were formally conducted, then, with a sigh of relief that I sincerely hope was not audible, I sank into the nearest chair and prayed that conversation might become general as soon as possible. After a few minutes I noticed that there was a distinct tension in the air and that all faces were turned in my direction, and, on looking round I discovered that a boy was standing at my elbow holding a large tray of bottles. I had not the faintest idea what to do. At the best of times it is difficult to know what to say on being asked 'What will you drink?', but to have to deal with deciding, pouring, and mixing was too much. I was so frantic about it that I could not even read what was on the bottles. Luckily I managed to catch my husband's eye just as things were becoming critical, and he came across and poured out something—to this day I don't know what it was—and the situation was eased.

As it grew slowly later and later I began to wonder if every one had forgotten about dinner, and it was not till 9.30 that the host suggested making a move. This habit of late dining was a thing to which I never became accustomed. It became increasingly difficult to make one drink spin out for two hours or so, and by the time we did move all appetite had vanished. On this occasion the appetite was non-existent for, although the meal was an excellent one and the conversation more or less easy, I was perpetually panicked as to whether and when I should leave the men to their brandy. Again at the critical moment I caught my husband's eye and retired with as much aplomb as possible to the nearest available room. This in itself was not easy, because there was no other woman with whom to make light conversation, and every word and jest that was repeated round the dining-table was clearly audible to me over the top of the flimsy match-board partition. However, they shortened the usual half-hour to suit the occasion, and joined me after a brief ten minutes. I cannot remember exactly what we did after that, but it was something like roulette, and the rest of the evening passed so pleasantly that I was hardly aware of the time when we decided to leave at about one o'clock.

Two days later my husband had to go out to the jungle for a day, and I found that I was completely alone for the first time. To begin with, it was so novel that I did not mind in the least. The fact that I could not speak to the servants did not worry me at all, for my husband had given all the instructions he could think of before he left, and ordered the meals for the day. But as the hours wore on I began to realize that this was to be my lot for five whole months during the rains, day in and day out. It was such a frightful thought that I hardly appreciated the full portent of it; it seemed to be an impossibility and very remote, although in actuality only six weeks distant. At about five o'clock, very bored with my own company, I decided to go down to the Club and play a game of tennis or golf. On arrival there I found one gloomy-looking individual whom I had never seen before seated in one of the empty chairs in front of the Club house. As there was no one else to do it, we introduced ourselves and embarked upon a polite conversation about nothing in particular. At one time he made what I then considered to be rather a singular remark. 'How long have you been up here? Oh, you'll soon find that every one in the north is a bit queer.' As he was only a visitor from Bangkok, I immediately assumed that every one in that city must be a little strange if he was a typical person, and the conversation became more and more mono-syllabic. After about half an hour I ventured a suggestion that people were a bit late in coming down, and was more than startled to be told that there was no one else in the place, the entire population having returned to their work in the jungle, so we had better play a single on the tennis court. This we

Some have wonderful profiles.

While some like the strenuous side of the game.

And a few have confidence.

Some have style.

Some play for the thrill.

And some love the smell of the grass.

Tennis at the club.

did for about an hour, and retired in the end worn out with the exercise after hitting a series of rockets and boundaries that defied even the highest wire netting and raced to the furthest extent of the polo field. I fear that the standard of play was not very high; at least it did not appear so to my eye so fresh from England. After this we retired to consume enormous lime-squashes in a comparatively gloomy silence, all my efforts of conversation meeting with a blank 'Yes' or 'No'. At eight o'clock I had had about enough of it so decided to make tracks for home, and as I rounded the corner I waved good-bye to my illuminating companion who by this time had exchanged his drink for one of a more stimulating nature, and whose facial expression was, if possible, a shade more gloomy.

In the few days that elapsed before our departure for the jungle I saw very little of the actual town. Lampang in itself was not a particularly interesting place, apart from the old wall and one or two ruined *wats* or temples, and when my husband was not there I did not feel much like exploring by myself. But one thing that I was beginning to realize, and that pretty forcibly, was the dismal prospect of heartrending loneliness that stared me in the face, coming rapidly nearer and nearer with each succeeding day. It was not a previous lack of knowledge that brought it home to me so vividly now, for my husband had always described it graphically to me in letters, and I had always known more or less what kind of a life it was. But never in my wildest dreams or most fertile imaginings did I get within a mile of the reality, or rather the actuality of my own reactions under such conditions.

Noel Wynyard, *Durian: A Siamese Interlude*, Oxford University Press, London, 1939, pp. 34–9.

Daily Life

EUROPEANS in South-East Asia were usually birds of passage. The main exceptions to this were those Dutch, mainly on Java, who settled with their families and established sizeable communities which had an air of permanence. To some extent, the Spanish did the same. Elsewhere, individuals might spend their lives in the region. Some stayed on after retirement. Others married into the local community and lived lives which uneasily bridged the racial and cultural divide. However, most Europeans lived in South-East Asia with the expectation of eventually returning to their homeland. The men were usually employed by the colonial government or by private enterprise, generally under contracts which provided their return passage. The women were generally wives and family, although during the twentieth century the number of women employed in their own right increased; usually as missionaries, teachers, nurses, and secretarial staff. The main expansion in this category occurred after the Second World War.

Daily life, therefore, involved employment for the men, and domestic management and chores for the women. Both roles could be challenging; both could be tedious, as the following passages reveal. Many spent long periods of isolation from other Europeans (see, for example, Passages 14 and 15). Most were supported by an existing European social structure, the men, even when away from other European contact, having the responsibilities and satisfactions of their employment to provide their lives with direction and purpose. It was the women who were more likely to find time heavy on their hands, unless they found activity which was rewarding and interesting (see, for example, Passages 24 and 25). In this sense, our examples may not be typical. Women who wrote memoirs, letters, or books were likely to have the resource and character to make the best of their situation.

In the following passages we meet a varied gallery of Europeans pursuing at work and at home, lives which were more humdrum and routine than family and friends in Europe probably imagined.

13
Domestic Content

MARGARET BROOKE

For Ranee Margaret Brooke (Passages 3 and 8), in the early years of her marriage, daily life in Sarawak was idyllic, disturbed only when some crisis called Rajah Charles away. The following passage refers to the period soon after her arrival in 1870.

A ND so the days went on, placidly and happily. At daybreak I would rise to watch my husband start out for his morning ride. After he had gone I would stay on the verandah watching the miracle of beauty which is sunrise in Sarawak. So long would I gaze, entranced, upon the scene, that I had often to hurry considerably over my toilet in order to be in time for the Rajah's return about eight o'clock. At that hour the Datus, those delightful Malay chiefs (my husband's ministers), would arrive at the Astana to escort the Rajah to the Court House across the river, where, assisted by Mr. Crookshank, he dispensed law and order to his subjects. Their departure from the Astana was most picturesque. As the Rajah stepped outside the porch, Subu would unfurl the large yellow state umbrella over his head and they would set forth. Behind His Highness walked his Malay ministers in their rich robes and beautiful turbans, they, in turn, being followed by the usual retinue of subordinate Malays. They looked to me so very biblical, those dear, kind, grave Hadjis, as they marched along with their slow and stately tread. I used to feel as though I had just taken leave of Abraham, or Jacob, or Esau! Bless their hearts, they have all now left the world. Some day, who knows, I may find them in spirit to welcome me in the land beyond the sun....

The Rajah returned from the Court House at noon, when breakfast was served, after which he rested, as is customary

The dining room at the Astana, *c.*1900. From S. Baring-Gould and
C. A. Bampfylde, *A History of Sarawak Under Its Two White Rajahs
1839–1908*, Henry Sotheran, London, 1909.

during the hottest hours of the day. At five o'clock we took
tea together on the verandah. Then we would go for a paddle
excursion up and down the river. At eight we dined in the
enormous dining-room (so large and empty for two solitary
souls!), waited upon by Talip, our butler, and four young
Malay boys, their bare feet making their movements as silent
as if they had been ghosts.

Margaret Brooke, *Good Morning and Good Night*, Constable, London,
1934, pp. 56–7.

14
Domestic Vicissitudes

EMILY INNES

Emily Innes's days (see Passage 4) were far from idyllic. Langat may have housed the Sultan of Selangor, but it was a poor place, although Emily may have emphasized its squalor. Nevertheless, she coped with the problems of isolation and deprivation, as well as with her somewhat ineffective husband. In this extract she describes the vicissitudes of colonial life as it undoubtedly was for many women in the backwaters of empire in the mid–1870s.

W E soon settled down in Langat to our every-day life. Indeed, there was not much to settle down to, which made the operation the quicker. I passed my days in my bare wooden bedroom, sometimes trying to teach myself to read or write Malay, anon mending clothes and house-linen, generally to the accompaniment of a murmur of voices from the Court-room. Mending the clothes is a task thrown upon the 'mem' (mistress) by Eastern servants when there is no ayah, although before the Tuan's (master's) marriage, all his mending is cheerfully done for him by his 'boy.'

The 'boy's' tactics to avoid betraying to the mem that he knows how to sew are amusing. If engaging himself to a new mem who knows nothing about him, he will roundly swear that he never had a needle in his hand in his life; while if he has been the Tuan's servant in his bachelor days and therefore cannot deny his sewing powers, he will keep any garment entrusted to him many weeks, and finally return it so badly mended that the last state of that garment is worse than the first. As a matter of fact, I believe all Malay men of the lower class can sew neatly. The women sometimes weave the material for their own sarongs, but having done that, hand them to the men to be sewn. The women, in fact, when they do any work at all, which was not often the case at Langat, seem to do all the hardest part, and may be seen digging in their gardens or pounding rice, while the men sleep in the shade.

Mending the clothes gave me plenty to do, for we never wore anything that would not wash, and they came back from the tender mercies of the Klang dhoby once a fortnight in a sad state, however new or good they might have been when they reached him. The mending, if done properly, would have taken three of me to execute; as it was, I did what I could, and let the rest go. I preferred this state of things, strange as it may appear, very much to the trouble of having an ayah. My English relations were always urging upon me that it would be a great comfort to me to have an ayah; but I knew better. They fancied it must be a safeguard and an addition to one's respectability; but in reality the reverse is the case.

The women who go out as ayahs in Malaya are the most degraded in the land. They are ready to steal, lie, drink, poison their master and mistress, or join in a plot for murdering them at any moment.... This does not happen in Singapore, where the class of ayahs is a shade more respectable; but in Malaya, as in England, the best servants cannot be induced, for love or money, to bury themselves in desolate wilds such as Langat.

Often my peaceful occupations were disturbed by natives prowling round the house, who descried me in my room and shouted 'Tabek, mem!' at me. I used to dislike this a good deal, but could not conceal the top of my head from them unless by shutting the shutters; and as long as they saw the top of my head and thus knew I was in the room, they would continue to shout. Sometimes, wishing to put an end to the annoyance, I went to the window, and said in a snubbing manner: 'Tabek, what is it you want? I am very busy.' Then those outside looked most hurt, and shocked at what they evidently considered my bad manners, while on turning away from the window I found the room full of others, squatting on the floor as if they had taken root, and filling the air with a detestable smell of cocoanut-oil and 'moist unpleasant bodies.'

It was of no use to give these women the broadest hints that one preferred their room to their company. At first, I sometimes said to them, 'Now, good-morning; I have to bathe and change my dress.' They replied, 'Good-morning,' but, instead of going, they settled themselves down more comfortably than ever, while their brightening eyes and smiling faces showed that they thought they were in great luck at having come just when so delightful an entertainment was about to begin.

It was the same with the men in our sitting-room. They would call and sit squatting on the floor for hours, saying nothing, and seeming quite contented to stare at us. On one occasion I remember it was particularly awkward; the Resident was with us, and we had fresh pork for dinner, a most unusual treat. Two strange rajas had come to see the Resident, and would not go away. I told the Resident dinner was quite ready, but as it consisted of pork, we were afraid of hurting the rajas' feelings by having it put on the table. 'I will soon settle that,' said the Resident, and turned to the rajas, saying, with a bow of dismissal, 'Pray excuse us; we are going to dinner.' But the rajas were not to be so beaten; they merely said, 'Tuan,' and sat on placidly. Presently somebody apologized to them for not inviting them to join our meal, as the habits of Malays and English in the matter of feeding were very different. To this they replied politely that they believed the habits of the English were in every respect superior to those of the Malays (!), and that with our permission, although their religion forbade them to join us, they would have much pleasure in looking on. In short, it was impossible to make them stir, and there they sat, all through dinner, while pork was eaten and alcoholic liquors were circulated round the table that would have made the Prophet's hair stand on end.

I gave orders to the Malay policeman on guard that he was not to allow strangers to come round to the back of the house, but it was of no avail. He thought it his duty to walk to and fro in front of the house, while my persecutors came from everywhere but the front. One only of these visits proved rather amusing. Three Chinawomen, wives of shop-keepers, came one day and asked an audience of me. They explained that they were going to be had up by the police for gambling without a license, and they wished me to beg the Tuan to let them off from their punishment (a fine). They assured me that they had not really gambled, but were only playing 'a little child's game' at cards, merely for amusement; and one of them let me see clearly in her hand a dollar, which I am quite sure from her manner she would with the slightest encouragement have put into mine. Somehow, instead of rousing my indignation, the idea of a low Chinawoman's thinking she could bribe me with dollars to pervert justice in Langat amused me excessively, and for a moment I was tempted to lead her on till she had committed herself; but recollecting that it would be more easy to excite her suspicions than to allay them, I forbore, and treated her and her companions instead to an harangue on the subject of English justice and English law, the effect of which was, I felt, considerably marred by the broken Malay in which it was uttered.

Sometimes I had to jump up suddenly from my work when a comparatively cool breeze swept through the room. This in the tropics is a warning that a shower is impending. Looking out of the window over the plain, we became aware of a thick wall of white mist, like cotton-wool, advancing towards us, blotting out the landscape as it came. It was then about a couple of miles off. We heard a noise like a distant waterfall, and we saw the cotton-wool gaining first one clump of shrubs and then another, with incredible swiftness. Then it reached the herd of buffaloes in the middle distance, and enveloped them; the breeze freshened; everything in the room, unless we had occupied the previous minutes in making all secure, flew up into the air or out at the doorway, and there was barely time to rush to the window, unhook the shutters and shut and bolt them with frantic haste, before the storm burst on the house with a roar like that of Niagara, and a violence that seemed likely to batter down the frail roof.

If I wished to go from one room to another during a storm, I had to put on galoshes, hat, and ulster, tuck up my skirts and make a rush for it. The open doorways in all directions left even the middle of the house liable to incursions of rain. And such rain! However, we soon grew accustomed to it; so much so that when I returned to England, after four years of tropical climates, the silence—the quiet, modest demeanour—of the English rain was one of the things that struck me most. It seemed strange to me that one should have to look out of the window in order to know whether it was raining or not. In Langat when it rained no one in the house could possibly have remained unconscious of the fact. We could often not hear each other's loudest shouts a few yards off....

Our lives were extremely dull—especially mine. We tried to get books from the Circulating Library in Singapore, but failed because there were only two Europeans (our two selves) in the district, and there was no regular communication at all between Langat and the outside world. We had hoped that these facts would have been thought strong reasons why a point should be stretched in our favour; but it was not so. We received a printed paper to be filled in, containing questions, one of which was: 'Which is the leading member of the European community at Langat?'—a question which was amusing under the circumstances.

Having failed in this direction, we sent home for books and newspapers. We ordered six of the latter, besides several magazines, to be constantly sent to us, but from various causes we did not reap the full benefit of this arrangement. Our papers, especially the illustrated ones, were more often than not stolen, or delayed for months, on the way; and of those that did eventually reach our hands, the greater part had the post-marks on them: 'Missent to Bombay,' 'Missent to Hong-Kong,' 'Missent to Deli,' and so forth. Postal officials seemed to be under the impression that 'Singapore,' which was part of our address, must be an Indian name, while Langat was often confounded with Langkat, near Deli, in Sumatra.

Some of the day was got rid of by bathing two or three times, and the consequent dressing and undressing. But, as a Singapore lady once remarked to me: 'What is the use of dressing three times a day if there is no one to look at you when it is done?'

Some more time was disposed of in eating and drinking—or rather in sitting at the table and looking at food—for the debilitating effects of the climate and want of exercise did not leave us much appetite. There were still many hours during which we either had nothing to do, or could do nothing, from heat, ennui, and mosquitoes. These latter, after visiting us by tens at a time during the day, rose up at sunset in their thousands from the swamp with an audible hum like that of a distant swarm of bees. In the evening we escaped them by taking refuge in the 'mosquito-house.'

This was a sort of large square cage made of wooden bars with mosquito-net nailed to it; it had a door, and if we managed to pop in and shut the door very quickly behind us, we were tolerably comfortable inside (except for the intense heat) for the rest of the evening. The cage contained a couple of rattan lounges, and a small table; on the latter we put our lamp and our books or work, while thousands of baffled insects of all kinds swarmed on the netting outside, gazing into our Eden like so many Peris, and thirsting for our blood. I should often have liked to do my sewing in the mosquito-house in the daytime, but could not, because it had been erected in the Court-room, the only room large enough to hold it; and it would not have done for me to be in the Court-room while cases were being tried. It would have distracted the attention of the witnesses, and would besides have had an unofficial look, even more in the eyes of Malays, if possible, than of Europeans, as the former, like all savages, jealously exclude their women, wherever they can, from all concerns of life, except the purely domestic.

We walked on the mud-path every day in the year, when the weather permitted it, and when Mr. Innes was at home. If he was away, I walked on the mud-path alone. We never quite reached the pitch of heroism necessary to 'do the mud-path' more than once per day, though doubtless it would have been good for our health if we had.

'Smoking the mosquitoes.' From Isabella Bird, *The Golden Chersonese and the Way Thither*, John Murray, London, 1883.

* * *

IT was during this second year that we began to send home to a co-operative store for groceries, tinned meats, drinkables, etc., instead of sending for them, as formerly, from Singapore. We found at the end of the year that we had made a saving of £80 by this means, allowing for loss of money in exchange and loss of interest during four or five months, while the 'goods' were far superior, from being fresher and the tins in better condition.

We absolutely found it cheaper to send for lard from England for cooking purposes, than to order tins of ghee from Malacca or Singapore. This seems most unnatural, as the ghee was prepared in the Malay country itself, and was used by all the poor people round, so that it ought to have been cheap; but what made it expensive to us was that it was almost invariably sent to us in a leaky tin, and by the time it reached us had nearly all leaked out. We paid, if I recollect rightly, thirty shillings for each tin; but often there was not more than five shillings' worth of ghee remaining. Redress—from a jungle—is unattainable; the only reply we got to our complaints being an assurance that 'the goods at the time of embarkation were in perfect order.' Perhaps they were; the tins may have been knocked into holes by rough treatment on board the steamers.

The first co-operative store that we tried was not a success. Although its bill reached us duly, thus proving that our correct address was known at the store, the cases were all addressed wrongly or insufficiently, whereby some of them went to Langkat in Sumatra, and remained there unclaimed for six months, while others went on to Hong Kong. Eventually they all reached us, but in a sad condition. The things had been packed by some one evidently ignorant of tropical climates. Hams, tongues, tinned fish, flesh, and vegetables had all been put pell-mell together in coarse salt. Of course the salt had melted, and left the tins rusted and leaking, and the hams., etc., damp and rattling about in a half-empty chest. We wrote to complain, and received only insolence in return, so I need not say we did not patronize *that* store again; but we found the Civil Service Supply Association, to which we next applied, most satisfactory, and continued to deal with it till we left the East finally.

It was, of course, necessary to look ahead and send one's order four or five months before the things were wanted; but this was but a slight inconvenience. At first, until we learnt to allow several weeks for delay in executing the order, we were rather apt to run out of stores. On several occasions we were reduced to some bottles of mustard, some pickles, and anchovy sauce. The principle which regulated the survival of things in our store-room was just the opposite of that which regulates the world according to Darwin: it was the survival of the unfittest (for the purpose for which they were designed—*i.e.*, to be eaten). I was sometimes very nearly reduced to feeding Mr. Innes on the diet recommended by Grumio as good for the temper—namely, 'the mustard without the beef.'

We did not always send at once to Malacca or Singapore when our store-room was empty, as we hoped the stores from England might arrive at any moment by native boat. Mr. Innes astonished me by his genius for cooking on one of these emergencies. There was nothing but fowls to be had, and we were so tired of these that we both agreed it was of no use to have them cooked. So he ordered a large dish of rice to be boiled, and some eggs; and with these, and some mustard, anchovy sauce, capers, olives, pickles, and various other condiments that lingered on the shelves, he produced a most delicious dish. If we had only written down, at the time, the quantities and names of the things which he put in, I believe the recipe would have been an invaluable one to housekeepers in the East, and he might have been immortalized by calling it after himself.

We found this hot climate was quite a touchstone for butter. Whether what we received under that name was really oleo-margarine, butterine, or some other composition, I know not; but on opening a tin we generally found the upper half was full of oil, and the lower half of grey or white fat, which latter had sometimes a bad smell. The Co-operative butter was, however, better, being fresher from home.

We were also able to grow a few vegetables in our garden at the hill, which were a great comfort to us. The principal kinds were sweet potatoes or yams, caladium, tapioca (the root of which boiled is a little like a potato), a kind of spinach, a kind of haricot-bean, Indian corn, and brinjal or egg-plant. We also succeeded in producing some tiny cucumbers from seed bought at Malacca, but they did not flourish.

I was much aggrieved once by a mistake made by a shop-man in Singapore. I had ordered, as usual, four dozen tins of condensed milk and four dozen tins of biscuits (we never had bread, as there was no yeast to be had in the country). The shopman jumbled these two orders together, and sent me four dozen tins of 'milk biscuits.' The consequence was that for a whole month I was deprived of my solitary comfort and pick-me-up—namely, my afternoon cup of tea. I drank *café noir* at breakfast, and tried it again at five o'clock, but found it was neither refreshing nor wholesome at that hour, as it prevented my sleeping at night. We tried tea without milk, and with lemon, but we did not care for it.

This seems to me now, and probably will seem to others who 'live at home at ease,' but a trifling grievance; but my experience is, that the less you have to eat the more you think about it, especially if you have nothing else to think about.

Emily Innes, *The Chersonese with the Gilding Off*, 2 vols., Richard Bentley & Sons, London, 1885; reprinted in 1 vol. by Oxford University Press, Kuala Lumpur, 1974 and 1993, Vol. 1, pp. 21–38 and Vol. 2, pp. 25–33.

15
Loneliness

NOEL WYNYARD

Noel Wynyard (Passages 5 and 12), alone in a large bungalow up-country in northern Thailand during the rains, found the solitude hard to bear. Her many servants were not companions and their presence only emphasized her loneliness. In an effort to occupy her time and her mind, she tried to learn the language, but the days dragged, even the Club offering little solace as most members were away.

THE loneliness that may be experienced in an up-country station is so entirely different from anything that touches the lives of those who, living in England, are always in some form or other busy, that a description conveying to such even a part of the absolute negation of the interests, the action, the companionship, and the gaiety known to them, is an extremely difficult undertaking. Loneliness plays so great a part in the life of a woman out there that its description, however, must be attempted.

Some are unaffected by it; some become inured to it; but for any one whose nature is in any way sensitive or imaginative I am convinced that it is nothing far short of a dragging hell, and needs a will of iron to defeat it. It is a mental state. It is not the effect of, nor is it affected by, things physical, other than illness. Illness, of course, with its accompanying depression, aggravates the state almost to madness. There can be few conditions more utterly unbearable than loneliness to one who feels and is conscious of it in every fibre of her being and who knows her efforts to combat it are unavailing and herself beaten by it. It is not the sort of thing that can be eradicated; putting it in the background on every possible occasion seems to make it reappear the more frequently; the airing of it, as psychologists would have us do, entirely fails to lessen it. One wakes each morning to the realization of yet another day alone; no one to speak to, no one to discuss things with, however trivial, no one to play a round of golf, or a game of squash with; no word of English to be heard, nothing to be heard except the annoying sing-song tones of a barbaric language and the paralysingly insistent roar of the rain and the splashing of the deluge from the roof, the noises of which cannot be shut out of a house whose windows are slatted boards. As one wakes to this realization one begins to wonder in an all-absorbing way just what is there left of purpose in life for such an unfortunate individual. Then comes self-pity, the beginning of the end of all happiness.

It may be dulled temporarily by influences made for that sole purpose, which will, for the time, get the upper hand. In other words, we can force ourselves to interests which will act as soporifics. The interests must be primarily of a mental nature. Things like weaving or painting—painting that is forced, a time-killer, and not done with the creative stimulus and loving hand of an artist—are useless, because they become mechanical unless rooted in an intense interest. If this is absent, there is no reason for the work, no object in it, nor any spur in the form of competition or example.

In England, if one is suffering from intense loneliness, there are a thousand distractions if one wants to use them: a walk, a ride, a drive in the car, a theatre, a cinema, a library, news and concerts on the wireless, even a gossip or squabble with some friend: all these things are at every one's command, but in an up-country station during the rainy months hardly a single one is. The only thing to be done is to read, to lose one's whole identity in a book and, for the time being, to forget that one is alone. But even this has its drawbacks in a place where literature is hard to come by, where there is a small library of ancient books of limited selection, with a few new books that annually swell the shelves of crime and sport. A library run for and kept by a total membership of ten, most of whom are absent in the jungle with the best books, is soon exhausted.

If one is merely solitary and a bit bored, physical activity will get the better of the ennui; a game of golf or squash will induce a feeling of lassitude. When the body is in that state the mind is also less active. But for real loneliness, that is for ever in the foreground of one's consciousness, touching one everywhere and always, one must occupy the mind so fully as to exclude the one thing that fills it already. How to do this, how to numb the agonizing feeling of aloneness by a concentration on something that one knows all the time to be designed to replace it, is beyond my experience....

I shall never forget the first time that, standing on the veranda of my house within 100 yards of the railway line, I watched my husband depart for the jungle on a six weeks' trip. He was waving 'Good-bye' from the back of a train that crept slowly across the plain, to disappear within fifteen minutes over the hill with a triumphant shriek from its beastly little funnel. The bottom seemed to have fallen out of everything; I was most horribly alone with nothing to do nor any wish to do it; I was not on the telephone; I was a mile and a half from the town, whose only European occupant at the time was a woman; and here I was to remain for six weeks.

People have often said, 'How nervous you must have been'. But the nervousness was nothing as compared with the fearful ennui of my own company. Before me was a vista of six weeks' black blankness which nothing could penetrate. If I had been one of those who thought about it differently, who are unaffected by it, things might have been easier; as it was, the prospect was appalling to me.

I started by feeling completely numb and useless, but, as the days dragged by, this began to give way to a feeling of helplessness. From this I rallied myself into a desire to be able at any rate to make myself understood by the servants. So I hunted round and managed to find a very decorative little Siamese-cum-Philipino girl named Juanita, who could speak good English, also Siamese, Lao, and a smattering of three other languages. She had, of course, no idea of how to teach, as she had previously been employed as a nursemaid, in which capacity she had once been to England. At the moment she was pedalling a bicycle-taxi for hire round the town. But she was most bright and intelligent, with perfect manners, and she agreed to come for an hour a day to try to drum some of the rudiments of the language into me, and also to give any orders to the servants that were necessary and do odd pieces of interpretation to shopkeepers and others. Her interpretations to the cook and boys often caused minor troubles, as I am convinced she often misunderstood me, and the cook her. . . .

All this time I whiled away the hours in compiling a dictionary of my own with phonetics beside each word. They were my own phonetics and were completely unintelligible to other people and, after a time, to myself, as I found my own ideas on the subject changed from day to day. I took down whole phrases that I was in constant need of using, such as, 'Boy! tell the cook this food is uneatable and if he doesn't give me better I shall sack him', and 'Bring my bath water', and 'Start the car'. Whole phrases I learnt and whole phrases were often muddled up, with the result that my boy used often to get such messages as: 'Sack the cook, and if he's not eatable bring a bath.'

So as to make the days seem less long, I seldom got up before 9.30, had breakfast at ten, after which I would have my lesson. I am one of those people who like to take their meals either entirely alone or not alone. I could never accustom myself to the prevailing formality of being waited upon by one or two servants who were neither within the room and part of one's company nor without and cut off. They would be hidden behind a screen, or would be outside the door, round which they would periodically peer, and one was incessantly conscious of this subservient and irksome supervision that lurked unseen until the last mouthful had been watchfully swallowed, when it would pounce into the open, exchange courses, and once more slink behind its camouflaging screen. All this in silent-footed attentiveness and competence, with a hushed but uneasy tranquillity inside the room that was rudely broken immediately on the boy's crossing the threshold by a loud howl to the cook signifying my readiness for the next course. All meals alone soon became a nightmarish burden to me, and I never had more than was strictly necessary.

My knowledge of certain restricted phrases and my lack of

knowledge of further vocabulary often got me into difficulties. I shall never forget once when I had been ill with one of the usual internal troubles of the East. After I had been alone for about three weeks, I was laid up and had been in bed for about three days before I called in the local doctor, a little Siamese who allowed me to take nothing but liquids. I was lying there feeling very sorry for myself, when there was a knock at the door, and in trooped the boy, the cook, and the cook's helper, who proceeded, to the best of my knowledge to ask me what it was I was allowed to eat. The thought of food at that moment was nauseating, and the effort required to remember what there was in the store-cupboard and then to translate it into words understandable to this grim row of menials was more than I could summon up, and if my English-speaking neighbour had not arrived at that moment to inquire of the boy as to the state of my health and had not helped me out with the translation, heaven knows with just what I should have been served.

The weather was such, and the days were so hot, that it was impossible to go out until about five o'clock. The morning I used to while away as I have explained; then I would have luncheon, after which I would rest until tea-time, change leisurely and drive down to the Club. The car was an extremely ancient Austin Twelve, and was liable to break down at any time. I used to take a coolie with me in the back in case of emergencies and also to swing the starting-handle, as the self-starter, when it worked at all, was more liable to jam than to move the engine. This coolie was a perfect fool. If any breakdown had occurred, he would have been of very little use, as he made no attempt ever to understand a single word of my halting speech, which doubly handicapped me, because, in any emergency, it would have been quite useless for me to have tried to do anything to the inside of the car, as I knew nothing about it. I was fortunate enough not to be stranded on the road with him more than once. Most of my journeys were done after dark to and from the Club or a dinner party, after which a midnight walk along a road with an unsavoury reputation would not have been genial; the coolie would have had to remain with the car to prevent pilfering of tools, tyres, dynamos and all removable parts, until assistance had been summoned, and where to get suitable assistance at that time of night I had no idea. So each time I set forth on an expedition alone, I would tender a prayer to the god of roads to see me safely home again, and he answered me every time except once. This time it was during the day and help was handy.

At the Club there was a certain choice of amusements, mostly depending upon the state of the weather. Billiards, which came to be my stand-by, did not; but it was often too hot for squash or too wet for golf and tennis. Golf I could play by myself if no one else was in station and if the weather permitted, but tennis I hardly ever played as it took third place to golf and squash and needed three other people.

The rains were not what I had expected them to be. Instead of the dull, grey days of England, we had brilliant sunshine followed by sudden, violent storms. The town was bounded to the south by low hills, which were turned by the

Driving along a trunk road. (Steven Tan)

sun glancing from and through great masses of clouds into every imaginable shade of colour. Looking from my veranda I would see them smoky-black beneath lowering rain-clouds; shivering, opalescent in the steam of a recent storm; silver-grey on the near face of some mountain valley, and dark green on the far; golden in the sun; purple in the twilight; rose-coloured on a stormy dawn; always changing, always kaleidoscopic. At times enticing with the charm of their meek tranquillity; at others forbidding, menacing with a merciless threat. Always there was an appeal; to pleasure or to daring, to quiescence or hazard.

Lying in a long chair watching one evening the play of the sinking sun on these hills, the only beautiful natural feature of that ugly countryside, I was suddenly aware of a roar as of an express train. Turning round, I saw a solid sheet of rain approaching far quicker than a man could have run, pouring from a great black cloud which it seemed to race and out-run even though there was no breath of wind. Then it was on me. From the shelter of the eaves of the house I could see that the falling raindrops were like pieces of coloured glass reflecting the lights of the rainbow. A rainbow, seemingly so near that I had but to stretch out a hand and touch it, formed itself into a complete circle whose foot nearly touched my knees. Perhaps this was due to the upflung spray of the water cascading off the roof on to the concrete veranda, but whatever its cause there it was, the only rainbow I have seen entire except for those sometimes to be seen in the spray of a wave breaking over the prow of a ship. It was an amazing sight, the diamonds and the rainbow and, like all things too good almost to be true, was soon nothing but an exquisite memory. The cloud, racing after the rain as though it would re-swallow it, blotted out the sun, making tallow of the diamonds and oblivion of the rainbow.

Noel Wynyard, *Durian: A Siamese Interlude*, Oxford University Press, London, 1939, pp. 82–93.

16
Mynheer at Home

H. W. PONDER

The Dutch were numerous enough in Java to create a stable European society which in the larger centres reflected the domestic values of the Netherlands. This passage begins with a portrait of the somewhat phlegmatic Dutch colonial middle class at home in their tropical suburbia in the 1930s, living lives of humdrum comfort. It is a world away from the frontier loneliness of northern Thailand or of Langat in the 1870s. The Dutch settled in Java in a way the British did not settle in their colonies, and even in Java the English kept very much to themselves and acted, as far as possible, as though they were in an English colony, a point made by Mrs Ponder. (See also Hubert Banner's comments in Passages 17 and 37.)

ALTHOUGH Java and Malaya are next-door neighbours, and both are tropic colonies, the life that Europeans live in each of them is absolutely different.

The most notable difference of all has nothing whatever to do, so far as one can see, with the essential difference in nationality, for nationality does not explain why it is that Malaya, except for babies and tiny tots up to six or seven, is empty of European children, whereas in Java they abound. It is difficult to see why the fact of being born Dutch should render children immune to the tropic sun; or why, on the other hand, the British child should be more susceptible to it.

Both colonies are close to the Equator: on sea-level they have much the same climate; if anything, Singapore is rather cooler than Batavia. Yet it is the firm conviction of the British in Malaya that children cannot possibly be brought up there; and the equally firm conviction of the Dutch that their youngsters will be every bit as happy and healthy in Java as they would in Europe. And the fine healthy young Hollanders, sunburnt and sturdy and full of life, that you see on all sides as soon as you land in Java certainly give the lie conclusively to the theory that healthy children cannot be reared in the tropics.

In Malaya the sun is regarded as the child's most dangerous enemy. It is only in the early mornings and late afternoons that the Chinese 'amahs' (nurses) are allowed to shepherd their charges out of doors. And even then the poor mites are made ridiculous as well as miserably uncomfortable by their fond parents' insistence on their wearing sun-helmets. The sight of a toddler of two or three years old, half extinguished by a pipeclayed 'topee' big enough for its father, is a sight to make angels weep. Can it be that we conservative Britons have yet to discover that Malaya is not India, and that in its totally different climate sunstroke is unknown?

The pity of this sunless treatment is that it turns the children into pasty-faced, peevish, pathetic little creatures, who seem to grow pastier and more peevish every day, until the time comes when (to everybody's relief) their mothers take them off to England, to deposit them with accommodating grandparents, and come back without them.

One sometimes wonders (quite in a whisper!) whether this custom of 'dumping' the children at home was really instituted for their benefit at all? It certainly does leave Mother so delightfully free for her busy life of bridge from ten till one, sleep from two to four, tea-dance, golf or more bridge, cocktails (known here as 'pahits'), dinner, dance—and so to bed; which is roughly the routine of the average Malayan British matron.

Dutch parents, on the other hand, regard the sun as a friend, not as an enemy. Their children run about and ride their bicycles in the sunshine, bareheaded, barearmed, and barelegged, not only in the hills, but in the towns on sea-level, and they thrive on it.

By way of demonstrating their confidence in the East Indies as a place in which to bring up children, the Dutch authorities have transported there the selfsame system of State education that is in operation in Holland. There are schools in every European town in Java, housed in admirably planned modern buildings, with spacious, lofty classrooms open to the air, and glorious gardens and playgrounds shaded by great jungle trees.

The curriculum is precisely the same as that in use in the Netherlands, with the addition of the necessary extra languages. There are primary, secondary, and technical schools, and several universities; and it is possible to qualify in most of the professions without leaving the East at all. It is noteworthy, however, that, in order to keep up the standard, it is considered desirable that all teachers and professors should be imported from Europe, rather than that they should qualify on the spot. They are very highly paid, and the cost to the government of the whole education system in Java is one of its heaviest commitments.

There are also a great many fine Roman Catholic schools and colleges, and all nationalities, including the Chinese, attend both these and the government schools.

The children's special festival among the Dutch—the day when Santa Claus arrives and there is a present for everybody—is not Christmas Day, but the feast of St. Nicholas, on the 5th of December; and in the schools in Java it is a very great day indeed.

For weeks beforehand the devoted teaching staffs have been scouring the local 'tokos' (shops) for presents and prizes, which are laid out in impressive array in one of the classrooms, each having been chosen with due regard to the special tastes of the lucky recipient; and all heart-burnings being saved by a tactful arrangement according to which, though everybody cannot very well win a prize, every one at least has a present; and, after all, there is really very little difference, when we are very young.

The most entertaining part of it all is the immense earnestness with which the good Dutch enter into the 'play-acting' part of the affair. They are the last sort of people of whom you would expect it, but perhaps even their matter-of-factness is infected by the native love of dressing up. So on the morning of the great day, Santa Claus, who is always an important local citizen, sets out, in full regalia of red robe and long white beard, in an open car, with almost the solemnity of an episcopal visitation, on a tour of the schools. He is accompanied by his black servant, 'Piet,' who carries a capacious sack, into which custom ordains that all really bad little boys and girls will certainly be thrust if their school record is beyond forgiveness, unless Santa's fatherly heart is touched, as, fortunately, it invariably is....

Dutchwomen are wonderful housewives, as all the world knows, and happily they have brought their talent for home-making with them to the Far East. I have read (and chuckled over) novels about Java, in which the heroine (obviously 'no better than she should be,' but the authors assure us that we could scarcely expect anything else in that 'awful climate') lived a limp, perspiring life, all languor and lovers, perpetually arrayed in a kimono.

I am sorry to disappoint you, but the Dutchwoman in Java isn't in the least like that. On the contrary, like the virtuous lady in the Bible, she looks well to the ways of her household; and if you should happen to catch sight of her in her kimono, she is pretty sure to be either on her way to a bath (we have several a day in Java) after some especially strenuous piece of activity in the kitchen, or else she has donned it for the afternoon siesta, which is the custom here, as in so many other hot countries.

I have never yet come across a Dutch housewife who had fallen into the fatal habit of leaving everything to the 'boys,' which is so dangerously easy to acquire where labour is plentiful and fairly efficient. She has one goal in Java as she has in Holland, and that is 'Perfection.' And because modern Dutch homes in the East Indies are very charming, and she has everything to hand to make them more so, it may be that her housepride is, if anything, even greater than it is in her home country.

The new Colonial Dutch style of architecture is designed on an altogether more modest scale than the old. But it is just as good of its kind. The rooms are lofty, the floors tiled, and the windows large; there are usually bathrooms to each bedroom, set-in basins, and all the most shining and up-to-date of electrical devices.

Every bride migrating to the East is quite certain to bring some old family china with her. Brass, Oriental pottery, Chinese embroidery, Batik, and all such decorative adjuncts are plentiful and by no means dear, on the spot; so that the Dutch matron's task of making the 'Home Beautiful' in Java is a happy one.

Every house has its 'voorgalerij,' a wide front veranda, which is really a sitting-room open to the air on three sides. This voorgalerij is the pride, the shop window, as it were, of every house large and small, for, having no front wall, except perhaps a stone railing and pillars, it is in full view from the road. The walls are hung with highly polished brass, and old blue plates and dishes. There are deep armchairs and lounges, covered with soft, inviting cushions; tall palms, and masses of maidenhair fern in pots, and jars of crimson and flame-coloured cannas (for whatever flowers there may or may not be in your garden, the canna is always in evidence all the year round).

At night the houses look even more alluring; and if you walk along the road in the European quarter of any town after sundown you will see every voorgalerij aglow with deep orange or rose-colour or gold, from lights shining softly through native-made silk lampshades.

Gates of any kind are the exception rather than the rule at the entrance to Dutch homes in Java, and the fences or hedges that enclose them are usually quite low. The gardens, like the houses, are their owners' pride. It is easy to make them beautiful, for labour is cheap, and the Javanese native, a descendant of countless generations of cultivators, is a gardener by instinct.

So the householder has no diffidence or shyness at all in exhibiting his garden, with the open voorgalerij of his house in the background, to the gaze of the passer-by. Nor has he any of our British exclusiveness in regard to himself or his family. You will be sure to see them sitting reading or sewing by the light of standard lamps (shaded like those in the veranda) in the garden after dinner. And when the sacred hours of the siesta (from two to four in the afternoon) are over, tea is usually carried out by the house-boys, and dispensed by mevrouw at a little table under the trees, or in the shade of a big, gaily striped umbrella.

As soon as mijnheer arrives home from business (for him, good man, there is no afternoon sleep) he has a bath, and dons pyjamas. And then, when he has finished a leisurely tea, he will stroll, as often as not, down the drive, and stand at the entrance smoking a large cigar, affording the populace ample opportunity to appraise his often very garish taste in 'slumber wear,' which, by the way, in deference to this little weakness of his for disporting himself in it in public, is invariably starched.

The Dutchman's tropical kit is not quite the same as that of the Englishman. He eschews the collar and tie of our convention, and the jacket of his white drill suit, instead of the usual turn-down collar and lapels, has a stiff, straight band fitting tight round the neck like a bandsman's uniform. It is known as a 'badjoe toetoep' (literally, a 'shut-up jacket'), or 'toetoep,' for short, and is fastened round the neck with two brass studs.

That is to say, it is designed to be so fastened. But 'India' (as Java is most often called by the Dutch, to the great puzzlement at first of the English visitor) is a warm country, and Dutch necks are seldom slender. So it is rare indeed to see a toetoep that does not gape widely apart at the neck, with two bright brass studs adorning one side, and two empty studholes on the other....

A Java bathroom is quite unlike any other. It has a concrete floor, and a large bath (tiled or concrete, according to the sumptuousness or otherwise of the owner's quarters) in one corner. But the bath itself is a delusion and a snare; it is, in short, not a bath at all, but a tank, from which the bather, standing on the concrete floor, is expected to pour water over himself with the dipper provided for the purpose (which varies from a delightful utensil of highly polished brass, or brass-bound teak, down to mere aluminium, galvanized iron, or enamel). It is a method of bathing learned from the natives, and is a very much pleasanter one than it sounds, in a warm climate.

'A first attempt at an "Indian" bath.' From
W. S. Caine, *A Trip Round the World in 1887–8*,
George Routledge and Sons, London, 1888.

It should be impressed upon strangers to the country that
to try to get into this bath is extremely unwise. They will
probably skid, they may possibly drown; and they will certainly
be most unpopular if they ever happen to mention that total
immersion is their chosen method of bathing in an hotel
bathroom!

It seems a natural sequence from bath to breakfast, and a
Dutch breakfast as served in Java is so unlike any other that it
unquestionably deserves a place in any picture of life in the
island. It is not, like the famous rijst-tafel, a recognized entertainment, but an entirely domestic affair,—so very Dutch
that it is met with in its true form only at houses and hotels
where no English are catered for, and where, if they do
come, they must do as Holland does. It is, as I said, a family

affair, and as such it must be served at a communal table, even though at the same hotel you may eat your other meals as unsociably as you please in your own undiluted company.

Down the middle of a long table, side by side, are set a number of large dishes; on about one in every three there is a square loaf of white bread cut up into thick slices. The other dishes are filled with wafer-thin slices of cold delicacies, such as liver-, garlic-, and blood-sausage, ham, tongue, smoked fish, and (most important of all) cheese; all the peculiar edibles, in fact, that garnish the windows of German or Dutch 'delikatessen' shops.

Like the rijst-tafel, a Dutch breakfast has its own technique. The correct procedure is first to help yourself (always with a knife and fork, for to use 'fingers' would be considered most indelicate) to a slice of bread; then to dip (also with your own knife) into the deep dish into which the butter has been melted and allowed to set; and lastly, having buttered the bread, to pile on it a generous selection of the sliced dainties. The result is known as a 'Boterham,' and is eaten with the knife and fork; and I am afraid it must be added that local custom appears to dictate that it should be consumed in mouthfuls whose generosity is not at all conducive to polite breakfast-table conversation.

A fried egg may also be placed on the Boterham, and eaten in the same way; and it is curious to note that although custom forbids bread to be taken in the fingers, it permits the finger and thumb to be dipped into the open 'cellars' of salt and pepper (for which no spoons are ever provided), unless the point of a knife or the handle of a fork is preferred by the more fastidious....

* * *

There are other contrasts between Java and Malaya beside the reaction of their respective children to the tropic sunshine. The whole 'atmosphere' is different. There is a homeliness and simplicity about Dutch life in Java that is entirely lacking in the British colony over the way. The Dutch love their homes and really 'live' in them, not, as do so many English in the East, regarding them merely as places to sleep in. This homeliness is especially noticeable in the country towns; there is something pleasant and old-fashioned about life in them, despite all their modern comforts, a restfulness sadly rare in these days. The Dutch are 'domesticated,' as the English used to be a generation or two ago. You will often see young married couples out for walks in the cool of the evening, with 'Vader' pushing the baby's pram, and perhaps a youngster, the next size larger, toddling at 'Moeder's' side.

The reason is that the Dutch really 'settle' in Java as we do (or used to do) in Australia and South Africa and New Zealand. They are not, like the English in Malaya, perpetually recovering from one 'leave' or getting ready for the next, with always at the back of their minds the thought of retiring to England as soon as ever they have qualified for a pension.

It seems to me a strange ambition. And the problem of why anyone should ever want to leave the eternal summer of Malaya for the almost eternal winter of England remains unanswerable! Half of the unlucky optimists die of pneumonia before they have enjoyed that longed-for retirement for a year, but even that doesn't seem to teach the poor dears common sense! The Dutch have to serve a very much longer term of years before they are granted their first leave, so that from the beginning their roots strike deeper.

I am afraid that one could go on indefinitely with these rather invidious comparisons. They are certainly somewhat odious to our British *amour-propre*, but they are none the less intriguing. It would be so interesting to know, for instance, why the Dutchmen and Dutchwomen of Java use that most practical and economic steed, the 'push-bike,' on every possible occasion, while we English would rather die (or leave the country, 'broke') than be seen on one. It is painful to reflect that the only possible reason can be that the one community is sensible, and that the other is foolishly snobbish.

There is a marked contrast, too, in the accommodation available in the two colonies. If business or pleasure takes you to either Singapore or Penang, unless you are prepared to become a householder you have only two exorbitantly expensive hotels and a few indifferent boarding houses to choose from; whereas in Batavia or Soerabaya there are small, moderate-priced hotels in almost every street. There are these admirable hotels, too, in every country town in Java; in Malaya there are only the government resthouses, with their curious regulations restricting the length of your stay....

It is not only in contrasts between Java and Malaya that the student of international manners will find entertainment, but also in comparing the triangle of colonies, British, French, and Dutch, in this south-east corner of Asia.

Near neighbours as they are, they have developed on strikingly divergent lines, and national qualities in each case, mingling with local conditions, have combined to produce three strangely characteristic blends.

The French, passionately home-loving, regarding all absence from their beloved country as exile, have created, wherever it was possible, a little bit of *la belle France* in the Far East; and if a Frenchman could be dropped from some magic carpet straight into Saigon or Pnom-penh he might well rub his eyes and think himself at home again. There are the same wide boulevards, with patches of gracious shade thrown by avenues of tall trees. There are the same cafés, with their little tables in the open air. There are the same glass-fronted restaurants, with their creamy, lace-trimmed blinds and, best of all, inside are the savoury dishes and goodly wines of France. But there also, sad to say, too often, are the same small and stuffy rooms, the microscopic towels, and the bath-room almost as hard of access as Mount Everest. I have even been in hotels in Indo-China where the 'boys' used it as a broom cupboard! France has done so many admirable things in this Asiatic colony of hers it does seem a thousand pities that she saw fit to import her peculiar notions of domestic hygiene with the rest.

Then the Dutch, those painstaking, orderly, methodical people—the race that a recent writer has described as sharing with the Scandinavian peoples the distinction of being the most civilized in present-day Europe—have made of Java, as nearly as may be, the perfect colony. It is a sort of tropical Holland, but a Holland modified and adapted to its new environment with all the skill that human brains could devise.

And the English. Well, being English, we never bothered to design our colony at all. It simply 'growed.' Singapore and Penang just straggled along the water fronts as occasion and commercial interests demanded, and there they stayed. Every now and then an imposing (and very costly) building is put up wherever there happens to be room for it, and the result is (especially at Singapore) a heterogeneous jumble of godowns, blocking out the sea for miles, along what might have been one of the most beautiful sea fronts in the Empire, and Chinese streets that are all tangled up with imposing European shops and banks and offices.

In the matter of language, too, the characteristics of the three nations clearly show themselves. The Dutch learn languages as a matter of course when they are young, and learn them fairly easily. The English learn them only when they must, and learn them painfully. But the French (except in rare cases) learn them not at all. Thus it is that the Dutchman in the East has always learnt English at school, and so is quite at his ease when he visits British Malaya; but it would be hard to find an Englishman in Malaya who could return the compliment. The English as well as the Dutch civil servants are compelled to pass examinations in the Malay language, so that members of the Malayan Civil Service all know it fairly well; the Dutch, both men and women, speak it fluently. But it has to be confessed that the Malay spoken by all English people, except those who have learned it compulsorily, is about on a par with our very worst schoolroom French; and I am sorry to say that there are few of my countrywomen who know more than a dozen or so words of the crudest 'bazaar' Malay, picked up from their Chinese servants.

But we can take heart of grace. The French in Indo-China are even worse! They have not only refrained altogether from attempting to learn Annamese or Tonkinese (the languages most in use), on account of their admittedly great difficulty (for both belong to the Chinese group of languages), but they went a step farther, and insisted upon the poor, despised, ignorant natives learning to speak French. The astonishing thing is, that though the natives of that part of the world are by no means to be classed as 'quick at the uptake,' many of them do speak it after a fashion, and quite as well on the whole as the average Englishman.

The British population in Java mixes but little socially with the Dutch, and keeps very much to itself. It does its best to live exactly the same life as that lived in all British colonies throughout the East. It plays bridge and golf, meets at the English clubs, drinks pahits, and signs 'chits,' though this last practice it cannot indulge to quite the same airy extent as in a British colony. For the Dutch tend to look askance at the 'chit' system, and the word 'CONTANT' (cash) looms in large letters from the walls of most garages and many other establishments throughout Java.

H. W. Ponder, *Java Pageant*, Seeley Service & Co, London, n.d., pp. 250–8, 260–1, and 272–4.

17
Young Englishmen in Java

HUBERT S. BANNER

There was a small British business community in Java. As is made clear by Hubert Banner, for twelve years one of their number, their situation differed from that of the Dutch. In this extract, he explains this to his readers and describes something of the life-style of the young Englishmen employed as junior managers in British commercial and banking establishments in Java. Forbidden to marry during their first ten years or so of service, they formed a bachelor community with little in common with the Dutch described in Passage 16.

THE junior newly out from Home generally begins by residing in a hotel, on monthly terms, but as soon as his fellows have had sufficient time to sum him up and decide that he is companionable, it is usual for him to be invited to join a 'Mess.' A Mess, it should be explained, is simply a house taken by several men together and run on communal lines. All general expenses such as rent, wages, food, and drinks—everything, that is to say, except personal servants and laundry—are pooled and equally divided, each member receiving a monthly 'mess-bill' from the Mess President.

The cost of living in Java varies, as elsewhere, with the individual. But, taken all round, for the British Community it is high—much higher, if the truth be told, than for the Dutch. For the position of Java in relation to Holland is analagous to that of Australia, rather than of India or Malaya, in relation to Great Britain. It mainly attracts, that is to say, what we should call the 'emigrant class' of Dutchman, whereas our Crown Colonies make their chief appeal to the administrative class. The British, too, are so few in numbers—they do not reach four figures—that they are forced to a constant round of entertainment, and the junior, given officially to understand that he must keep up the standard, usually finds himself up to the neck in debt before many months have elapsed. A salary which looked royal to the youth thinking in terms of bed-sitting rooms and a weekly visit to the cinema takes on a totally different aspect when it has to cover club-bills running to £10 or £12 a month. The choice lies very definitely between a 'good time' on an income spent up to the hilt, and a 'mute inglorious existence' as a social recluse. Java has no half way.

If asked to name the minimum salary at which it is fair to bring a youngster out, I would set it at £500 per annum. The banks, unless I am misinformed, are sending out their new men at about £600 per annum, which enables them to keep up the compulsory standard of living without plunging into debt. The banks have, moreover, a rule whereby no staff man may marry until he has completed ten years' service, except in extraordinary circumstances. Marriage may be taken as roughly doubling the cost of living, and the climate does not, as a rule, agree with Englishwomen.

The views I have expressed above on the question of salaries drew, when they appeared in the Press, a certain amount of criticism. Letters were written in which it was pointed out as 'palpable to the meanest intelligence,' that a junior bent on learning the rudiments of his business and the local tongues will have little time for running up big club-bills; that my suggestion was tantamount to recommending $500 per month as a commencing-salary in the Straits; and that there are hundreds of young Dutchmen going out to Java on a salary of £250 per annum.

To this—prefacing my answer, however, with the observation that my remarks are directed a little higher than to the 'meanest intelligence'—I would reply as follows:

I have yet to meet the junior, however conscientious, who will devote *all* his evenings to study when the Club lights are beckoning. And even *one* Club night when things are really 'humming'—one solitary really 'dirty night'—can be sufficient to make the end of the month a thing to be dreaded. Secondly, conditions in the Straits and in Java are entirely different. Singapore, for example, is large enough to allow of a youngster living his own life without let or hindrance. Not so Java, where the British communities are so small that the doings of each individual are perpetually under the 'spot-light,' and small-minded tittle-tattle is as rife as in an English country parish. Thirdly, the young Dutchman on £250 a year does not enter into the question at all. He joins no clubs and plays no games; his evening meal usually consists of bread, with cheese or a sardine. As already pointed out, he is in most cases a product of the 'emigrant class,' pure and simple.

And finally, are we to take it as ideal that young men should go out on a salary calculated on their exact living-expenses, so that they have no chance to put by a little, month by month? I think we may assume that the banks know very well what they are doing when they start their men at £600 a year, and that they do it because *it pays*.

Hubert S. Banner, *Romantic Java as It Was & Is*, Seeley Service & Co.,
London, 1927, pp. 248–54.

18
A French Outpost in Indo-China

SYDNEY J. LEGENDRE

The Europeans who lived in remote corners of empire often developed eccentricities of manner and lost the ability to deal easily
with strangers. Often, the official in a remote posting was there
because he had failed elsewhere: even if that were not the case, he
nevertheless often believed that he had been passed over and his
resentment was made evident to visitors. The characters that the
Americans, Sydney and Gertrude Legendre, met on their journey
through the interior of Indo-China demonstrated this. They were
leading an expedition collecting specimens for the American
Museum of Natural History, New York. On their arrival at
Lai Chau, an outpost on the border of Vietnam and Laos and not
far from China, suspicion gave way to hospitality. But, as they discovered elsewhere, officialdom could also be boorish and difficult.

WHEN I had finished reading, the captain and commandant who had been surveying us with critical
eyes asked what our plans were, and how long we
intended to stay. We replied that a week or ten days would
probably suffice to make our collection.

'Have you camping equipment? Because, if not, there is a
native hotel here,' the captain said. The captain had a long
scar over one eye and an unpleasant manner. I did not like
him at first, but he afterward proved to be a very nice fellow.
The commandant, who had until now remained silent, suggested that there might possibly be an empty villa which
could be put at our disposal. Scarface, seeing which way the
wind blew, said that he was sure that there was, and as an
extra friendly gesture asked us to have dinner with the doctor
that evening. We had never seen the doctor, nor had he

indicated in any manner that he expected us to dinner. Nevertheless, we accepted this holiday from the bep's cooking with pleasure.

The house that we had been given was a palace. It consisted of three rooms, one of which was a bath. These chambers opened into one another through wide doorways in which doors had never swung, and they appeared to be perfect apartments for a communistic settlement. The hills of Lai Chau are dotted with these pink, blue and white villas which the French have brought with them from the sunny coasts of the Riviera. As long as they remain one-storied and a little rambling, they are delightful, but when an attempt is made at towered splendor the effect in a tropical setting is excruciatingly painful. Ours, fortunately, was of the attractive type. It was surrounded by a wide veranda of which one end ran off into a smaller building housing the bep and a massive brick stove, out of which, he assured us, would come the finest bread in Indo-China.

A loud, shrill creaking that tore at our nerves announced the arrival of the solid-wooden-wheeled buffalo cart that was bringing our luggage from the piroques. The case marked 'city clothes box' (because it held our white linens) was thrown open, and, arrayed in the splendor from within, we set off to the doctor's for dinner.

Dr. Palmas, the French doctor in charge of this post, was one of the most charming men that I have ever met, and with an interest in life and people that had not been dulled by his eight years' sojourn. 'He is the life of the post,' the captain said, as he introduced us. I later learned that he meant exactly that. It was the doctor who prevented the silent hostilities that grow up so often between men isolated in far-away places. It was the doctor who kept their minds alive and interested in international news, preventing them from stagnating—and from the worse hell of brooding over fancied wrongs and imagined injustices. With it all he had a manner so gracious, a spirit so gay and a charm so binding that I hope some day to have the pleasure of seeing him again. Should

106

you ever be in Indo-China and have the opportunity of meeting Doctor Palmas, do not fail to grasp it.

Now that we had taken the initial plunge into the social life of Lai Chau, the captain hastened to invite us to luncheon the following day. The walls of his living room, dining room and bedroom were alive with pictures of naked women, portrayed in the act of eating chocolates out of large beribboned boxes, reading magazines while lying on sumptuous beds, and cavorting about on lawns, while plastered-haired young men lying about in spotless flannels tempted them with glasses of champagne. Conversation proved to be a supreme test of one's knowledge of French, for the topics consisted principally of wives, mistresses and how *sympathique* the third wife of the native chief was. As everyone knows, French is the perfect language for such a discourse, with its host of expressions, each possessing a subtlety of meaning and a delicate shading that permits its use at exactly the right moment without the subject becoming vulgar. When I attempted one or two labored sentences, I realized from the expressions about the table that I had definitely not used the right phrase, and accordingly, squelched, I lapsed into silence. But the silence was equally embarrassing and to save 'face' I asked that we might be excused to go specimen hunting. A minute later I bit my tongue off for having made this statement, as I remembered that my gun was broken, and without a gun I automatically became camera man for the afternoon. This seemed to me catastrophical, for there is nothing that I dislike more than taking pictures.

As we left the villa the guardian of the prison waylaid us and demanded that we dine with him that evening....

* * *

Behind this important mass of business paraphernalia sat a fat, important looking little man who, on our entrance, picked up a letter, read it, shook his head, stroked his chin, and then rang for his secretary to whom he spoke rapidly in a very loud voice as he asked him to transfer his balance of ten million francs to another bank. The secretary, only too bewildered by the request, was about to ask what ten million francs, when the commissaire waved him out of the room and, turning to us, asked us what we wanted. What we really wanted to do was to laugh, but then our chance of obtaining piroques and men would have been nil, for without the aid of the government such a thing is impossible. Accordingly, Gertrude explained who we were and asked if he had not been advised of our arrival by the government. As he said no, the secretary who had gone out a minute before entered with a file of correspondence. Placing this on the desk, he said in a loud voice: 'There are the letters about the Legendre Indo-China Expedition that you were reading the other day.'

The fool at the desk roared, 'I never saw them before, I never saw them before!' and picking them up commenced reading them. At last turning to us, he said: 'I knew nothing about your expedition until now. My secretary is so stupid that I am forced to do all the work myself and as a result I occasionally overlook something. Unfortunately, I am leaving on a tour of my province tomorrow. The people wish to see me and ask my advice, so I will leave you in charge of my assistant.'

When the assistant entered I had proof of the saying about birds of a feather flocking together. A narrow, cross-eyed, opium-smoking, betel-chewing Frenchman was the assistant, whose one pleasure in life seemed to be to say no to every request.

Sydney J. Legendre, *Land of the White Parasol*, Rich & Cowen, London, n.d., pp. 95–7 and 168–9.

19
A Distant Corner of Empire

HERMANN NORDEN

Hermann Norden visited a French military post in the highlands of northern Vietnam in the late 1920s. The commandant and the sergeant and corporal of the military garrison were the only European men. The commandant had with him his wife and daughter, and Norden remarks on the beneficial influence Madame Walzer exercised in this remote outpost.

W E reached the post at five in the evening. It had taken the whole day to cover the thirty-eight miles between Laotschai and Hoang Su Phi. The post is strongly fortified and is one of the large posts of the district. The sergeant and corporal are Europeans and there are twenty-four native *tirailleurs*. Beyond the spiked walls and the barracks are two cottages; one is the guest-house. In the other, the living quarters of the commandant, I was surprised to find Madame Walzer and the two-year-old daughter of the house. Surprised, because I knew about the governmental policy of banning the officers' families from the strictly military posts: but Madame Walzer had been installed before the commandant-general had issued his edict, and since the captain was due to leave this post soon she had been permitted to remain.

Though the general's reasons for the prohibition are readily understandable, Madame Walzer's attitude toward the native women and theirs toward her showed what the presence of a sympathetic European woman can mean in the native life. While I was making notes from the captain's data book I was startled by a succession of reports that sounded like gunshots, but which proved to be only fire-crackers. The preparations for Tet had been pursuing me ever since I left Hanoi, and here at last was the great festival itself. On this first day of Tet the wives of the *tirailleurs* had come to visit the wife of the commandant; had come to make gifts and to

109

receive them. In front of the house stood two dozen women of the Man, Meo, and Nung tribes, each with one baby and some with two tied on their backs.

The first European to greet them was two-year-old Renée. Infant Europe welcomed infant Asia; the one in fuzzy white coat and cap and carried in the arms of her Nung nurse; the others, slung on their mothers' backs, their black heads covered with coloured silk caps from the corners of which dangled silver buttons, bells, fish—'devil-chasers' all.

Madame Walzer followed the nurse and baby into the veranda. She received gifts of eggs and oranges, made gifts in return, and in her talk with the women showed that they were definite personalities to her. Each one she knew by the husband's number—the local manner of designating the *tirailleurs*, because of the difficulty in pronouncing the native names. For each woman she had a special word. 'Bonjour, Madame 194. Et voilà, Madame 65! How nice that your husband has been made a soldier of the first class. Oh, Madame 39, you must come and teach my cook some of your recipes. My husband says that you cook so well that Monsieur 39 grows too fat to climb the mountains easily.'

Hermann Norden, *A Wanderer in Indo-China*, H. F. Witherby and G. Witherby, London, 1931, pp. 131–3.

20
In Remotest Burma

C. M. ENRIQUEZ

Major C. M. Enriquez of the Kachin Rifles and a Fellow of the Royal Geographical Society was for a time at Sadon in northern Burma, close to the Burmese–Chinese border. The civilian administrator was Assistant Superintendent T. M. Wilson, whose wife and four daughters shared his life in this remote but spectacular region. The daughters, however, were shortly to be sent away for their education: separations were a part of colonial life. Yet the compensations of such a life are clear from the following passage. Wilson and his wife were so identified with Sadon that Enriquez could call it 'The World of the Wilsons'.

SADON is the kingdom of Mr T. F. Wilson, who has ruled it as Assistant Superintendent for thirteen years. His kindness and hospitality, and his deep knowledge of the strange people with whom he deals, have won him a very special position. Like Scott, he is an acknowledged authority on Kachin affairs, and he has given the Kachin military venture his earnest support. Both he and Mrs Wilson seem to know every villager individually. My pleasantest duty in Sadon was to entertain Mrs Wilson and her four charming little daughters to tea. These four little girls, now excitedly awaiting impending adventures in Europe, reminded me of shy, eager fledgelings about to leave their nest.

Sadon has an elevation of 4600 feet. The fort (Fort Harrison) occupies a bare hill-top, and commands a splendid view all round, especially to the east across the valley to high mountains culminating in Tabu Bum (11,000 feet). It is a wonderful panorama, serene and calm, and endowed with an ever-changing beauty as the shadows move across the uplands from dawn to dusk. The Chinese frontier follows the lofty sky-line. . . .

At Wawchon Wilson has built a snug little house of solid stone—a safe refuge from a rain-storm which came racing, black and threatening, over the hills just as we arrived. We were, however, lucky to get twenty-four hours' rain safely over during a period scheduled for halt. When at last the clouds passed away we found the hill-tops powdered with snow. That evening a large snake, apparently a viper, entered the house, no doubt to escape the cold. Luckily the whining of one of the dogs called our attention to it.

The hamadryad occurs here, and I met people in Sima, Bhamo and the Gauri country who have personally been attacked by them. In Sadon the clouded leopard is fairly common—a beautiful beast with a coat marked like grey variegated marble. At Wawchon I saw a splendid pine-marten on the road.

The birds of Sadon are a study in themselves. Numbers of tits and small babblers, apparently of several different kinds, travel together in large flocks. Some are extremely small, and the flock moves furtively through the foliage like shadows. I had not time to identify them. Near Bum Katawng I obtained specimens (male and female) of the exquisite Dabry's scarlet sun-bird which had been caught with lime, and which two little fiends were wearing alive in their button-holes. Kachin boys often decorate themselves thus with live birds. The victims are usually bulbuls. The male of Dabry's sun-bird is iridescent blue and lilac on the crown, nape and throat, crimson on the back and shoulders, and scarlet on the breast. The belly and rump are yellow. The female is olive on head, neck and throat, with touches of shining blue, and stains of red. The breast is scarlet, and the belly and rump yellow, as in the male, but a little less brilliant. The tongues of these tiny birds, which live on honey, are hardly thicker than a butterfly's proboscis.

The road to the Kambai-ti Pass can be seen fourteen miles away zigzagging up to the Chinese frontier. There are said to be pines on the top. Wilson went up to visit boundary pillars, and was walking for some miles in snow. Unfortunately I could not go with him as I had to visit the neighbouring villages of Luhtawng and Singai. These expeditions were, however, delightful. The weather was utterly gorgeous after the rain. It was a pleasure to sit basking in the sun with a coat on. The atmosphere was brilliant, and the hills were washed with fresh and lovely colours. On the distant peaks beyond the Triangle, and also close above us on the uplands of Kau Lyang Bum, new snow lay glistening in the sunshine.

C. M. Enriquez, *A Burmese Arcady*, J. B. Lipicott Company, Philadelphia, 1923, pp. 231 and 236–7.

21
A Rubber Planter's Day

LADISLAO SZÉKELY

For Europeans employed on the rubber plantations of Malaya and Sumatra in the 1920s and 1930s the work was monotonous, hard and demanding. In this extract from *Tropic Fever*, Székely is making his first visit to the town since his arrival in Sumatra three years before. The 'tukang ajer' was the servant who carried water; a 'mandur' was an overseer; the 'tuan besar' or 'great lord' was the manager; Székely was still a little tuan, or under-manager; Kartinah was his native mistress who managed the household.

THE train ran over iron bridges and high slopes at a speed of thirty to forty kilometres. Sometimes it puffed vigorously and gave forth soot and sparks. Sometimes it also stopped because a stray buffalo herd happened to be wandering over the tracks. But the kareta sewahs had now become superfluous, you no longer had to be jerked and shaken in those miserable little wooden boxes. The town could be reached comfortably by the railroad in four hours. Later there would also be fast trains provided with dining cars, refrigerators and cold beer. For the present, however, travelling even like this was very pleasant, much better than in the kareta sewah.

I was using the railway for the first time. I had not sat in a train or seen a locomotive for three years. Not for three years since the day I had accompanied Peter to the harbour at Belawan. Since then I had only trotted through the virgin forest and had had neither time nor opportunity to leave the plantation. For always I had been obliged to work. The cruel merciless work was the most important commandment. From morning till night, day in, day out, year in, year out, I toiled. One could get accustomed to the climate. That is to say, one could get accustomed to it, but endure it one never could. Lord, how lovely a bit of spring or autumn would be. And even a little winter! ... Summer, everlasting summer,

A rubber plantation. (Steven Tan)

heat, sweating, headaches, bad digestion. How good a little rest would be!

In the morning at half-past five the tom-tom rang. At eleven o'clock: again the tom-tom. Lunch, At half-past twelve: tom-tom—work began again. One sweated incessantly, the air was scorching, the sun was scorching in the whitish-blue sky, and under one's sun helmet the sweat poured down in streams. The coolies were lazy and one must yell at them. One must for the boss would be coming. He, too, sweated; he, too, suffered from bad digestion. He grumbled and always found something to criticize. The mandurs forcibly and without any conviction bawled at the coolies. They did not understand why there was so much hurry. They did not know what rationalization was. They had never heard of a calculation whose compass may not be exceeded. They only knew that the big tuan had scolded the little tuan, that the little tuan bawled at them and that they, in turn, must bawl at the coolies. And the coolies stood in endless rows and pulled along the clippers, cutting the eagerly growing weeds.

A five-thirty the tom-tom rang again. This meant the cessation of work, and you could go home. Tired and exhausted the coolies dragged themselves along, they lay down beside the water-ditches, in the mud, parched with thirst.

And the little tuan trotted home, poured the putrid water over his body, sank down on the long-chair, and did not know what to do. The European mail had arrived. He ought to open the letters. He ought also to read the paper. Ought to settle with the Chinese store-keeper. On God, I am tired!—he would groan—tomorrow, tomorrow I'll settle everything, now I must first stretch myself out in the long-chair.

And then the mandurs came to get their instructions for tomorrow's work, and the white man would say: 'Wait back there, I'll call you.' The mandurs would retire outside the servants' quarters where they squatted and waited patiently. The heat had not abated although the sun was already setting. But the burning earth exhaled the absorbed heat. The red, loamy soil was dry and cracked.

Chickens were scratching around the house: 'Tukang ajer, dammit! Do chase those wretched creatures away!...'

Was I getting nervy? To hell.... Why should they be scratching just out there ...' Tuan, shall I bring tea?' Kartinah enquired softly. 'No!...' Then all was quiet again.... 'Shall I get beer?' Kartinah timidly ventured another question ... 'Get out of here!....' And Kartinah would slip out obediently. 'The white man is crazy,' she would say outside to the men and women servants, 'you want to bring him some refreshment, and he roars like a tiger.....'

To hell with the mandurs.... Of course I'll settle them, it just worries me that they're here. What I had to do was to check the accounts, arrange the coolie divisions and make plans with the mandurs. The accounts were not correct. Outcry. The mandur got confused. Great confusion. Start all over again. The mandur could neither read nor write. His head, too, was aching, he could no longer reckon how many men he had had and what work they had done.... 'Get off to your home! We'll work it out tomorrow morning!...'

I cursed the whole bunch ... 'Kartinah! Beer!....'

'There,' Kartinah would say in the back premises to the tukang ajer, 'now he wants beer after all! When I offered it to him, he wouldn't have any. Aren't the white men crazy people?!... Yes, yes, it's coming!' she called in to me and then, with a loud report, she pulled the mouldy cork out of the bottle. The beer tasted of cork. Phew! Oh, how I longed for a glass of beer fresh from the barrel! And a few anchovy rings with it, and a salt stick, very crisp, with caraway seeds. And a portion of veal goulash with sour cucumber in the Restaurant of the Apostles.... And oh, for a refreshing cold bath. To be able to lie in a tub of clear cold water! Not always merely to spray yourself with the lukewarm, putrid brew! If only it had been possible for me to bathe over there in the Buruwang. Even though the river water was putrid and not very cold. But it was impossible: it was full of crocodiles and spirochates, or whatever those things are called. These civilization had not yet extirpated....

Then, of a sudden, the sun disappeared. The darkness fell quickly. The kerosene lamps must be lit. We out here on the plantation had as yet no electric light, only the clerks at the head office had that privilege. The kerosene lamp was warm, it threw out heat like a stove. And mosquitoes came swarming in to the open veranda, and one had no choice but to retire to the room hung with mosquito-netting, a terribly hot kind of cage with no air in it.

What use were stone house, fine streets and those damned tennis courts? They should rid us of the heat and the mosquitoes, that would be more to the point! Now I ought to open the letters. God, how hot I was. Even sitting down I was soaking wet with perspiration. And yet the temperature was only thirty-eight. A little more than in the first drying-chamber of a Turkish bath. But day after day it was like that, and one got sick of it.... No, I did not feel inclined to read the mail. Tomorrow morning, perhaps then it would be cooler, and I then, too, would be a little more rested.

And the next morning the same humdrum business began all over again. Tom-tom. Start work. Divide up the coolies, settle the accounts that were not finished the night before. But when one has had a good sleep, the accounts will tally at once.

The coolies were digging water-trenches and pruning the weeds, and again the sun was terribly scorching, again the big tuan was in a bad mood and scolded.

But the old man had now been roasting in the equatorial sun for twenty-one years, so that he had, after all, some hereditary rights. He was certainly entitled to a fit of tropic frenzy.

And thus it went on, one day the same as a another. Only on the first and the sixteenth was Hari Besar.

But now I had three days' leave, I was going to the city to see the dentist. After three years I was leaving the plantation for the first time. It was the first time since the kareta sewah had lumbered off with me and carried me from the virgin forest to the city. For three days now no tom-tom would

117

plague me, no mandur, no coolie and no bad-tempered tuan besar. For three days I should be my own master, could sleep as long as I wished, could sit down outside the hotel at night and drink ice-cooled beer, and for once talk with people other than the inhabitants of Kwala Batu.... Not that I did not like the Kwala Batu comrades, but—God knows I was pretty sick of them! And they of me. We knew one another inside and out. Had nothing new to say to one another. Always the same thing: this coolie commited this or that offence, that mandur treated himself to this or that, the boss said that, this fellow or that has been deceived by his nyay with the tukang ajer, or another by his with the coachman.... Well, now I would manage to see other people, proper cultivated city people....

Ladislao Székely, *Tropic Fever*, Harper & Brothers, New York, 1937; reprinted by Oxford University Press, Kuala Lumpur, 1979, pp. 275–80.

22
Planters and Officials in Vietnam

ROLAND DORGELES

In this passage, Roland Dorgeles writes of the French rubber planters in Vietnam and their similarly circumscribed lives: though he does so as an observer and not with the passionate intensity of experience one finds in Székely. He also comments on the eccentricities of outstation French officials deprived of social contact with other Europeans.

' *ALLEZ, hop!'*
My companion leaped lightly from his carriage and scaled the wooden stair of his bungalow in three strides. He had covered acres of plantation; he had stopped for a moment to inspect the labor of a clearing-squad, burning a corner of brush in which the bamboos were popping

118

like musketry; he had run in to see one of his section chiefs, a young Frenchman shivering with fever; he had made a halt at the factory, where he had examined the vats and had passed through the drying-sheds. He had been out since early dawn and was returning only at high noon, when an irresistible languor stretches the coolies out like dead men, under the thatched roofs of their shelters.

At the sound of wheels, a boy had dashed to the phonograph and set it going. We entered the house, greeted by jazz. My young host looked at me and laughed.

'Are you surprised! I have trained one of my Annamites; the instant I come back, the orchestra must strike up. I take my brandy and soda to music. I have tiffin to music; I sip my coffee to music. Then half an hour of siesta, and off to work again. In this way, I have no time for reflection, you see.'

I saw, and I admired. He was a tall chap, substantial in both body and soul, the traditional planter of travel-tales—tanned face, white helmet, shirt-sleeves rolled up on sinewy arms, calves bare under shorts, heavy boots, a horn-handled knife at his belt.

On a concession of twenty-five thousand acres, he is in sole charge. He is the only person to give orders and assume responsibility. Thirty-two hundred coolies, seven hundred thousand rubber-trees, a factory, transportation of the rubber—all this he has to run, keep up, develop, attend to, entirely alone, without being able even to consult any one, whatever emergency may arise. The directors and shareholders of the enterprise care only for dividends. Do they even so much as know where their plantations are! 'Somewhere over there in Cochin-China!'

Coolies desert, storms wash out the road, overseers take to their beds, the rubber-trees die, those that have been tapped too young turn sickly. Paris cables to ask why production is lower than last month. There is nothing for it but to work harder than ever. The gangs are pushed. 'Every coolie must handle five hundred trees a day!' The number of vats is increased, a new drying-shed is constructed, a watchful eye is

119

kept on the storehouses where the grainy sheets of crude rubber are stacked. At the end of the day, the manager goes
home, utterly done up.

This is the bad hour. On the table in a little ivory frame is
the photograph of a woman and child; they had to be left
behind in France. It is good to look at them; strength comes
back. But it is not wise to look too long—a mere glance—for
depression sets in quickly. So in order that the master need
not think, Nam selects a record at random and winds the
crank. Such is the nightly festival. The exile, hands thrust
deep into his pockets, strides up and down the veranda,
whistling off his blues.

'No time for reflection, you see.'

One requires a rugged constitution to live that kind of life,
but something else is necessary; more important is the other
sort of health—health of spirit. The section heads and assistants
may fall sick and lose courage; the manager is not permitted
to do so. Who would take his place? He is not only the head
but the motive power. His energy makes the whole machine
run. His will, his faith, his joy in his work, brace all the others.

'Little So-and-so is down, is he? All right. I'll go to see
him at once.'

At the other end of the plantation, in his wooden house, is
a twenty-five-year-old colonial, delirious, hollow-eyed, jaun-
diced, and wringing with perspiration even under his fan. Or
perhaps he is not even sick, but ennui has taken hold of him,
misery at being so far away, so solitary, losing his youth out
here, cut off from every one he loves. Quinine is no remedy
for this type of fever.

'So things are bad, are they? Come along, old chap. Buck
up! Look here; I've an idea! I'm going to take you home to
luncheon.'

The manager talks to him, discusses prospects, hums
snatches of the airs the phonograph grinds off, and opens a
bottle of champagne.

'Clink! Here's to your next leave of absence, hey?'

His junior is visibly cheered and returns to his post in that
vast melancholy wood, where thousands of trees stand in

straight lines, and every tree holds out its latex-cup, like a mendicant.

It is always hard in the beginning. Later on you get used to it. Perhaps the ties with the past weaken. Other roots are put out that hold you to the land of your choice. A whole new life opens. Evenings will come, to be sure, when, lost among these red lands in which the brick-colored dust clings thickly to the boots, you will experience again the old feeling of isolation, but less sharply than before. You take your rifle and go hunting. There are plenty of deer and tigers. Or else you go off and forget your troubles for two days at Saigon, dancing at the Continental, visiting the Chinese restaurants at Cholon, the theater if a play is being given. Then back to your station and into harness again, face to face with the daily struggle and the ever-unattained goal!...

The fascination of the unknown and the hope of making money some day are the incentives. There is all the mysterious seduction of this country, which cannot be forgotten by any one who has ever known it. There is also, for many, the charm of a life that is certainly less commonplace than it would be in France, in suburban lodgings or some small provincial town. You have your own chalet, servants, a good table, your rifle hanging on the wall between a pair of elephant's tusks, convenient transportation by autobus to the Rue Catinat. You are obeyed; you are somebody!

The novice allows himself to be tempted by the one hundred and fifty to two hundred piasters they offer him at the start. He looks on this fifteen hundred or two thousand francs a month as a bonanza. He has no idea of the prices asked by the Chinese grocer. As for the veteran, habit fetches him back. Where else would he go? When he was suffocating on his balcony over there in Indo-China, in those March days when skies are heavy with storms that never break, he feverishly counted the weeks and thought only of France, 'the finest colony.' He laid plans and perhaps swore that he never would return. But in France the accumulated piasters slip rapidly away. Pleasures are soon exhausted. The old friends of other days are no longer to be found; their ideas, their tasks, their concerns, have ceased to be of interest. Among the repatriated there are those who even have a feeling of something akin to degradation. The astute 'boy,' taken along, is not slow to observe the metamorphosis in his masters. 'Monsieurs, maybe so, draw water at pump,' he will relate in his own jargon after his return. 'Madames, maybe so, cook all same *bep.*'

All this hurts, and finally you begin counting the days again. French life seems banal. What you miss is the colony. It was good to come home, but you are content to leave. Why are the outward-bound voyages, by the Messageries Maritimes, always gayer than the homeward-bound ones? Out there you find your house again, your servants, your friends. You tackle your work once more. You get tired and keep on struggling. Success comes to some—a lucky fall of the dice, a concession obtained, a fortunate speculation. It does not take so very many piasters, at ten francs, to fill a woolen stocking. Or perhaps a day comes when in some small post a group of men in white stand round a freshly opened grave between two pandanus-palms.

The free life of the colonies!...

In met many of these exiled Frenchmen between the shores of the Red River and the soft banks of the Mekong. They have been forgotten, off on their farms, at their little posts, in forest cabins, where they live eternally alone, among the natives, meeting a white person only by accident. For the harassed city-dweller, the word 'solitude' evokes a thought of composure and relaxation. But what does it mean to those who endure it months and years?

At a distance, I find the life they all lead still more romantic. There was a little inspector of militia, commander of a somnolent port, with books and magazines piled up on all his chairs and tables. There was a Belgian engineer, whose rustic dwelling was planted on a mountain near the railway-line, whose only companion was a large gibbon, which he had taught to smoke. There was that astounding missionary, the only white man in the region, who had organized a band among his Muong converts and had these children of the forest playing hymns and military marches. There was a young forest inspector from the outskirts of Paris; until the war, he had never got beyond the quarter of the Temple, and then he had taken a flying leap to the Annamese forests, where he now lived alone with his wife in the heart of the jungle, thinking of nothing but hunting. And there was that scientist who worked for months on end in the swamps of the Plaine des Joncs, in a veritable cloud of mosquitos.

Their complexions become tanned, their tastes shift, their manners change; but let a Frenchman come on the scene, and immediately they resume their former personalities, as one might put on a coat. There are only a few whose minds are actually affected by this solitary existence, but they are harmless lunatics, put on earth, one might almost believe, to make copy for transient writers. The former government official who turned hermit and who now lives in retirement on a little island in the gulf of Siam, where he trades nobody knows what with the Chinese, is one of them. He visits the coast only on very special occasions, for instance, at election-time, when he exults in casting one ballot for his forgotten hero, the assassin Ravachol. Is he crazy? Not a bit of it. He is, on the contrary, exceedingly cultivated and intelligent and is rational enough to be making himself rich, and he amuses himself addressing complaints to the governor in Latin.

It is true that one also meets imbeciles, like the simpleton with a Gascon accent who accosted me in the little hotel at Cantho. His whole eloquence consisted in repeating with naïve indignation:

'Everything is going to hell, I tell you. Imagine not having the right to thrash my "boy" if I please! The rod, sir; that is what is needed!'

But those old ex-regulars who believed in educating the *nhaque* with a cane have now become rare. No absinthe was offered me when I put in an appearance. Instead, on arriving at some remote little station, I noticed on the tables the latest Paris reviews and parcels of books forwarded from Hanoi or Saigon. What endurance these men must have to bear the burden of their every-day life without growing weak or bitter! It is true that they are not all real exiles from the world. In the district seats and larger trading-centers, besides the administrator or the resident, there are always a few Europeans, some of whom are married. There is sure to be one business man, one customs officer, one settler, one police official. But in spite of these associations, may there not often be moral solitude as hard to bear as the other kind?

I remember, for instance, being the guest of one evening in a modest drawing-room at a lonely substation. There was no electric fan, only the punka of other days with a 'boy,' half asleep, pulling the cord. Big lamps, which made the air all the more stifling, furnished the sole illumination. The deputy, who had not been expecting me, hastily invited in a few Frenchmen of the neighborhood, including the local police officer.

I have never met a person so dull and so cumbersome as this mustachioed sergeant. The deputy, a discerning chap who knew the natives perfectly, could not get a word in edgewise nor answer a single one of my questions. Every time the lout would break in with his tiresome, 'I'll tell you all about that.'

He talked with his mouth full, gravy smeared over his face, and he wore me out with his tales. He was one of those colonials who spend twenty years in a country and leave it without having seen or understood anything. The deputy sat looking at me with an expression of despair. At dessert the sergeant, now in full swing, undertook to figure as a wit. He seized the champagne-bottle to fill our glasses again and indulged in various tavern pleasantries, first moaning as the champagne came out and then pretending to milk the bottle. He finished by announcing:

'Mr. Deputy, now you can add this bottle to your curio collection and tell people that it refreshed six men; it will be the greatest treasure in the collection!'

At last some duty called him away, and we obtained a moment of respite. With a faint smile the deputy remarked, 'My sole friend!'

And it was the sad truth. The settler seldom left his land;

the representative of the Department of Public Works was a bird of passage; the customs officer often was away. But the sergeant came regularly every evening, and the young administrator was actually glad to see him: he was somebody; at least he was a white man!

Roland Dorgeles, *On the Mandarin Road*, The Century Press, New York and London, 1926, pp. 188–92, 195–7, 200–1, and 205–9.

23
A French Settler in the Philippines

PAUL P. DE LA GIRONIERE

Married couples had their partner and family as a defence against loneliness. However, given the state of medical knowledge in the nineteenth century, it was a fragile defence. The death scenes in the nineteenth century novel drew on hard fact, and tropical South-East Asia was at least as hazardous to health as London or Paris, while the death of a loved one in so remote and alien a place was probably more crushing a blow. The Frenchman Paul de la Gironiere spent twenty years in the Philippines in the first half of the nineteenth century. At the time to which this extract refers he was a successful planter at a place called Jala-Jala, where he grew sugar-cane, coffee, and rice. His brother, Henry, managed a highly successful coffee plantation; his wife, Anna had, after twelve years of marriage, produced a son, also named Henry. Let Gironiere continue the story.

M Y brother—my poor Henry—committed some imprudences, and was suddenly attacked with an intermittent fever, which in a few days carried him off.
My Anna and I shed abundance of tears, for we both loved Henry with the warmest affection. For several years we had lived together; he participated in all our labours, our troubles, and our pleasures. He was the only relative I had in the Philippines. . . .

Some who remained.

I had gathered in my sugar-cane crop, which was most abundant, and my plantations were finished, when, wishing to procure some amusement for my wife, I proposed to go and spend some time at the house of her sister Josephine, for whom she entertained the warmest affection. She, with great pleasure, agreed to do so. We set out with out dear little Henry and his nurse, and took up our quarters at the house of my brother-in-law, Don Julian Calderon, then residing in a pretty country-house on the banks of the river Pasig, half a league from Manilla.

Of the three sisters of my wife, Josephine was the one for whom I had the most affection: I loved her as I did my own sister. The day of our arrival was one of rejoicing. All our friends at Manilla came to see us, and Anna was so pleased in seeing our little Henry admired that her health seemed to have improved considerably; but this apparent amelioration lasted but a few days, and soon, to my grief, I saw that she was growing worse than ever. I sent for the only medical man in Manilla in whom I had confidence, my friend Genu. He came frequently to see her, and after six weeks of constant attention, he advised me to take her back to my residence near the lake, where persons attacked with the same malady as my dear Anna had often recovered. As she herself wished to return, I appointed a day for our departure. A commodious boat, with good rowers, was ready for us on the Pasig, at the end of my brother in-law's garden; and a numerous assemblage of our friends accompanied us to the water's edge. The moment of separation was one of most melancholy feelings to us all. The countenance of each seemed to ask: 'Shall we meet again?' My sister-in-law Josephine, in a flood of tears, threw herself into Anna's arms. I had great difficulty in separating them; but we were obliged to set out. I took my wife into the boat, and then those two sisters, who had always maintained towards each other the most tender love, addressed with their voices their last adieus, while promising not to be long separated, and that they would see each other very soon.

Those painful adieus and the sufferings of my wife caused the trip, which we had often previously made with the greatest gaiety, to be melancholy and silent. On our arrival, I did not look on Jala-Jala with the usual feelings of satisfaction. I had my poor patient placed in bed, and did not quit her room, hoping by my continual care to afford her some relief in her sufferings. But, alas! from day to day the malady made fearful progress. I was in despair. I wrote to Josephine, and sent a boat to Manilla for her to come and take care of her sister, who was most anxious to see her. The boat returned without her; but a letter from kind-hearted Josephine informed me that she was herself dangerously ill, and confined to her room, and could not even leave her bed; that she was very sorry for it, but I might assure Anna that they would soon be re-united, never again to be separated.

Fifty days—longer to me than a century—had scarcely elapsed since our return to Jala-Jala than all my hopes vanished. Death was approaching with rapid strides, and the fatal moment was at hand when I was to be separated from her whom I loved with such intensity. She preserved her senses to the last, and saw my profound melancholy, and my features altered by grief; and finding her last hour was near, she called me to her, and said: 'Adieu, my beloved Paul, adieu. Console thyself—we shall meet again in Heaven! Preserve thyself for the sake of our dear boy. When I shall be no more, return home to thy own country, to see thy aged mother. Never marry again, except in France, if thy mother requires thee to do so. Do not marry in the Philippines, for thou wilt never find a companion here to love thee as I have loved.' These words were the last which this good and gentle angel spoke. The most sacred ties, the tenderest and purest union, were then severed—my Anna was no more! I held her lifeless body clasped in my arms, as if I hoped by my caresses to recall her to life; but, alas! her destiny was decided! ...

For several days I continued in a thorough depression, unable to attend to anything, except to the cares which my son, then my only remaining consolation, required. Three weeks elapsed before I quitted the room in which my poor wife had expired. I then received a note from Josephine, in which she stated that her illness had grown worse. The note ended with these words: 'Come, my dear Paul; come to me: we shall weep together. I feel that your presence will afford some consolation.'

I did not hesitate to comply with the request of dear Josephine, for whom I entertained an affection as if for my own sister. My presence might prove a solace to her, and I myself felt that it would prove to me a great consolation to see a person who had so sincerely loved my Anna. The hope of being useful to her re-animated my courage a little. I left my house under the care of Prosper Vidie, an excellent friend, who during the last days of my wife's life had not quitted me, and departed, accompanied by my son.

After the first emotion which Josephine and I felt on meeting, and when we both had shed abundant tears, I examined her state. It required a strong effort on my part to conceal from her my anxiety, on finding her labouring under a most serious malady, and which gave me grounds for fearing that a fresh misfortune was not far distant. Alas! my forebodings were correct; for eight days afterwards poor Josephine expired in my arms, after the most poignant sufferings. What abundant sources of woe in so short a space of time! It required a constitution strong as mine was to bear up against such a number of sorrows, and not to fail under the burthen.

Paul P. de la Gironiere, *Twenty Years in the Philippines*, James Vizetkelly and Henry Vizetkelly, London, 1854, pp. 234 and 238–43.

24

Mrs Pryer in Sabah

NICHOLAS TARLING

Married women often led lonely and tedious lives, surrounded by servants who by their presence prevented them from doing more than issue instructions, as in the case of Noel Wynyard. How she coped depended on the woman's own character, interests, and inner resources, as we have already seen. Some were able to take an active interest in their husbands' affairs. Those who published are perhaps atypical, and this may be true also of those who wrote long descriptive letters and kept diaries. However, it is from these sources we get a glimpse of the day to day lives of the women concerned. Unfortunately, not written with an eye to publication, they contain much matter of a personal and family nature which tells us little about how they actually lived and much mundane repetitive material which tells us clearly that life was lived to a routine, as are most lives. The following extracts, therefore, are a selection which give some idea of what one woman experienced in her daily life.

Ada Pryer was the wife of Willam Pryer, founder of the town of Sandakan in North Borneo, now Sabah, and the British North Borneo Company's first Resident of the East Coast. In 1883, the year the Pryers married, Sandakan became the capital of North Borneo and W. H. Treacher moved there from the previous capital, Kudat. While in England in 1892, Pryer retired from the Company's service and formed the Development Corporation, which established an estate at the Byte, north of Sandakan. Until his death in 1899, he experimented with a number of crops. Ada Pryer's diary, as finally published a century later, begins in September 1893. Ada had published a book entitled *A Decade in Borneo* in 1893 so she also is perhaps not typical.

13th Oct [1893]:

JAMIE back from the Byte, called here for my letter to Willie—arrived at 12:30 noon cooked and had a meal and left for Kabeli at 2:15. A note from A. Walker who says they are getting rain at the Waterpark Estate almost daily.

14th Oct:

Willie returned by gobang from Kabeli: he had evidently had much more rain and thunder than we have had here in Sandakan. He is very well and quite satisfied with everything on the estate. We walked together to the Hughes returning to Claras' to dine and sleep.

15th Oct:

Rain last night and again this morning: a disagreeable warm muggy day: gardening vigorously this morning and planting out, pruning etc digging out all the gardenias and having them thrown away as they are most unsatisfactory get black blight which affects other plants and their blooming is most uncertain tho' I have given them great attention.

17th Oct:

Rain last night and again early this morning but it has cleared off a bit and allowed Willie to get comfortably to his gobang at Sea View from whence it takes him to the Byte. He left about 10am. At 11:30 there arrived a long letter from A. Walker, but nothing in it that needs attention especially as W. will be there in the next 4 or 5 hours, everything going on well. The migratory birds have arrived. There are a number of the lovely pure white egrets about following the cattle. Rain again at night.

18th Oct:

A soaking morning everything as damp and horrid as can be. Usop busy making me a bamboo frame to hang clothes on to dry over a charcoal fire, wish I had known about these convenient arrangements years ago it is such a nuisance when for days one can't dry ones clothes etc.

19th Oct:

No rain last night but it set in again at daylight today most tiresome, poor Willie will be in despair for men can't work in such weather, and it looks particularly bad Byte-wards. Feel as tho I shall have to retire to bed until all this rain is over or shall shut up the house and live by lamp light. Decidedly cold. Willie returned from the Byte about 2:30 the weather being so bad he was not able to do more than the Byte itself. He brought back with him a branch of coffee very fine large dark leaves and bunches of cherries clustering at every pair of leaves, biggest bunch of cherries nearly full size has 18; besides this, there are 5 other bunches, differing sizes, and 3 more showing diminutive blossoms.

20th Oct:

No rain, dull and cool, thunder prowling in the distance. Have been gardening vigorously and have exterminated all the hibiscus shrubs before importing new ones so as to get rid of the blight. Rain in the afternoon, fine later on. Usop has finished me the rottan stand over which to dry the damp clothes this rainy weather resembles a gigantic crinoline.

21st Oct:

Finer Day. Willie experimented on 1/2 oz. of gutta with Mr Collins 'Cervantine' the result being a very pure white colour. W. only took a very little gutta as the tree has a fruit on it and he wants the seed for planting. No doubt if there was still plenty of gutta in the country this 'cervantine' might be useful as it should command a high price the gutta prepared with it being a pure milk white far cleaner and nicer than any I have ever seen before. From fluid to a stiff congealed article it is easily simply and quickly converted....

2nd [Nov]:

A sprinkling of rain last night, we want it badly here today to lay dust and freshen up the gardens. Kabeli men come in for wages report sufficient rain on the Meade Estate. Lovely big coffee plants came across from Loong Piasow for Melenow, a thousand pities there were not plants like these put in at the Byte and Kabeli, old Hunter to blame for the horrid shrubby things that had to go in on these estates.

Pinson been up to see Willie on business, he voluntarily offered to put in $1000 if W. is starting a sugar mill.

3rd Nov:
    Ranee arrived from Singapore at 5.30am with mails of 29th Sept. Mrs Elton and Mrs v.d. Hoeven dined with us.

4th Nov:
    No rain yet, tho it looked cloudy last night. *Ranee* left at 11 am this morning for Europe. Mr and Mrs Hughes left us. We walked down to the Allards where we stopped and dined. A very dark night and we were very glad of the lantern to light us home. It rained heavily in the night.

5th Nov:
    Raining softly, does not seem likely to be a fine day.

6th Nov:
    A nice shower this morning from 6 to 7am but sun shining by 8. o.c. Willie starting for Melenow to see how Hartons

Another wet day.

coffee is doing. W. very pleased with the coffee which is looking healthy and vigorous. I walked up to see Mrs Hughes, it gets so soon dark now that I was glad of the light of the lantern which I made Allitian carry. We got back about 7:15.

7th Nov:

Walked down to Claras, was able to start early as it was a cloudy afternoon. Willie sent off to try and catch cattle. Returning from Claras' got caught in the rain and had to shelter in the club for a short time finally got home fairly well but the roads were dreadfully slippery and I was ankle deep in mud at some places. My face very swollen in consequence of a troublesome tooth. Sea pounding on the shore.

8th Nov:

Made my mind to have my horrid tooth out so sent for Dr Walker who took it out capitally. Mrs Rozzoli kindly came to help me through it. . . .

20th Dec:

Still no 'Memnon' and no news whatever about her. All sorts of speculations are rife as to what can have befallen her. Got out early as it was a cloudy afternoon. Went to the R.C. Mission and visited Mother Teresa and Fr. Verbrugge then to the Hughes whilst there the Shaws called and Mr Elton. Mrs S very elegant! After that made our way to the Allards, Clara not very well. Got home late and found poor A. Walker waiting for his dinner.

Henry Walker making all sorts of stupid muddles and mistakes over registering the mortgages on which we are making loans. Are told that the Banjer had such bad weather that a poor native woman died in consequence of sea sickness: also that the Ranee will be 3 days behind time as she had to lie by in consequence of bad weather. Went nowhere saw no one.

22nd Dec:

Rain again this morning at 5 am. Cleared off and sun came out at 7 am. so hope for a good day. A good day it was. Walked to the Allards.

23rd Dec:

Busy house cleaning 2nd day of it. Willie returned from the Byte. Went for a tramp on the Beatrice where it was quite dry and nice. No 'Memnon' nor any news of her, and no other steamer. People are beginning to talk of a famine. Potatoes have gone up from 6cts per catty to 12 cts and flour which is always 8cts has risen to 15 cts!!!

24th Dec:

A busy day making ready for Xmas. Went to church in the evening afterwards went to Govt. House and then to the Allards as he has fever and is rather bad. Dreadfully tired could hardly drag myself home with Willies assistance.

25th Dec:

Xmas day. Too done up to get to the early morning service, but was carried to church in the afternoon. The Pinsons and Rozzolis dined with us, a childrens party, they seemed to enjoy themselves much. The Allards not able to come. Ah Zin got bitten in bed by a rat who invaded his tempat tidor the child caught the rat by his tail and he then bit Ah Zin thro' the finger a rather sore place.

26th Dec:

A duller day than we have been having lately, for, tho' we have had a good deal of rain, the mornings have cleared when the sun rose and the days for the most part been bright. They tell me the flour will only hold out for a day or so, so unless a steamer soon turns up with supplies we shall have no bread!

27 Dec:

Father Verbrugge brought his boys (22) to a Xmas supper at 6 o.c. Before the feed the boys band performed for us on the lawns in front of the house. They are quite self taught and it is surprising how well they play. They gave us quite a musical recital of eleven tunes, the time and tune were in all cases excellent. Dominic is the band master. They had Snap dragon and were much pleased with that style of 'new pudding' especially the small silver pieces hidden amongst the raisins. Fr. Verbrugge stayed and dined with us. Just as he was leaving the mata mata galups arrived on the scene with a bull's eye lantern a man and a note from Mr. Jones. On opening the note found it contained my lost pearl ring and Willie's gold sleeve links which disappeared whilst we were at Loong Piasow in Sept last. Very glad indeed to have my ring back again and hope now we may find the rest of the missing shirt studs. The links and the ring were found in the possession of a man called 'Morah' who said he bought them, for the ring he gave $10 cheap! I value it at $80 and would not sell it for less.

28th Dec:

The Javanese a set of thieves all round not a man amongst them to be trusted! The mata-matas galup came and walked off Mr. Gani the Javanese Gardener as he is suspected of making away with them. I await fresh developments.

Willie has left for the Byte. We are both feeling quite well and fit this morning.

No steamer and the flour in the place is exhausted so Ah Siong could not bring us bread this morning.

Vezeer Singh reports that his Sikh helper is missing. He saw him last at 2 pm yesterday, has enquired amongst their mutual friends but has not heard of him. Strange! Can he have lost himself in the jungle or been bitten by a poisonous snake? If he does not turn up told Vezeer Singh to report to the Sikh Sergeant at 1 pm.

29th Dec:

Vezeer Singh's friend turned up all right, he had gone benighted in the forest stupid man. Called on Mrs. Walker last night. No steamer. Hear the mata matas when they walked off Mr. Gani went and searched his cot and found some socks or stockings (Sarong kahki) and handkerchiefs of ours amongst his barangs. Persistent rain but not very heavy. My poor Willie will have a wretched time at the Byte.

No rain last night for which I am duly thankful! a nice cool morning that promises to turn into a fine day. Mme Rozzoli and Mrs and Miss Shaw called last night. Ah Siong bought flour to make me a little bread tomorrow as none can now be got, he gave 20cts a catty!!! '*Ranee*' in at last, she brings news that the 'Memnon' is in Singapore, she broke her shaft when not far outside Hong Kong and sailed down to Singapore. The 'Normanby' has gone down not far outside Singapore the Capt. and his child lost but his wife saved. The 'Calypso' who went to the assistance of the 'Normanby' broke her shaft Devonhurst to be up here directly to connect with Hong Kong as the 'Memnon' will be a month in dock for repairs. Received London and China Expresses of 3 Nov: 10th: 17th: 24th.

Walked down to Claras. Very done up.

31st

In bed all day. Mme Rozzoli came to comfort me. Willie arrived back from the Byte, all his news good. He bought a fine lot of Manila Hemp. The Chinese inclined to learn Hemp making after seeing Augustine at work. We hope it will prove a very remunerative employment for Chinese tenants etc. Fr. Verbrugge dined with us. So ends the old year which has bought us many blessings for which we should be thankful tho' it has not been without its days of worry, still, these are passed and gone and hope for the future remains with us. May our ambitions and desires which are closely linked with the success of our adopted country be abundantly fulfilled.

January 1894 New Years Day

Willie opened his mail, all the news proved satisfactory and we begin the New Year full of fresh hope that the day is not far distant when the prospects of success so long deferred will be fulfilled. Courage, faith and hope are ours.

Willie gone to Kabeli, Mr. & Mrs. Hughes and the Governor. Everything there looking very well. Made Manila Hemp before their eyes. Willie got back by 7.30 Mme Rozzoli spent the day with me.

2nd Jan:

Willie bad with an attack of indigestion. We couldn't go to Govt. House dance. My ring case came off Gani and Morah pleaded guilty, they each got a year. Willie went to Sandakan got much news.

3rd Jan:

Fine day, no rain last night. Willie better. Called on Beestons, Dr. Walkers and Rozzolis....

13th Jan:

Torrents and deluges of rain during the night, it is the heaviest rain fall we have yet had and that is saying a good deal!!! One tremendous peal of thunder in the night. Everything is as damp as tho' recently wrung out of water. We have had to take down and dry the curtains and every garment has had to be hung over the rattan frames beneath which we have had the little clay baskets with charcoal fires in them. The matches in the night would not ignite altho they had been dried during the day and the candle wick wd not burn either so we had to light a lamp. The No 2 boys has been wholly occupied this morning drying and turning about the clothes over the fires! When will this dreadful state of things cease? I wonder if the sun is shining anywhere in the world? How desperately I wish we could see it.

14th Jan:

It ceased raining at 5 pm and was fine until 1.30 am at which time the N.E. wind failing it started to rain again and has done so right on till 3.30 pm to day. The only things that like this weather are the caladiums which are all flourishing. Willie gone to the Byte in the s.l. 'Belle' weather too rough for the gobang. Ah Chee made efforts to get there by boat Thursday and Friday but couldn't manage it, the wind blew him up at Ah Hings garden. By some stupidity Ah Chee failed to go with Willie this morning as was proposed. Very stupid of him to let such an opportunity slip. Very busy writing all day enlarging 'A Decade in Borneo' I mean to try if I can to do anything with Malayan folklore. Rain till about 3 o.c. when it cleared off so I was able to get out for a walk. Met Willie just back from the Byte, below the Barn Hill.

15th Jan:

A fine morning with sunshine, tho' of a rather watery character; delightful, we do hope the rains are now over for this season. They have been quite abnormal. I append the rain fall from the Byte which speaks for itself.

7th Jan	80	–	8th Jan	2:25
9th "	1:30	–	10th "	6:60
11th "	11:–	–	12th "	8:-
13th "	7:–	–	14th "	8

Total 44 inches 95 !!!!!!!!!!!! in eight days only.

A good day: went for a prowl about the town and met a good many people we wanted to see. *Banjermassing* left for Singapore. Roads had dried up considerably.

16th Jan:

Glorious fresh bright morning. No rain last night. Willie left for the Byte in his gobang. Towards mid-day clouded over to the S. but the N.E. wind dispersed the cloud. Busy copying out my chapter on Dusuns. The orchid men brought up the Palawan orchids and started to make a rough house for them. Everything is dropping to pieces from the effects of the long continued wet weather, boxes photo frames, the backs off hair brushes etc. no gum or glue can hold. Had a regular turn out airing all the clothes. The garden is dreadful no flowers and all the plants looking bad after the lashing of the incessant rain. Mrs. Hughes writes me that the Arensburg Tobacco Co. have determined to open a second Estate. Goodluck be with them and great success they can afford it and have good Managers to send up.

17th Jan:

A good day, my dear Willie will be revelling in the fine weather and getting no end of work done at the Byte. Mme Rozzoli Clara and Wilson came to see me. Afterwards went for a short walk and got wet through, only a short very sharp shower.

18th Jan:

Rained hard last night, for how long don't know. A fine morning....

Nicholas Tarling (ed.), *Mrs Pryer in Sabah*, University of Auckland Centre for Asian Studies, Resource Papers No. 1, Auckland, 1989, pp. 8–9, 12, 19–21, and 24–5.

25
A Missionary Wife in Sarawak

HARRIETTE McDOUGALL

Harriette McDougall was wife of the Right Reverend Francis Thomas McDougall, who arrived in Sarawak in 1848 to set up the Anglican mission there and who became the first Bishop of Labuan and Sarawak in 1856. The English adventurer James Brooke had made himself Rajah of Sarawak in September 1841. His suppression, in conjunction with the Royal Navy, of Malay and Iban 'piracy' had gained him a knighthood in 1847 and had made him a public hero in England. The McDougalls thus arrived in a very recently established European community of which Harriette was the only 'lady' after the other missionary family which had travelled with them left in 1849. She was not the only European woman, but the others were servants or of lower social class and did not appear in the very small Sarawak society composed of the Rajah and his few young officers. Visiting naval officers enlarged that society from time to time. As the years passed, other wives arrived, but at the time these letters were written Harriette remained 'first lady'.

Harriette wrote two books about Sarawak, but of more immediacy are her letters to her family, no doubt self-censored as such letters are, but presenting, nevertheless, a lively picture of her life as she led it.

HARRIETTE McDougall to her Mother, Mrs. Bunyon [August 1849]

Now tonight I thought I should have a long quiet evening for writing as Frank, Parr & Brereton dine on board the Brig with Capt. Farquhar who gives his farewell dinner to Sarawak today, but No,—Mr. Vogors, a very gentlemanly nice person travelling for his health on board the 'Albatross' petitioned to come & spend the day with me & I have had two middies up to tea besides, they are sitting reading in the room & I shall have to sit up tonight and write after they are gone. We have Capt. Farquhar staying in the house with us, sick & under Frank's care whom he prefers to his new ship's

The Mission-house, Harriette McDougall's home. From Harriette McDougall, *Letters from Sarawak Addressed to a Child*, Grant & Griffiths, London, 1854.

141

doctor. He is a very sailor–like, frank, & merry man & quite a gentleman which is not always the case with sailors—what a constant dose of sailors I get here, some are nice fellows like my juvenile ideas of the set, some are rude vulgar creatures who care for nothing but drinking and smoking. We have had a midshipman, Dyer by name, staying with us during the expedition, sick of intermittent fever, when he first came I was afraid, & Frank too, that he wd die in the house, however with care & nursing he got quite well & was no trouble through our moving. I was very glad he recovered but such a disagreable inmate I never had, a regular cub without manners or politeness of any kind—I was truly glad when after 3 weeks of him his senior Officer carried him off to his ship the Royalist, but last Saturday to my dismay he returned & without asking leave & saying how long he meant to stay, coolly took up his quarters with us again, my spirit has been just a little (riled) at his impudence. Capt. Farquhar has his former bedroom but he said he should sleep on a sofa & *here* this is a common thing, so I still have the young gentleman hanging about the house, & both Frank & I have plainly let him see that we are tired of him, but he does not care a bit & presents himself at meals & stretches himself in an easy chair with a book. I sometimes think how annoyed you wld feel, dear Mama at such an inroad; Frank who takes things so easily & is the most hospitable creature in the world cannot always stand Mr Dyer, little, vulgar man that he is—*to me* he is quite a trial. I shall soon be moved to tell him that I cannot be tormented with him any longer, but after being really his nurse & so kind to him while he was ill I feel loath to spoil it all by being angry, for if the broadest hints are lost on him & last night every sofa in the bouse, 3 were occupied & we always have the house full in the day—well it is only tomorrow & we shall be quiet again, but for Mr Dyer I do not know when we shall be quit of him as the Royalist remains here another month—I expect we shall have to tell Capt. Everest to take him back to his ship....

I cannot write to dearest Nelly this mail. She must be contented to read yours & Fanny's letters & to receive the warmest of mental kisses—Ah happy Frances to have you with her during her confinement, Aunt & Emily to manage the house & a good nurse to care for the eldest. If I have a living baby this time I shall become quite a Nurse for these native ayahs cannot be trusted ... wld you believe there is no woman in this place who will undertake a nurse's situation or any place of servitude—they are far too grand, I shall have to send to Singapore for a nurse by November which is an expensive business inasmuch as servants require higher wages here than at Singapore 'because it is dull'—Mrs. Hentig pays her Ayah 10 dollars a month which is nearly £2.10 of English money—she feeds herself like all servants here. I am not at all sorry dearest Mother that I am to have another baby so soon, it will be a great addition to my cares but at the same time Harry wants a companion. . . .

* * *

Harriette McDougall to her mother, Mrs Bunyon
[August or September 1849]

A few nights ago I had an article on music in the Edinburgh Review, it was almost like going to a concert. I went to bed quite excited—the books are a trouble to us, [they] are obliged to be all taken down off the shelves and rubbed every week. The ... of ... mildew stands over the bindings of some at the Weeks [end]. We are going to put glass windows in our little library on the hill to preserve the books. The weather now is perfection, our heavy rain is gone & the air is still, cool & pleasant early in the morning, it is even a little chilly & I sometimes come from school at 12 o'clock without opening my umbrella, the sun is so shady [?] Parasols are a mockery to this sun when it does shine but it is like a furnace heat then. I never walk out, Frank goes about all day & so do the English with only a pith hat covered with white calico, but I do not let Harry go out in the sun. . . .

* * *

Harriette McDougall to Ellen Robson
[About September or October 1849]

I put Harry in the Holland frock & tried to fancy it was Charles [her elder son, at school in England], but the young scamp is not much like his brother ... he wears an enormous number of frocks—as for my making him trowsers it will be a long time before I shall give myself that trouble ... what a bad workman I am, but 7 children & the prospect of an 8th, a husband and a house require plenty of needles and thread....

[Mr Jackson a magistrate from Singapore came in the Albatross for Frank to doctor him].... I always said this house on the hill wld be a Hospital & I think it is a v. suitable part of our Mission ... the old religious houses were always hospitals ... it is some expense for instance when the 'Royalist' sailors were here ill at the boat under Frank's care they made a considerable inroad into our Port wine wh was really necessary for their health & we have now for some weeks been without any wine at all ourselves wh is more wanted in this climate than in a colder one & spirits proportionately nasty & unhealthy. There ought to be a medical man—a hospital—where is the money to come from? In twenty years I expect this place will be much more complete but at present it is under a disadvantage of a new colony, money is all spent on it without a visible return & Rajah has no resource to set things going....

* * *

Harriette McDougall to her sister Ellen Bunyon
[Sometime after November 5th 1849]

I always go by the path when passing the Churchyard & then I slip in & visit my baby's grave. Frank has sown all over it a little scarlet creeper & it is already nearly covered with the delicate leaves; there are also 3 young orange trees growing on it the seeds having been set there by Frank one day when he was eating an orange as he passed. It pleases me to see how often Frank goes there. I find it out by the care he takes of these little plants, sprinkling them with charcoal etc. We are going to have 2 small wooden crosses put, one at the head, the other at the foot of the little mound; but although I have drawn a great many patterns, I find [I have] not yet made one to Frank's fancy.... Now I am quite well, strong again, I quite enjoy myself—every day I go to school from 10/12, I have at present only 2 girls (Julia & Nancy) besides my 4 little adopted children—but these 6 occupy 2 hours pretty well. I used to find them tedious, but now Peter & Mary begin to read a little & I can talk to them better—then at 1st we are very merry, but I keep a *rattan* & very necessary it is; well at 12 I come home & order the dinner & visit my chicken house & scold the servants & then I paint or work, more generally the latter until 1/2 past 4 when I go out walking. Harry and Elizabeth go at 3 or 4 if the day is [fine] & I meet them on the hill where Harry amuses himself with riding on planks or grubbing up the sand etc, the workmen leave at 5 so I am pretty sure to find Frank there also & we go home by the garden & Babu the gardener cuts me a piece of sugar cane which I suck all the way home. Then we dine & Harry comes in after dinner in his nightgown, sits by me in his high-chair & has a book of pictures to look at till 1/2 past 7 when he goes to bed & Frank walks up and down the balcony & *smokes* a *cigar* & I read, we have tea at 8, prayers at 9 & then we go to bed. Indeed you will be shocked to hear how long I sleep i.e. from 10 till 7, then I get up & run to the bath house & have a famous cold bath but I have given up any early rising till I am very strong again. Here is a long letter all about myself, yet to you, my darling, I think it will be interesting. I fear I cannot write to dearest Fanny by this mail, I must write to Wotton, they sent me a family letter beginning with Uncle Bick [The Rev. Edward Bickersteth. His wife was sister to Mrs. Bunyon, Harriette's mother] down to Harriette & I have only 1 day more, the Nemesis steams off on Saturday. Adieu, my darling, can't you draw an *interior* for me of the drawing room at Stratton, at least the only one I care for, Ever your own loving sister.

Harriette McDougall.
Frank's best love, Ah, Nelly, he is so kind & good.

* * *

Harriette McDougall to Eliza Bunyon
[December 1857]

[Edith has cut two teeth and has two more coming.] One day she was so poorly with them I mustered up courage and lanced her gums myself with my penknife. I was in a great fright and felt it to my backbone, but now I shall never be afraid to do it again, it relieved her immensely ... she is very backward I think with her teeth—19 months old!

* * *

Harriette McDougall to Ellen Robson
February 10th [1858]

Frank was staying with Governor Edwards [Governor of Labuan], who has an English housekeeper and maid—her niece. The house was consequently made to look as English as possible, with white curtains, toilettes, bedroom carpets, which Frank highly appreciated and since he returned a week ago, he has proposed several things to me which I may perhaps do *in time*, but when you have all the sewing for self, children and house to do, *prettinesses* go to the wall. I have to cover my sofas & chairs, make pillows, cover mattresses etc. etc. There is no tailor in the place as there used to be before the Chinese insurrection. [She mentions the kneeler along the Communion rail and the altar cloth also.] Lizzy [Chambers] will help but she has to make shirts for her husband since she married—a virtue I have never attained to. She has also made a surplice and contemplates another, besides jackets and neckties. Frank buys his wardrobe, I only pretend to mend or put in a pocket or hem.

* * *

Harriette McDougall to Eliza Bunyon
[1858; middle of the year.

Someone ran amuck up & down the village ... the Court was cleared in a trice, Peter (Middleton) nearly lost Brooke

146

trying to shoot the man, the whole village turned out and
the Chinese shut up their shops in a twinkling, our servants
who were in the village came rushing up to the house—'shut
the doors Ma'm, people are all fighting.' 'Who is fighting?'
'Oh I don't know, but there is something dreadful the matter'
—I could have horse whipped them all round, they looked
as white as cowards could, and there was poor little
Mrs. Hacket, not knowing the ways of the world here, all in a
tremble crying & wringing her hands—I assured her it was
doubtless nothing, laid her on the sofa & sprinkled her with
eau-de-cologne. It might have been serious to her in her
condition. The man was shot down after seriously wounding
a poor Chinese carpenter whom Frank went forthwith to
sew up—he was cut something like Bertha last Feb.—but not
so deep & he is mending. Today we have had another rush to
our house, some row amongst the Chinese at the sago factory I fancy, but forth with every body coins a story.... Frank
shouts to the carpenters and Stahl to go back to their work
instead of running to the village with loaded guns, and drives
Owen back to school—and I administered ... a glass of port
wine to Mrs. Channon. [Rest illegible]

McDougall Papers, MSS Pac. s104, Rhodes House Library, Oxford.

26
A Missionary in Burma

HENRY PARK COCHRANE

Missionaries were among the poorer members of the European
community while still drawn from an educated social class which
was admitted to colonial society, though somewhat on the fringe of
it. They were, in a sense, like poor relatives. They could not be
disowned by Europeans of the official, commercial, and planter
sectors for that would lower their prestige and that of the European
community in general. It was a matter of keeping up appearances,
as well as a matter of practicality. And yet missionaries were

expected to work among the ordinary people. The American missionary, Henry Cochrane (Passages 6 and 9), faced this dilemma when serving in Burma at the end of the nineteenth century.

MUCH has been said and written about 'living like the natives'.

Many have maintained that the missionaries should abandon their former mode of living, and adopt the customs and costume of the people among whom they labour. It is said that old maids know the most about the proper way to bring up children. It is interesting to note that advocates of this theory of missionary methods are men who never have been out of their native land, and have spent but little of their time in informing themselves as to the habits of uncivilized peoples. Prospective missionaries will do well to provide themselves with the customary outfit,—to meet their needs while finding an answer to the many-sided question,— how *do* the natives live?

For the present we will confine our investigations to Burma. Let us visit one of the native houses, and see for ourselves. Running the gauntlet of several snarling pariah dogs, we pass through the muddy door-yard, littered with banana leaves, munched sugar-cane, and waste from various sources. The house is set up on posts, several feet from the ground, affording a shady place below, to be shared by the family and the domestic animals. The floor overhead is of split bamboo or thin boards, with wide cracks through which all sweepings fall, and *kun*-chewers lazily spit without troubling themselves to get up. At the back part of the house a corner is partitioned off for the cook-room, the stove being a very shallow box filled with earth. The cooking is done in earthen chatties over the smoky open fires. Near the cook-room is an open space where household utensils are washed and the babies bathed, the water falling through the open floor to the ground below. Month after month and year after year this filthy habit goes on, forming a cesspool from which a foul stench arises, offensive to nostrils and dangerous to health. This foul pool is a paradise for their ducks, its slime being tracked all over the place. The house is small, its thatched roof coming down so low as hardly to leave room for a full-sized door. Many of these homes have no outbuildings whatever, trusting to the pariah dogs and the crows,—the village scavengers,—to keep the premises in a sanitary condition. Some of the well-to-do Burmans live in larger better houses; showing that not only is it impracticable for Europeans to live like the natives, but that natives when able, find it wise to live like Europeans. This is a tropical climate, with the temperature at 112° in the shade on the day these words were written. It would be almost suicidal for Europeans to attempt to live in such houses, even under the best sanitary conditions possible. Missionaries have lived for a time in such houses, from force of circumstances, but always to the detriment of health, sometimes with very serious consequences. To a stranger, European 'bungalows' in the tropics seem needlessly large. 'Globe-trotters' in general, and sometimes representatives of missionary societies, it is to be feared, visiting the tropics in the coolest season,—carry away this impression with them. In New England there is a saying 'You must summer him and winter him' to find out the real worth of a man or beast. Could all who visit the tropics, or presume to write of conditions in the tropics,—spend a whole year in such a climate critics would be few, and funds for seemingly expensive, though necessary buildings less grudgingly given.

They who urge that Europeans should *clothe* like the natives would surely allow exceptions to the rule, on closer study of native habits.

Among some of the tribes of Burma the question of wardrobe and latest style would be easily solved. Clothing like such natives would greatly reduce the expense for 'outfit.' Two strips of cotton cloth, one for the head, the other for the loins, would meet all requirements even on state occasions. But apart from all questions of common decency, it is to be seriously doubted whether the European would enjoy 'sailing under bare poles' in a tropical sun.

The railway trains are provided with first, second, and third-class compartments. Officials and wealthy business men travel first-class. Less fortunate Europeans, and people of mixed race but with European habits travel second-class. Natives, as a rule, go third-class,—but the rule has many exceptions. Not to speak of well-to-do Burmans and Chinese, who, though unobjectionable in dress,—are inveterate smokers, the 'chetties,' or money-lenders invariably travel second-class. They are the wealthiest men in the country, but with the exception of coolies,—they wear the least clothing and are the most offensive in their habits. The missionaries, whether on private or mission business, being unable to bear the expense of the higher class, and striving to save for the society which they represent, travel second-class. Now that many very objectionable natives have taken to riding second-class, it is no longer respectable for Europeans, except on rare occasions when the train is not crowded. For my own part, I seriously doubt whether this habit, on the part of American missionaries, of taking an inferior place among so-called 'Europeans,' is a wise policy.

Henry Park Cochrane, *Among the Burmans: A Record of Fifteen Years of Work and Its Fruitage*, Fleming H. Revell Company, New York, 1904, pp. 26–30.

Social and Community Life

THE social life of Europeans in colonial South-East Asia was at once more active and frenetic than many of them would have enjoyed at home, yet more confined and incestuous. Again, circumstances varied according to time and place. Emily Innes in muddy, isolated Langat in the mid-1870s had practically no social life; Ada Pryer in Sandakan, the North Borneo capital in 1893, had a more interesting social life. Harriette McDougall, as the one European 'lady' in Sarawak, for many years was confined to the role of hostess in an otherwise all-male society. Other European women of lower social class lived in Sarawak, but she could not mix with them socially as equals. Only when other female missionaries and the wives of government officers and the wife of the manager of the Borneo Company arrived did her social circle expand. Margaret Brooke's social horizon was circumscribed by her position as Ranee. As the twentieth century progressed, social restrictions based on occupation and class became less rigid; those based on race persisted, although cultural differences also accounted for the awkwardness experienced at social occasions where Europeans mixed with other races.

Men also faced social barriers, based more upon occupational hierarchies than those imposed by social class. Men in plantation communities like those described by Székely and Lulofs (Passages 28 and 29) came from a variety of national and social backgrounds. Székely, for example, was a Hungarian working in a Dutch colony. Social structure was imposed by the hierarchies of management. Even those were of little consequence in a remote outpost where only two or three Europeans lived. Conversely, a small community could

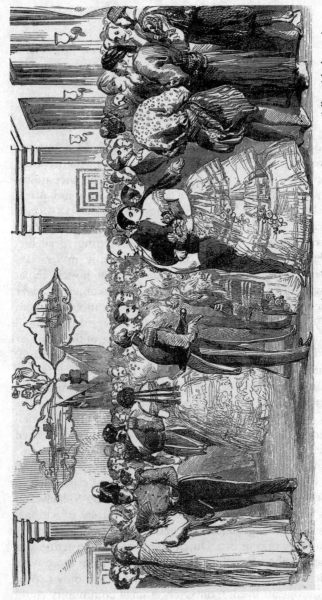

Balls, garden parties, and formal gatherings were occasions where the European community met socially with the native élite.

also be rent by jealousy, intrigue, and ill-feeling which divided the community socially. At the risk of being accused of sexism, it does appear that such divisions were more frequent when wives appeared on the scene, as may be seen in Passages 34 and 35.

The centre of European activity in any colonial outpost was the Club. Although it probably reached its apotheosis among the British, European social and sporting clubs were to be found throughout South-East Asia. The Club was where Europeans, who in their occupational and public life had to maintain a facade of correctness, probity, and superiority, could relax among their fellows, lower their guard and do and say things unacceptable outside its bounds. It was this as much as racial feeling which excluded even Europeanized natives from the Club. The local staff of the club were a different matter. Like servants in households, they were part of the background: and, for the most part, they appear to have accepted the antics of their masters with a mixture of indifference and bemused tolerance, as being the way Europeans behaved. A large proportion of the following passages refer to the Club because for so many Europeans in colonial South-East Asia the Club was the social centre.

In larger European communities, as found in cities like Batavia, Bangkok, Saigon, and Singapore, social occasions were more varied, especially as the twentieth century progressed. Hotels held dances and eating out at the major hotels was popular. The arrival of the automobile made possible excursions and picnics on a scale not possible before. In Singapore, as we see from Buckley (Passage 38), the British passion for amateur dramatics found early expression. And everywhere the Europeans played sport, usually centred on the Club. Tennis courts were established wherever possible. The British found cricket adaptive to the tropics and by the 1930s other sports were increasingly popular. Government, the military, and the commercial and banking houses employed a large number of young bachelors who formed teams and competed. Finally, horse racing attracted a following from all races and classes in the major centres and could cause dissension in a small European community (Passage 31).

The European population, married and unmarried, was largely a young one and relatively well paid. It had leisure, because servants carried out the household chores and minded any children, so that an active social life was easily sustained. In contrast to the limitations upon social life imposed in the pioneering stage of colonialism, the image of European social life that has persisted in the modern mind is based upon this later period—the 1920s and 1930s—and immediately post-war.

Many Europeans led more varied social lives than these passages suggest. Those in Government were required to attend important state occasions, like the ball to entertain Lord Dalhousie, the Governor-General of India, illustrated here. On many occasions leading members of the native communities would be invited to garden parties and formal gatherings; in return they would entertain leading members of the foreign community. This was particularly so where traditional ruling structures survived, as in the Malay States, or where leading Chinese merchants in Singapore entertained for reasons which were at once social, political, and commercial. Europeans might also be invited to Asian weddings or were expected to pay their respects on important occasions like Chinese New Year or the Muslim celebrations ending the fasting month of Ramadan. District officers and commercial agents were also involved in similar functions at the local level. Although in this volume we are concerned with the social life of Europeans among Europeans, this cross-cultural dimension is evident in some of the passages. However, many Europeans found these occasions stilted and uncomfortable and more a duty than a pleasure. Thus, European social life has been defined as just that: occasions when Europeans socialized amongst themselves.

Nevertheless, intimate relationships did develop between Europeans and Asians, in particular between European men and Asian women, and produced what Alec Waugh in 1930 called the problem of 'the brown woman' (Alec Waugh, *Hot*

Countries, The Literary Guild, New York, 1930, pp. 198–9). He was referring to the practice of white men taking local mistresses. Condemned by Christian churches and missionaries, it was a practice widely tolerated; even encouraged in some instances. The obverse, local men taking white mistresses, evoked outrage in the few instances it occurred; nor was the marriage of white women to Asian men condoned. Full legal marriages between white men and local women were also rare and usually condemned the couple to social marginalization on the fringes of white society.

These instances would appear to reflect racialist attitudes amongst white colonials, and they did. But mixed marriages were equally abhorrent to Asian communities, so that mixed couples might be accepted by neither community; and their offspring, as Eurasians, were also of neither one community nor another. Nevertheless, liaisons occurred and attitudes towards them were not uniform, differing according to both time and place. To generalize, miscegenation appears to have been more acceptable in the Philippines, where by the end of the Spanish period there was a large *mestizo* population and where Filipinos and Spaniards shared a common religion in Christianity; and also in French Indo-China, where, officially, cultural assimilation was the policy and French citizenship could be acquired by accultured natives.

Attitudes everywhere were affected by the size and stability of the European community. Until the late nineteenth century, there were few European women, especially in remote areas, and relationships between European men and local women were common. Some employers regarded it as desirable for a new man to acquire a 'sleeping dictionary' who would introduce him to the language and customs of the country; especially as marriage was not commonly permitted during the first ten years of employment. Sexual relations between Asians and Europeans have been also power relations. The dominant white males in colonial society claimed almost a proprietary right over the women of the colonized. This was not so much a racial matter as one of power and prestige and might be found within the class structure of European societies. Moreover, the sexual mores and customs of at least some Asian peoples were freer and less guilt-ridden than those of Europe, women's role was often subservient and forms of concubinage socially acceptable. It was inevitable that liaisons occurred. It was a fact of European life and society in South-East Asia—at once condoned and condemned (for Malaya, for example, see 'European Men and Asian Women', Chapter 8 of John G. Butcher, *The British in Malaya 1880–1941*, pp. 193–222. Also the short stories of Somerset Maugham. See, too, Passage 40).

The relationship between European and Asian women was also a power relationship. European wives who would not have considered employing servants at home, found themselves mistresses of households of servants (see, for example, Noel Wynyard's comments in Passage 12). Where a servant was retained for many years, strong bonds could develop. As is often the case, emotions and feelings are given expression more readily in fiction than in other writing. It is an aspect of the European experience that is easily forgotten, and so we have an example from Madelon Lulof's novel *Rubber* (Passage 41).

27
Christmas Festivities in Northern Thailand

NOEL WYNYARD

Noel Wynyard (Passages 5, 12, and 15) attended with her husband the Christmas festivities at their Club in northern Thailand, where the largely bachelor company behaved in the manner which might be expected; presided over a more decorous dinner party at home; and enjoyed a moment of triumph at the clay pigeon shoot. Read in conjunction with Passage 15 we can appreciate why she anticipated with such eagerness the round of social activities at Christmas and New Year.

TIME was slowly drawing on towards Christmas, and with it work seemed to increase. I had heard for years of the famous parties that took place at this time of year, and longed to take part in all the festivities; but things did not look very hopeful, in fact if work went to schedule we should be about as far away from station as was possible on Christmas Day. In the end however, we found ourselves aboard the train, and actually arrived in station late on Christmas Eve.

We boarded the train early in the morning when it was distinctly cold, and I am afraid that my trousered legs rather agitated several elderly gentlemen who were travelling north for a holiday from their comparatively civilized town of Bangkok; but they had to put up with being shocked, for I had no clothes that were both warm and feminine. As we had contemplated a Christmas in the jungle, all our stores had been dispatched there, and we arrived home after a month's absence to find a depressingly cheerless house, and a very empty larder. This in the ordinary circumstances would not have mattered in the least had we been alone, but we had, unfortunately for him, picked up a stray guest on the train

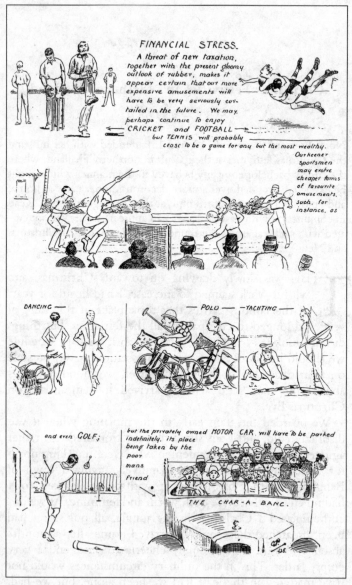

The importance of sporting activities to expatriates in the inter-war period is demonstrated in this cartoon.

who had been invited to take part in the festivities by some one who had inadvertently forgotten to arrange quarters for him. We did what we could, but I am afraid that we were only able to entertain him very frugally, although he was a perfect guest and most polite about it.

Gathered together that evening at the Club, we totalled about twenty-five, of whom twenty-two were men. This seemed a tremendous number, as the average was not more than five to ten at the outside, but when one accepted it as almost the entire white population of the up-country, with a few visitors from Bangkok to swell the numbers, it was not a very great company of exiles. After a great deal of chat and a countless number of rounds of drinks we dispersed to our own houses to dinner, and a moderately early bed in preparation for to-morrow's festivities.

In the morning we all met again at the Club, where things were soon in full swing. Some people were practising polo, others were engaged in golf, squash, or billiards competitions, and the inevitable few were gathered in 'the circle' having a few hairs from the dog's back. One of the things that struck me most about the life generally was the enormous amount of liquor that was consumed. One always hears of the East as a sink of iniquity and reads of tough guys whose lives are made up of licentiousness, the seduction of others' wives, a little murder, and a lot of delirium tremens. Some places may own such a reputation, but certainly not this part of the world, where I was startled to find drinks sunk not by the glass, but almost, as it were, by the bottle with very little appreciable effect. I found this rather disconcerting, as the few women who were there were expected to do their little bit to avoid an up-stage reputation. Seeing that one drink of anything alcoholic gave me a strange feeling in the region of the knees, I thought out a plan of action whereby, with sleight-of-hand practice, I might be able to hold my own with the best and get away with it. My first essay in the art, however, was perceived by my husband, who gave me the most devastating glare, at which I abandoned my rather clumsy efforts, gathering that such a thing was not done.

After that I used to have two drinks, become quite hilarious and no doubt imbecile, go to bed with a splitting headache and rue the morn. How one must suffer to be conventional.

It was Christmas Day, and dinner at night was a grand show held at the Club. Hors-d'œuvres, soup, turkey, plum pudding, and dessert, laced with sherry, beer, champagne, whisky in some cases, and a variety of liqueurs. The long table was decorated with crackers, flowers, and balloons, and the fun was fast and furious. Speeches, mostly unheard or howled down, toasts, invariably drunk with the greatest enthusiasm, songs and recitations of excellent mimicry kept us going until midnight, when we all repaired to the airless squash-court, there to dance to the strains of the gramophone. With only a meagre proportion of women to men, the floor was almost entirely occupied by braces of men. Most men are poor dancers, empire-builders that is to say, but when many pairs of empire-builders get under weigh together on a squash-court floor on Christmas night, dancing may start, but prancing and hopping follows, Soccer barges soon hold sway (very much the sway) until Rugger reigns triumphant over all. In the intervals of dancing more than half the company was seated on the floor, backs to the wall, gulping their drinks, an irresistible lure. Just before the International a concerted rush was made by the standers, each at their chosen sitter, whose feet were seized and dragged thus in a sitting position to the other end of the court. Kicking, howling, struggling, bewailing capsized drinks, some were soon sitting on the heads of their respective attackers, whilst the one phlegmatic and unroused person present was enabled to reach the wall *sans peur, sans reproche*, but drink *á la main*. Then Rugger. After several mighty scrums nothing was left but a writhing mass of humanity laughing weakly on the floor, from which wives finally extricated husbands and set off for home leaving the brighter bachelor element to continue the party in their own unhampered style. A few hours later, I am told, they decided to retire to bed also, and one, the owner of a large car, offered several others a lift, but found that he was incapable of giving it to them owing to the idiosyncrasies of the steering, which persisted in taking him anywhere but on the road. The wheel was handed over to one of the passengers in little better condition, and he in turn ceded to another, but during the exchange of seats the owner had inadvertently been forgotten, and had been left vacillating in an uncertain manner in the middle of the road. The new driver, instead of putting his foot on to the brake at a hairpin bend, missed it and rammed home the accelerator, which was just too bad, as the car bounded on the same tack and careered wildly into the nearest house, entirely annihilating it. At that, slightly sobered, they began to look round for the owner, and remembered that they had forgotten him. So within ten minutes of leaving, they were back with his car smashed, but just runnable, and a lame explanation.

Two or three evenings before the New Year we decided to give a dinner in our bungalow, as we had been out in the jungle so much and had therefore had very little chance of entertaining. The main rooms were not large enough to hold every one, so we arranged to have dinner on the balcony. The house itself was one of the nicest up-country, constructed of stone and concrete instead of the usual hot wood; not only was it cooler in itself, but it was situated in an excellent position over a mile out of the town on the edge of the *padi*-fields, looking straight across on to the low range of hills that surrounded the plain. The square balcony stuck out over the porch, and directly in front of it was a large lotus-lily pond covered at this season with a mass of waxen flowers. We were so exposed that the night air was fresh and cool, unlike the stuffy, shut-in houses in the town, and the air was faintly scented with the smell of flowering shrubs in the garden below.

The light problem was rather difficult, as there was no roof from which we could hang lamps; however, we found a solution by erecting light poles at regular intervals all round the rail of the veranda, between which was stretched a wire, that suspended dozens of brilliantly coloured Chinese lanterns.

The effect was really lovely, for they gave out only faint diffused light, just enough to enable us to dine in comfort and yet not so bright as to detract attention from the quiet splendour of the night. Swaying gently to and fro in the wind, they looked like large golden Cape gooseberries. The difficult thing about a dinner party in the East is the similarity of the food. The menu always seems to be the same: soup, fish, duck, and ice-cream; variety being almost impossible to achieve owing to the limitation of the cook's knowledge and the impossibility of obtaining anything out of the ordinary. In the normal course of events this would not be too bad—that is if the dinner were a pre-arranged show—but in the East things are so informal that one may order dinner for two on leaving for the Club at five o'clock, and return three or four hours later with six extra people, and the admirable cook, instead of giving notice, provides a perfect meal in the space of about half an hour.

After much cogitation, we finally decided on a menu. Pumpkin soup, a delicious *consommé*, pale orange in colour, and foolproof from the cook's point of view. Two large dishes of a particular kind of fish cooked in Chinese fashion, served whole, beautifully decorated and masked with a highly spiced sauce. The *pièce de résistance* was a boned goose. I have never seen a better piece of culinary achievement outside London; even the legs and wings were stuffed, and the contours were so religiously observed that no one guessed that it was more than the ordinary roast bird until it was carved.

It was glazed and beautifully ornamented, and when served with potatoes and vegetables proved a very popular dish. The sweet was chocolate russe, which was followed by dessert and home-made crystallized fruit, tangerines, grapes, litchis, and mangosteens. Coffee was made from a particular recipe as drunk by the Dutch and learned in Sumatra. It all sounds rather rich and sweet in comparison with the ordinary English dinner, especially for the male guests, who formed a large majority that night, but at least two hours had been spent in the customary manner before dinner in consuming drinks, of which gin was the chief constituent and appetiser, and in eating a variety of hors-d'œuvres that are salty and spiced enough to make even the most hardened palate desire something sweet.

The decoration of the table took a considerable time. Not only were there large central vases to arrange, but the entire surface of the table was intricately patterned with tiny blossoms of all colours woven into fantastic designs. The green organdie mats gave a good foundation, and we were able to carry out the embroidered design in mauve, orchid-like water-lilies, various coloured leaves and little circles of tiny yellow daisies. Groups of pale pink hibiscus stood at each corner, and small, sweet-scented lilies outlined the border. Although there were but ten guests, an enormous amount of preparation was necessary; three cooks worked hard all day, and in the evening four boys were needed to keep things going smoothly without any annoying waits.

After dinner we danced for a bit, but this became a little tiring, as there were only two women to ten men; then some one suggested *vingt-et-un*, but it was more than half an hour before we were able to muster the guests, who were, by this time, clustered round the open brick fire (one of two of its kind in the station) at the end of the room. The fireplace emptied, the rest of us in the room were able to be warmed by the glow, for it was very cold, well below 50°, and the day had been hot. Seated at the *vingt-et-un* table, I agreed to the proposed stakes without giving them a thought, and, taking the bank for the first round, managed to lose £3 in the same number of minutes. Luckily for me, I about evened this out by the end of the evening.

The clay-pigeon shoot was one of the best sporting events, and amongst the men was keenly looked forward to. The cups provided were for inter-firm, inter-station, and individual merits. It was held one morning, and the whole station turned out to watch. As most people were keen game-shots, big scores were expected, but, contrary to expectations, nobody did very much, and I think I am right in saying that four birds out of ten singles was the greatest tally of the morning. I was sitting watching the preparations, talking to one who was astounded to learn that I owned and could

use a revolver larger than his own—in fact, my father's old
Army .455. He disbelieved me in no uncertain nor quite polite
terms, and scoffingly asked me if I could use a twelve-bore. I
gave a nervous 'Yes', remembering the one occasion I had
had one in my hands some time before in England, when
two rabbits stared at the scattering ground 3 yards away for a
second before bolting to safety.

He immediately pressed a gun upon me, telling me to
show him. I couldn't retire. The shooting had not yet started
and I had no idea what a clay pigeon looked like. I had a
confused notion of a china decoy pushed up from the bowels
of the earth on the end of a stick by the coolie in the pit
behind the tin shield. The range was about 10 yards, so,
though in no way confident, I had hopes. If I held the gun to
my shoulder with the safety-catch off and then gave the
command for the bird to appear, it should be easy enough,
and I was told that some beginners often shot that way, and
even older hands. It was allowed.

I took a firm stance with my right leg at an acute angle to
the ground, the gun weighing ten times its normal, a cold,
leaden feeling in my inside, barrels wavering between one
end of the tin and the other, and intimated that I was ready.
Some one behind me gave the word. There was a loud snap
and a wild whirring as a black object whistled through the air
giving me the fright of my life. My jangled nerves jerked
both my arms; there was a deafening explosion and I was
conscious of pain as though a large blacksmith had hit me
with a larger hammer hard on the right biceps. A chorus of
acclamation broke from the bystanders, and a quiet voice
behind me said: 'Well done, but hold the gun tight into
your shoulder next time.' My husband was evidently under
the delusion that I was contemplating having another shot,
to show, I suppose, that my first *gaffe* was, after all, only
a *gaffe* and not habitual to me. Strange gun, and all
that. Nerves, due to the crowd. With a feeling of hurt that
a loving husband should ask his wife to make another fool
of herself, I looked pleadingly at him and said: 'What again?
Not me.'

'Go on, you must have the other barrel.' He said it smilingly.

That smile irritated a bit. 'Was that the pigeon?' I asked.

'Of course it was. What d'you think?' He found the situation amusing.

'You great ass, why didn't you warn me it whistled out into the air like a confounded rocket? It scared a year's growth out of me. I might have killed some one.' Definitely peeved I was.

'Hush! Don't let on. It looked like a dam' fine shot.'

'Did I hit it, then?' Not so peeved now.

'Of course you did. Now do it again.'

This time I knew what was coming and prepared myself for the hideous roar and kick with dread. I hugged the gun into my shoulder with all my strength and breathed deeply. The word was given. Again the snap and the whirr. I pulled the nearest trigger at once. There was a click. I looked up and saw no black object where a bird should have been soaring into the sky over to starboard. Instead, out of the corner of my eye, I caught sight of something hurtling low over the ground on my port quarter. By this time nothing about clay-pigeon shooting had power to surprise me. I was irritated instead and, with a spasmodic jerk, pulled the other trigger. I could only just reach it, but the effort to do so must have rightly aligned the gun, for I opened my eyes to find myself being borne down upon by a small crowd of congratulatory onlookers. I had apparently smashed the other bird too! With one cheek pale with excitement and the other reddening from the hard-hitting, beastly gun, I approached my scorner very scornful and handed him the gun. All I could find to say was: 'Nice gun. Thanks.' I think he still thinks I can shoot!

With gaiety, fun, and games, and very late parties night after night, time passed rapidly towards New Year, when people began fading away back to their work in the jungle, in Chiengmai, and down in Bangkok.

Noel Wynyard, *Durian: A Siamese Interlude*, Oxford University Press, London, 1939, pp. 158–68.

28
Cabaret Night at Kwala Batu

LADISLAO SZÉKELY

The planters' club at Kwala Batu in East Sumatra, described here
by Ladislao Székely (Passages, 2, 10, and 21) was predominantly
male, although two senior managers were married. The presence of
these two ladies had some effect upon the manners of the men, but
on the evening in question the Club was to enjoy for the first time in
its history a performance by two Australian dancers, the first young,
attractive white women its members had seen for a long time.

THE Club was festively decorated. Three funny oil
lamps and sixteen Japanese lanterns, suspended on
wires, shed a lavish light over the scene. The wooden
pillars that supported the roof of palm trees were draped in
red cloth; the stage decorated with red–white–and–blue flags,
and five kitchen lamps with mirrors illuminated the platform.
On the wall, wreathed with palm leaves, hung a picture of
Queen Wilhelmina in her youth.

Over the entrance, a transparency made of cardboard and
red paper bore the inscription 'Welcome.' ... As the hall had
no ceiling, the sooty rafters unfortunately caught one's eye:
Nothing could be done about that for the present, and
besides the place was thus more airy. Only, when there was a
breeze, the soot fell into the glasses. This lack of beauty, however, was balanced by the bar, which was filled to the last
inch with every sort of drink, and by the huge chest standing
behind the bar, whose capacious interior contained valuable
treasures. A large placard said that for the day's festive occasion, as a great exception, ice had been procured so that ice-
cooled drinks were obtainable, and this could truly be
considered as a special achievement in this God-forsaken
region.

From the standpoint of moral conduct, too, the Club
Committee had taken special precautions. Large placards
beside the piano invited the honourable members, with due
consideration for the evening, to refrain from pouring drinks

into the piano and, as long as the ladies were present, to undo only two buttons of their shirts.

When Dwars and I arrived, the Club was still empty. The white-clad, Javan-Malay staff of the Club were still squatting sleepily in the corners. The *mandur*, the black head-boy, was just holding his final inspection of glasses and drinks.

The evening promised to be a good one. The two Turner Sisters had arrived for a starring performance: they were to delight the public with modern and classical dances. Nothing like it had ever been done in Kwala Batu. White dancers out here in the wilds!

Dwars was excited about the coming entertainment.

Now the first carriage, a sulky, drove up. Two planters, their white suits buttoned to the chin, climbed out. Then came a second and a third carriage. The Club began noisily to fill. The carriages brought a constant stream of well-shaven men in dazzling white suits. All of them were young, all longed for a little diversion, for some life, for white women.

Dwars introduced me to my new colleagues. They shook me by the hand, asked what sort of a crossing from Europe I had had, and how life was at home now. 'At home' meant not so much in Germany, in Holland, in England or in Hungary: 'at home' was simply Europe. The old home. The cool country, where there was spring, summer, autumn and winter. Where had stood the cradle of the whites. Frontiers, languages and customs had become blurred in this assembly. Here all were Europeans of one nationality: they were whites. The country that spelled their home was Europe.

Now Passé, the little Frenchman, ran to the piano and drew a snappy ragtime out the hoarse old instrument. Gryseels, that 'original,' tried to drown the music with his powerful bass. And Van der Werff felt himself called to transform a ragtime into a war dance of the natives. Von Markenheim alone, popularly dubbed 'Crown Prince,' watched the goings-on of these plebeians with aristocratic contempt. When he was still a lieutenant in the Guards ... Woods, who had been a sailor on an English boat and was exceedingly proud of the snakes and ballet-girls tattooed on his arms and chest, had been vying with Rossier as to who could drink the most whiskey, and Rossier as a Belgian had not been able to keep up with the Briton; soon after the start he had succumbed and now lay sound asleep on the billiard table.

Gradually the notabilities also arrived. A Ford with a sickly wheeze rattled to a halt outside the club house: Mr. Schweers and his wife. Fourteen years ago, straddling on beams, with axe in hand, he had earned his daily bread. Today he was Head Manager, Tuan Besar, a big tuan.

'His share of the profits last year amounted to one hundred and forty thousand guilders,' Dwars whispered in my ear. 'He can barely read and write, but that isn't important out here. Here you've got to talk big and have a hard grip.'

Mrs. Schweers was a corpulent, chubby-faced Dutch beauty of uncertain age. Full of pride and regal dignity, she gazed about her.

The hilarity abated for a while. The shirts which had been unbuttoned lower than was permitted were fastened: a *mem*, a white woman, had arrived, and she was entitled to a proper respect.

Now my employer, Mr. Klaassen, the man who had promised to teach me good manners, made his appearance. His shirt had five buttons. Ours had six. For we were only little tuans; *tuwan ketjils*. The one—the big tuan—commands, and the other—the little tuan—carries out the command. And that makes all the difference. Not only at work, but socially too. A big tuan who thinks something of his position, will not immediately associate with little tuans, not even if the big tuan was a coachman at home and the little tuan a Count. If a little tuan is suddenly made a big tuan, the situation changes immediately. The comrade with whom one was on friendly terms, straight away becomes a common, arrogant Tuan Besar, in whose presence one must stand at attention.

My boss was joining the Schweers couple. The people of rank held together.

The 'Controller' of the district with his wife had also

arrived. His white shirt was adorned with white lacings. He was a regular Tuan Besar! He belonged to the Government, he was the Supreme Judge of the district, the commander-in-chief of the armed force and of the constabulary, the so-called 'elder brother of the radshas.' It was the law that gave him this title, and it signified that it would be advisable for the radshas to follow the orders and counsels of their elder brother.

The Controller had been transferred here from the island of Nias. There he had been the only European in the whole region, and now he was obviously enjoying his civilized surroundings. His wife was a pale, delicate creature who dropped asleep every few moments. Starting up when she had been dozing, her glance would always meet the reproachful glance of her husband, and her tired eyes would gaze imploring at the strong, healthy man. She looked as if she would ask his forgiveness for daring to be sick, for having dared to get malaria on the marshy island of Nias, for having lost her first child on the island of Timor among the Alfurs when her husband was on an expedition, when there was no doctor within three days' journey—she had had hysteria when she had to make the little coffin with her own hands and bury the child. The poor woman seemed to be asking forgiveness because she knew that she was a burden to her big, strong husband who wanted to become 'Assistant Resident,' 'Resident,' and finally Governor.

Terhall, too, made his appearance. He was neither a big tuan, nor a little tuan. He was a quill-driver, the guardian of secret documents, and so he did not belong to the little tuans of the plantation. But neither did he belong to the big ones.

Finally the attraction of the evening arrived in a flower-wreathed, squeaking and puffing Ford. The President of the Club, a Tuan Besar from the neighborhood, hurried out courteously to welcome the two pretty Australian girls. Laughing in high spirits, they climbed out of the parade car and, utterly unembarrassed, their glances roamed over the suddenly silent farmers, who gaped at them with covetous eyes. The President strode proudly beside the smiling artistes and led them to the store-room which had been transformed into a cloak room. The *tapeur*, too, a half-caste Indian, aroused considerable attention in his dinner jacket which was an unaccustomed sight here. Through the wilds was suddenly wafted the breath of fashionable life, scent, make-up, a dinner jacket ... ! Von Markenheim's tired eyes beamed....

The young people took their seats, the hall grew silent, and only the barefooted club boys went on serving, soundless as phantoms.

The music started with an old, well-known tango tune. On the billiard table Rossier awoke for a second, snored and went on sleeping.

The curtain went up: the girls appeared dressed as cowboys. With loud shouts the enthusiastic crowd clapped their hands. The girls performed a wild west tango, clanking their spurs and waving their broad-brimmed hats. The curtain fell and boisterous applause surged through the hall. The tapeur hammered like a maniac on the pitifully weak piano.

Other numbers followed. Dressed now as rococo ladies, now as milkmaids, now as chimney-sweeps, the sisters whirled round, dancing the tango, a ragtime and sentimental waltzes as long as their strength held out. The public in its enthusiasm banged on the tables and shouted for beer.

Rossier woke up, thinking there must be some scuffle in progress.

Mr. Schweers' wife stood up with an indignant look and, enraged, began talking at the wife of the Controller, who acted as if she were listening, but to herself thought how much better she would feel lying in bed at home and sleeping. Mr. Schweers and the Controller, forgetting their dignity, roared like maniacs, while Mrs. Schweers dragged the small, limp Controller's wife after her. The men followed them whether they liked it or not, but in going they peered covetously back at the dancing girls.

Presently the engine of the croaking old Ford began moving and the car rattled off into the dark night.

'Well, at last the air is clear,' Dwars rejoiced, 'thank God the proudies have gone.'

The party scattered. The older ones retired to the bar, the younger ones sent delegates to the cloak room and invited the artistes to spend the rest of the evening in their company. The boys cleared the tables, swept away the débris and collected the bottles that had been thrown about.

Ladislao Székely, *Tropic Fever*, Harper & Brothers, New York, 1937; reprinted by Oxford University Press, Kuala Lumpur, 1979, pp. 83–9.

29
A Club Night at Randjah

MADELON H. LULOFS

Madelon Lulofs (Passage 11) writes from a woman's perspective and with an eye to the social relationships that existed in a planter community. The club evening she describes is at Randjah, the district centre, some 48 kilometres from Tumbuk Tinggih, the plantation where Frank Versteegh was overseer and Van der Meulen was manager. The story is told from the point of view of Frank's wife, Marian, who had recently had a baby. She had been pregnant when they first arrived in Sumatra and this was their first visit to the club for five months and her first opportunity in that time to meet another white woman.

S HE was glad they were going to the club, where they would see people other than those of their own estate, and where she would be able to talk to a woman. It was five months since Frank and she had been away from Tumbuk Tinggih. But as they came nearer Randjah, when they saw its lights, and when at last they pulled up before the club with its bright gasolene lamps, a sudden timidity surged through her. She felt nervous at the thought of having to enter the club and appear among so many people, and all of a sudden she became conscious of the fact that five months of loneliness had made her shy of her fellows.

She pressed Frank's arm nervously and stepped out a little

too hurriedly. In front of the wide steps that ran along the whole front of the club, they parted from Van der Meulen.

Pulling up his trousers and closing the two upper buttons of his coat, he said: 'Well, Versteegh, when I want to go home, I'll let you know. Don't let's make it too late, what? Till later.'

He strode up the steps, and joined the circle of managers who were seated round the large table in the veranda. Marian and Frank found seats next to a married pair, the Spoors, whom they had met in the hospital when Marian had been there for Bobby's birth.

The vast club was still quiet. In the dancing hall the musicians, who had come from Medan, were tuning their instruments. Two bachelors sat at the bar on high stools. Two assistants were playing billiards quietly and reflectively, unless the ball refused to roll as they wanted, when they swore aloud. A servant was leaning lazily against the wall writing figures on a slate and announcing them aloud in a monotonous, indifferent voice. The lamps hissed in the silence. The air was close and heavy. Myriads of insects swarmed in, circled round the lights, and dropped with singed wings upon the cement floor.

Then the place grew more animated. More and more buggies drew up soundlessly on their rubber tyres. Several Fords stopped noisily before the wide steps. Most of them belonged to managers, and one or two had been hired by planters who lived far away. The men came in rather shyly and looked at once to see whether there were ladies.

Of the hundred and forty assistants who were members, fifteen had married recently, and this had altogether changed club life. Formerly the planters entered noisily, and often more than half drunk. It was their club, a meeting place for men. Mrs. Stoops, who had been the one woman in the company apart from the nurse, scarcely ever showed herself. Five or six years of loneliness had taught them to drink, to swear, and to fight. They had become rough and coarse.

And suddenly, during the last year, fifteen pairs of gloves had appeared in their circle. The men had felt that they must

172

somehow restrain themselves and get back to the atmosphere they had known in Holland long ago. And as a result they were uncertain of themselves. They did not know how to behave, and each of them had his own way of expressing his shyness as he came in. One of them stroked his damp hair. Another passed his finger between his collar and his neck. A third put his hands in his pockets nonchalantly and talked loudly. Others crept in half hiding behind those who had arrived before them. But all of them kept moving about until they found a table where friends or acquaintances were already established.

Once they were seated, they regained their self-confidence. They shouted loudly for beer, poured down the first few glasses one after the other, and then talked about work, about the price of rubber, the coolies, the bosses. There was never any other theme.

The members of the club kept strictly to their own groups. There were the two inspectors, Van Hemert and Terheide with his wife. Then there were the managers with their wives, the unmarried assistants, and the married assistants. Most of the married assistants were awkward and shy. They walked in a little shamefacedly behind their wives, avoiding the circle of noisy bachelors in whom they suspected mockery. Besides, they were afraid that in the eloquence born of drink the bachelors might say rather too much about the past and about festive celebrations with sundry black Poppies and Minahs. They felt that they had been dragged out of the herd existence which had kept them in a safe circle.

Until the arrival of the women, they had all been united. They had lived the same kind of life—rubber, beer, a house-keeper. Their rough comradeship had been the basis of a social order notorious no doubt for wild drinking bouts, but with unwritten laws of loyalty and honesty. They had formed a society of adventurers which recognized only two author-ities: their bosses and the government officials who carried out the labour inspection. But with the arrival of the women all this had changed. The adventurers were now husbands and fathers, responsible for a wife and for children, and they had been drawn together by a new conception of duty and by narrower ideas of decency. The women had made the first breach in the close wall that had for years surrounded the planters' world.

The club was filling rapidly. Everywhere planters were sitting; their white starched coats, which were always half unbuttoned at work, except in the presence of the boss, were carefully closed right up to the neck.

With one or two exceptions, the women were badly dressed. They wore home-made frocks of cheap silk from the little shops in Randjah. Nearly all of them had a child, and all of them had faded as a result of the climate. All of them had had a hard struggle during the first year to pay off the club accounts of their husbands.

They came to the club, not to show themselves, but to break the deadly monotony of their lives. Every day began at half-past five and ended at nine. They all lived like well disciplined soldiers. Every day the same things were said. The boss had been in the section or had not. A coolie had run away or had died. The little boy or the little girl had been nice or had not. A thief had carried away a chicken. The milk had gone sour. The water-carrier had broken another glass.

Once in a while there would be a visit from a colleague, but this did not happen often. Everybody was too busy, and the distances were too great for a horse or a buggy. And if they did meet, the conversation was invariably about work, about rubber, which had become the soil, the content, the future of their lives.

Their evenings at the club were their only gleams of brightness. They got away from the estate for once. There was music. There were other people than those they saw every day. Sometimes there were pastries from Medan or fresh ham and cheese from the refrigerator, if a mail boat had just arrived. And sometimes there was a new wife. Then they all stared themselves blind looking at her fresh pink cheeks and her bright eyes and her new fashioned clothes. She would bring the latest news, the latest melodies, and a whiff of the old land after which they all hungered.

Suddenly the steady hum of voices ceased. Frank and Marian glanced up simultaneously: all eyes were fixed on the entrance, outside which an immense luxury car had stopped noiselessly. Van Hemert rushed towards the entrance and stood at the porter's side. Stoops, the chief manager, squeezed out of the door of the car. He was followed by two Americans, his guests, and then Van Hemert held out his hand to Mrs. Stoops, who appeared in the full splendour of a rustling silk gown direct from Paris.

The silence in the ballroom grew tense. Everybody had risen, and from each table came a discreet greeting as Stoops passed: while Mrs. Stoops bestowed benevolent nods left and right. The pair moved towards the little table reserved for them, which carried a vase of flowers to distinguish it.

The hush continued; the atmosphere remained uneasy. There were some whispered comments on Mrs. Stoops's new toilette, and on the massive necklace of diamonds that encircled her fat throat.

Stoops was sanguine and corpulent. His face perpetually glistened with perspiration. His moustaches were yellow. His clothes were ill-fitting—he was, in fact, a typical Deli planter of the old school. He ordered beer immediately.

After exchanging a few polite phrases with the newcomers, Van Hemert rejoined the Terheides at his own table. Between Van Hemert and Terheide, who were both fiercely ambitious, there was waged a silent, merciless competition. Van Hemert came from an old and wealthy family, and was intelligent. Terheide was a self-made man of the lower middle-class, and much less able. Soon Stoops would leave for Europe, and one of the two would be his successor.

Their enmity was carefully hidden and they behaved towards each other not merely correctly, but even with warmth and friendliness. Only when they were in private did they allow their animosity to show. During his last furlough, Terheide had married a girl from an impoverished family belonging to the lower ranks of the Dutch nobility.

Gradually tongues loosened again. The band played some out-of-date two-steps, but nobody danced. The empty

ball-room had a chilling effect on the musicians who, however, continued to play dance music throughout the evening.
As the consumption of alcohol increased, the atmosphere
grew gayer, and the conversation louder. Here and there
someone burst out singing. An occasional oath, followed by a
quick 'Sh, sh,' and a glance at the chief manager's table, fell
upon the air. But Stoops gazed round the room benignly, his
fat short fingers again and again encircling the beer glass
whose contents he poured down his throat in one gulp, to
have it replenished immediately. The terrific amount of
heavy, preserved beer he consumed seemed to have not the
slightest effect upon him. The only difference it made was
that the streamlets of perspiration ran faster and faster down
his face and over the folds of his neck.

Mrs. Stoops looked about her approvingly. Occasionally
she greeted someone with a friendly nod, sipped her lemonade, fanned herself, and glanced stealthily at her hand, where
brilliants flashed in the light. She had grown completely
accustomed to her position of absolute ruler in this little
community and had utterly forgotten the days when she
worked in a café in the Rembrandt Plein at Amsterdam, and
Stoops was a cigar maker's apprentice who had stepped on
board a steamer at Rotterdam to try his luck in the rubber
plantations. They were about to return to Europe with
something like a million guilders in their pockets.

One hour passed after the other. The evening, which had
been most unjustly described as a dance evening, brought little except the illusion of being 'out,' the breaking of a
monotonous routine. At half-past one Van der Meulen came
up to Frank and announced that he wanted to go home. He
was flushed and puffy-looking. His eyes were unsteady. Frank
and Marian rose.

'Will you sit in front, Mr. Van der Meulen? Or would you
prefer to sit at the back?'

'No, no. You sit with your wife. I'll be all right in front.
Come along, Amat. Home!'

As they drove through Randjah, Van der Meulen turned

round, took off his hat, mopped his head with his handkerchief, and sighed.

'Swilling like a pig again! Damn it! Headache tomorrow, of course. That's all you get from these rotten club nights. Good for nothing. No good whatever.'

Then he put on his hat again and lapsed into silence. Frank and Marian moved closer together. He put his arm round her. Her fingers crept into the palm of his hand. He kissed her quietly, and they laughed soundlessly, as though they were doing something forbidden. She nestled closer to him.

'I think the drive's the nicest part of the evening,' she whispered close to his ear.

There was nothing but darkness and the regular hum of the engine. Amat was a steady, cautious driver. Now and then he had to put on his brakes suddenly because of an ox-cart on the wrong side of the road—they always kept the wrong side of the road. When this happened, Van der Meulen muttered an oath, but gradually he grew silent. He fell asleep, and his sleep was so heavy that he did not notice his hat slide into his lap, or his head bang against the iron frame of the hood. He did not wake up even at the river crossing, although they had to wait half an hour for the ferryman. A heavy mist hung over the road through the forest. They advanced very slowly, Amat bending over the wheel, and staring with concentration through the glass that continually became opaque. When at last they stopped before the manager's house, Amat awakened Van der Meulen by pushing his arm.

'Tuan Besar! Tuan Besar!'

'Heh? What?' muttered Van der Meulen, gazing about him in bewilderment. 'Are we there? Oh! Fine!' Without another word, he got out, stumbled over his hat, which had fallen to the ground, picked it up, and toiled up the steps to the veranda.

Madelon H. Lulofs, *Rubber*, Cassell, London, 1933; reprinted by Oxford University Press, Singapore, 1987, pp. 100–7.

30
Social Life in a Burmese Outstation

BILL TYDD

In 1931, Bill Tydd was appointed Subdivisional Police Officer in Nyaunglebin, in the Pegu District in Burma. One of only two Europeans stationed in Nyaunglebin, he mixed socially with Burmese and Eurasians, and with forest officers who came in every few months from the jungle. A bachelor, Tydd led an active social life: although, as a police officer, he could not relax as completely as he might have wished.

UNLIKE Mandalay, social life in this small station was limited in scope but not in good will; moreover, in the absence of a European community of wives, tedious out-of-date conventions about calling and seating arrangements at dinner parties, were happily unknown. There were about a dozen officials in the place, most of them Burmese. Besides us two Europeans, there were two Eurasians and an Indian doctor. One of the Timber firms employed four European Forest Assistants in the North Pegu Yoma Reserve extracting teak. These employees had their headquarters in Nyaunglebin and would swell the club's membership noticeably, particularly the profits of the bar, whenever they came in for a few weeks rest from their arduous and lonely months of work in the jungle. Despite the small size of the station, the club was active, we had a tennis court, billiard table, library and bar. Tennis was played daily, weather permitting, and the billiard table was seldom out of use in the evenings. Several of us ran a regular, or as regular as work permitted, bridge four; the senior Magistrate, a Burman, was the best card player and collected most of the modest pecuniary gains; we all agreed that his obviously mis-spent youth made him quite unfit to grace the bench, where he had the power to dispense long prison sentences on others for their ill-gotten gains!

Occasionally, when the forest lads were in residence, we expatriates would call at the Railway Institute, five miles away. There were large railway works at Pyuntaza down the line and the Railway community, mainly Eurasian men and women, was large. The main event of the week there was the Saturday dance in their well-appointed Institute building, which was much grander than our little club. Anglo-Indians and Anglo-Burmese girls are attractive and have good figures when they are young but all too soon they seem doomed to acquire matronly shapes at an unnecessarily early age. However, there were always enough of the young shapely ones at these dances and nothing could hold us, particularly the girl-starved 'Jungle wallahs' from this particular honey pot. Our descent in relative strength on these dances was popular with the girls but, understandably, not with their regular boy-friends, who looked upon all of us as cursed intruders. My position as head of the police made it imperative that no serious unpleasantness spoilt these social occasions; so my own social activities were always handicapped by keeping an eye on the general situation. I was always relieved when the evening ended more or less amicably and I am glad to say that I was spared any serious incidents which could have had serious consequences, not least for myself.

We did also organise the occasional dance, on a smaller scale, at our own club and even got some of the ladies in Pegu to come up with their husbands for the night. Quite often, on these occasions, we would end the evening by bringing back to the bungalow up to a dozen unexpected guests for a midnight (more like post-midnight) dinner. The servants were marvellous on these occasions; within the hour they would produce, goodness knows how, a four course meal for all.

Bill Tydd, *Peacock Dreams*, BACSA, London, 1986, pp. 44–5.

31

Sabah Society in the 1890s

NICHOLAS TARLING

In Sandakan, the capital of British North Borneo, horse racing was
well established by 1893 and the Autumn Race meeting that year
attracted visitors from the territory's west coast. The week was
filled with social activities, described in the following extracts from
the diary of Ada Pryer (Passage 24). Unfortunately, they were
marred a little for her because her husband, as one of the race stewards, was involved in a dispute over the winner of the Charter Cup
(North Borneo was governed by a chartered company). Festivities
also marked Charter Day on 1 November, commemorating the
granting of a Royal Charter to the British North Borneo Company
in 1881. For most of the year, social life consisted of home visits for
tea or dinner. These state occasions were important for bringing
together this small newly established European community to celebrate its achievement, to renew its sense of common endeavour,
and to demonstrate its solidarity to the population it governed. The
local population itself participated in the Charter Day sports and
were eager spectators at the race meets.

September 1893
27th

Our Autumn Race meeting on the Beatrice course,
the 4th meeting. Four silver cups run for. The Gov-
ernors' won by Captain Barnett's 'Old Gold' Pavitt
jockey; Charter Cup Rialto came in first; Wild Mint second,
but an objection was raised to 'Rialto'. Club Cup won by
Pavitt 'Sultan'. 'Sultan' also won the Labuan Cup Fabris jockey.
Consolation stakes carried off by 'Normanhurst' young
Marcus jockey. Very successful meeting, course in good
order, fewer rows than usual. Visitors from West Coast,
Captain Peck, Little, Mr Thos Fergusson and Wise. We have
a tiffin, the Governor present, Mrs Creagh not well enough
to come but was carried to the course in a chair later. I omitted
to write that 'Paradox' won the Trial stakes, a young pony
that promises well, belongs to Allard. While at dinner got a
note from Weston Jarvis with 20 packages, over 14 piculs, of

sugar, largest consignment received so far. Chinese keen to buy Augustine only started his little wooden crusher the beginning of last month, very encouraging. Amanudeen getting on well with his wooden crusher. Hard up for buffaloes, which are very difficult to get. Clara sent me up a most wonderful basket of roses, great branches with lovely clusters of blossoms my tiffin table decoration of puffed white muslin and these red roses, much admired. Mrs Hughes also sent me a lovely basket of flowers very kind of her. Banjermasin arrived with 2 mails.

28th Sept.

Dance at Government House 13 ladies there: four ladies not present. Race stewards meeting to settle a dispute as to Rialtos getting the Charter Cup.

29th Sept.

Willie went to Loong Piasow and the Suan Lambah with Mr Roberts by launch. Dull cloudy day. Called on Mrs Fergusson. Went to the laying of the foundation stone of

Spectators at the races. Horse racing was an important event in the social calendar.

the future Cathedral by Governor Creagh: Mrs Creagh placed the donations on the stone. A long elaborate ceremony procession, band, harmonium, bunting, etc. The stone a fine handsome block well prepared, and the inscription cut and the lettering gilded very nicely. The stone for the building is being bought from Buli sim sim. Afterwards most of the persons went to the Parsonage, almost everyone attended the ceremony but Willie didn't get back quite in time. Later Mr Dunlop took Clara and me to the Club to see the Beaufort testimonial, a very handsome epergne of Chinese manufacture, silver work dragons and bamboo and tepai (pearl oyster shells) it is a pity the shells are not finer ones and the inscription is not satisfactory, on the whole however it is a very nice present.

Willie again attended the Race Stewards' meeting with regard to the 'Rialto' affair. A great pity that there are always such disputes and heart burning over these racing affairs....

30th Sept.

Willie gone to the Byte in Mr Roberts launch, took H. Walker and Little. Much interest evinced by the visitors in the sugar mill at Weston Jarvis, where sugar making was in active progress and a second mill nearing completion. Everything on the whole Waterpark estate looking very well. H. Walker and Little said our sugar was better than Chapmans'.

Went to a smoking concert at the Club in the evening. Hastings, myself and Mrs Dowell, with Jones and his—the performers. The Governor and Mrs Creagh there. W. had many discussions over the Charter Cup race affair, some hot language. Wilson's 'Rialto' got the cup by 8 votes to 4. Heard that the donations at the foundation stone laying the day before amounted to $208 not bad considering depressing times....

2nd Oct.

Mail day. Willie very busy writing the whole day. Masonic entertainment music and dancing at the Borneo Hotel. The

Governor and Mrs Creagh present. Mrs v.d. Hoeven and I the only ladies who sang. The Banjermasin waited for the affair to be over so that the West Coast guests might be present. They left the dance and went straight on board firing 3 guns when they started. A threatening evening but the strong wind blew the rain over and we had none.

31st Oct.

A shower of rain last night

Charter-day dance at Govt. House: 12 ladies present and three officers not there. A salute was fired at 12 o.c. and rockets let off from the 'Memnon' in the harbour, bells were rung etc.

November 1893

1st:

Charter day. Much display of bunting a salute at 12 noon. Aquatic and athletic sports: very hot day. Both of us much too tired and done up after last nights dance to get down to the town to see the sports. Mr & Mrs Hughes came to stay a few days with us. . . .

Nicholas Tarling (ed.), *Mrs Pryer in Sabah*, University of Auckland Centre for Asian Studies, Resource Papers No. 1, Auckland, 1989, pp. 6–7 and 11–12.

32

Celebrations in Kuching

FREDERICK BOYLE

In February 1863, Frederick Boyle, F.R.G.S., and his brother Arthur visited Sarawak as somewhat privileged tourists. They were detained in Singapore for nearly two months while waiting for Rajah James Brooke's steamer *Rainbow* to undergo repairs. Boyle's comment on Singapore social life is brief, succinct, and prefaces the passage below.

The two brothers travelled through Sarawak with the Rajah's

officers. In September, they returned to Kuching, the capital of Sarawak, and attended the festivities in Kuching to celebrate the twenty-second anniversary of Rajah James's accession to the Raj of Sarawak, after which the Rajah departed Sarawak for what turned out to be the last time. Boyle has a satirical turn of phrase and his description of Sarawak society has an almost Dickensian flavour. The presence of two Royal Navy ships at Kuching added to the company and provided the musicians. Unknown to Boyle, there was some irony in the event, for Bishop McDougall and Rajah James, who toasted each other's health so publicly, were setting the seal on a reconcilation after a major rift between Church and State. Nevertheless, for the small European community of Sarawak, established only twenty-two years, the event was a major state and social occasion.

D ECIDEDLY Singapore is the least sociable colony of England. No public amusement whatever exists there, and the English inhabitants rarely meet except in their warehouses or on horseback. Each family gives one dinner party in six months and a ball once a year; the military band plays three times a week upon the Esplanade; races occur once in the twelve months. The environs of the town are dangerously infested with tigers, and a mountain five miles distant is alive with them. Under these circumstances the community is naturally addicted to gin and grumbling, but nevertheless a traveller is sure to be hospitably received among them....

On arrival at Kuching, we found H.M.S. *Rifleman* still at anchor in the river, and further up lay H.M.S. *Pantaloon*. The *Rifleman* was waiting to convey the Rajah to Singapore, the first stage of his voyage to England; the *Pantaloon* had come in for want of something better to do. As the date of our return was quite unknown, the little bungalow in which we formerly resided had been given up to the use of Capt. Reid, of the *Rifleman*, and his officers. Accordingly we removed our impedimenta to another bungalow, which Sir James assigned to us, formerly occupied by Capt. Rodway, whom we had found at Bintulu. It was designed to celebrate the twenty-second anniversary of the Rajah's accession to the

Raj of Sarawak by great and unexampled festivities, and the invitations were issued to every white man in the country.

Already the preparations were going on bravely. Between Government-house and the little bungalow, an extensive building of 'ataps' had been hastily erected, calculated to accommodate a numerous supper party, and when the auspicious moment arrived on the evening of September 24, the interior decorations were of that class which may justly be characterized as dazzling. Flags, and flowers, and palm-leaves, and golden inscriptions, and Chinese lanterns, were displayed in wondrous profusion, with a result as of a hermit's verdant cell adorned 'with ten thousand additional lamps.' Except a few missionaries and out-station residents who could not leave their posts, all the rank and beauty of Sarawak assembled. Ladies were present to the number of eight, and the name of the gentlemen was legion. Under these favourable circumstances, the festive dance was sustained with the greatest perspiration; from the Raja downwards, we waltzed, and polked, and quadrilled in our very best manner. But one gentleman, who whirled round and about in the black-tailed coat of Europe, was the delight of all beholders and the glory of the scene. Our band of two fiddlers came from the *Rifleman*, and propounded most excellent music. The performers, however, seemed quite unable to play in time, unless their legs were permitted to go through a sort of endless hornpipe upon the brick floor—a proceeding which had a highly indecorous appearance till its necessity was explained.

At half-past eleven we adjourned to supper under the palm branches and Chinese lanterns and inscriptions. Then the bishop arose to propose Sir James Brooke's health and prosperity, and Sir James responded. I am not about to give an analysis of his speech; eloquence is not a very uncommon gift, and words are nothing; but let Englishmen look toward these islands, and see how glorious his *deeds* have been. From a population decimated by continual and merciless war, his subjects have become peaceful, orderly, and industrious; the savage Lanun pirates have been confined to their own seas; trade has settled in every river; law is justly administered to every class. The name of the Rajah of Sarawak is respected far beyond his little kingdom, and independent sovereigns appeal to his judgment and arbitration.

The supper passed off in a manner worthy of the occasion—with drawbacks of course; the rockets resolutely refused to go off, as was audibly announced by Capt. Reid's coxswain; and the Tuan Resident's bear spilt all the punch, which had been brewed with the strictest care in a bathing jar about four feet in height and three in diameter. When the three powers existing in Sarawak—the State, the Church, and the Borneo Company—had delivered a speech apiece, dancing recommenced, and, after the departure of the ladies, was continued in the shape of hornpipes until an uncertain hour of the morning.

Next day the Malay chiefs were assembled in the Court House, and we accompanied the Rajah thither. The building was crammed with ugly little yellow fellows arrayed in their gayest jackets, gold-worked sarongs, and embroidered trousers. The speech delivered by the Rajah was heard with the greatest attention, and it was interesting to observe how readily, and with what a flow of sensible words, the native chiefs responded to his address. Two days afterwards the *Rifleman* received her passenger and steamed down the river, enveloped in the smoke of her salute. Sir James Brooke, however, had made a promise to his subjects to return within two years.

Frederick Boyle, *Adventures among the Dyaks of Borneo*, Hurst & Blackett, London, 1965; reprinted by Antara Book Company, Kuala Lumpur, 1984, pp. 2 and 136–8.

33
Mrs McDougall Entertains

HARRIETTE McDOUGALL

Social life among the European community in Sarawak in the mid-nineteenth century was very much an exchange of visits amongst those government officers, missionaries and Borneo Company personnel senior enough to be regarded as society. Until 1856, Harriette McDougall, wife of Bishop Francis McDougall (Passage 25), had been the only woman in this society, but with the arrival of other female missionaries and the wives of young government officers she acquired female companionship. Nevertheless, the Rajah being unmarried, the Mission House was the centre of much of the settlement's social activity. These extracts from two of her letters tell us something of the social attitudes governing Sarawak society. Officers from visiting Royal Navy ships, like HMS *Spartan*, were welcome guests but added to her social responsibilities. The persons mentioned in these passages were of this small social circle: Arthur Crookshank was one of the Rajah's officers, Bertha his 17-year-old wife; Alan, about Bertha's age, was the brother of Annie Brooke, wife of the Rajah's nephew, John Brooke Brooke. The wedding of 9 September 1857 was that of the Revd Walter Chambers and Elizabeth Woolley, a lady missionary ten years his senior (Chambers was to succeed McDougall as Bishop. See Passage 34). Tidman was a young man in the Borneo Company. Crymble was the government treasurer. His marriage to Annie Brooke's lady's maid removed him from Sarawak society, as Harriette McDougall makes clear.

The letters are not in very good condition and not fully dated, although they can be placed fairly accurately from internal evidence. It is not always clear to whom they are addressed because of loss or damage.

HARRIETTE McDougall to Ellen Bunyon (?) (1856) 'My beloved Nelly' We are rather inundated with 'Spartans' just now. Sir W. Hoste being at Sadong with Rajah, his officers amuse themselves by trips and dinners at Sarawak. The ship is 14 miles down the river. Some of them are nice, some nasty, last night I had 3 to dinner, and the Crookshanks, and I wish you had seen Bertha Crookshank and Alan scampering about after dinner like 2 young kids ... in my large new verandah, playing hide and seek and shrieking with laughter.... But little Bertha is a wilful wight ... she is such a darling, so merry and charming that I am quite afraid of preaching too much to her.

* * *

Harriette McDougall to?
9 September (1857)

Our wedding went off very nicely (Chambers/Woolley) the Rajah's party also came to Church dressed in full uniform, Brooke's and St John's are very handsome. Fox, Charley Johnson & Rajah had also braided and gold thread about them, though not cocked hats and feathers and gold epaulettes—it made the assembly look distinguished.... Mr Koch played with great spirit ... we sat down 18 to breakfast, Arthur Crookshank (came) when we had nearly done and made 19. Capt. Skinner could not get away as the Steamer was being scraped at Santubong.... I put a ring in the cake, a little thing which Matilda Man gave me years ago, and it fell to Mr Tidman's share who was well laughed at, as also was Crymble for *not* getting it as he is to be married shortly to Addison, Mrs Brooke's lady's maid, by which match he shuts himself out for the future from our dinner tables. However I believe she is a very respectable well educated person from his rank in life and a pious woman who will, I hope, keep him in good order, so I think it will be no loss to him to take his proper place in Sarawak society in future....

McDougall Papers, MSS Pac. s104, Rhodes House Library, Oxford.

34

Bickering and Backbiting
in Sarawak Society

MARGARET BROOKE

As Ranee of Sarawak, Margaret Brooke (Passages 3, 8, and 13) was clearly first lady in the Kuching society of 1870; still a small society, as Passage 8 makes clear, excluding Europeans of a lower class, including, it should be noted, all missionaries other than the new Bishop, Walter Chambers, and his wife, whose marriage is mentioned in Passage 33. Rajah Charles was not a social being and was a creature of habit, so that social occasions at the Astana had a predictability his wife must have found more tedious than she admits. There was a presage of the jealousies and intrigues to which such a society was prone in Passage 8. In Sarawak they created and perpetuated a rift between Church and State.

ACCORDING to my husband's wish a certain time had to be devoted to social affairs, and he approved of my suggestion that I should hold a reception for our English friends once a week. So every Tuesday afternoon the English ladies, their husbands and the bachelor officials belonging to the Rajah's staff came to tea at the Astana. I cannot say our conversation was ever very exciting, but they were all very amiable. One thing surprised me greatly; they appeared to take little or no interest in the affairs relating to the country, but would wax quite enthusiastic when someone would announce how, with great good fortune, he had induced a small half-ripe strawberry to appear on a plant he had brought from England! With flowers it was just the same. 'Only think,' another would say. 'You know the red geranium shoots I brought from England? Well, I do believe we shall be able to get at least four blooms!' 'Really? How splendid!' the others would reply admiringly. This in the midst of the exquisite prodigality of the tropics.

They all wanted to be oh, so English! whilst I hankered after being oh, so Malay!

Now and again we would have dinner-parties, one nearly the counterpart of the other, to which the whole English community—some fifteen or sixteen in number—would be invited. After dinner there would be music in the drawing-room. The Rajah, knowing my love for the piano, had bought me an Erard, but alas! a few wet days would render one or two of its notes mute and my manifestations on the instrument would, in consequence, be somewhat marred! Happily, society in Sarawak was not highly critical. The music of the great Masters—even when played on a properly functioning piano!—would only have bored them. Several of our guests, however, could be depended upon to bring their songs (always the same) and thus contribute to the harmony of the evening. Even the Rajah would join in the fray! Mrs. Helms and the other ladies had given it as their profound conviction that he had a lovely tenor voice. The edict having gone forth, the Rajah would open the programme by singing with dignity and gravity 'La Donna e Mobile' to his own, and apparently everybody else's, satisfaction. Poor darling, he never sang in tune, and once, when we were alone, I hazarded the opinion that a little practice in *solfège* might do him good. He stared at me blankly, then remarked in an offended tone that if I did not like his singing he would not sing any more. I hastily apologized, took back my words, nothing more was said, and 'La Donna' remained on the programme at all our parties.

Truly, much is to be said in favour of the same programme pursuing its unerring course on the occasions of such social gatherings. Sarawak had never been known to falter or to fail! Desultory conversation filled in the interval between each item. One of the Borneo Company's agents was noted for his fine baritone voice and he would ring out 'The Village Blacksmith' to the delight of his friends, rendering with great delicacy and pathos the passage 'It sounds to him like her mother's voice singing in Paradise,' at which point the ladies could be relied upon to show their appreciation by tiny sniffs and gentle pattings of their eyes with their handkerchiefs. Our musical programme always ended with our good doctor, possessed of a tenor voice—'but not so good as the Rajah's'—inquiring 'Oh, don't you remember sweet Alice, Ben Bolt?'...

After lemonade for the ladies and brandy-and-soda for the men the guests would depart homewards, each expressing his, or her, appreciation of the evening in his, or her, accustomed way.

Doubtless many people could be found who would take exception to the sameness of our gatherings, but on the whole they were comfortable. We all of us knew exactly what to expect, and in the heat of such tropical evenings a change of programme might have been unduly exciting and bad for us!

The truth of the saying about a prophet being without honour in his own country was borne in upon me. My rôle was a modest one, for I had only to supply the accompaniments, and though I felt very pleased at the enjoyment of our guests and the delight they evinced in listening to the innocuous programme of songs, I was rather surprised (not being devoid of conceit!) that, in spite of one or two dumb notes in the bass or treble of our piano, caused by the damp climate, our guests never invited me to play a solo. Nor did I leave them in ignorance of my musical accomplishments but, being my own trumpeter, I dinned into their ears the fact that from my eighth birthday, right down my teens, musical celebrities had given me lessons and praised my performance.

* * *

(The Rajah was suddenly called upon to lead an expedition to Sibu, on the Rejang river, where the fort had been attacked by up-river Ibans. The attack had been repulsed, but the Rajah was determined to punish its perpetrators. Margaret Brooke was left in Kuching.)

At tea-time Mr. and Mrs. Crookshank often came to call. Mr. Crookshank, experienced in Sarawak affairs, made me understand that the Rajah was in no danger. Mrs. Helms came too, and whenever I was alone with her, she—being the mother of two young daughters, both born in Kuching—

191

considered it her duty to advise me regarding my condition, as I was expecting an infant in a few months' time. She warned me as to the dangers which might arise owing to certain precautions not being attended to, and once or twice during her kindly admonitions I felt Death almost staring me in the face. Never mind! She meant well. As for me, being young and healthy and knowing nothing of birth arrivals, my nerves did not get the better of my optimism on the subject.

Mrs. Chambers never put in an appearance during the Rajah's absence, on account of a certain amount of friction having arisen between Church and State. This is what took place.

On a Sunday before the Rajah departed for Fort Sibu, Bishop Chambers preached his first sermon as prelate in Kuching Church. The Rajah was present as well as most of his officials. Mrs. Chambers, who, on account of her dominating character and her airs and graces, had been given the nickname of 'Mrs. Proudie' by those who resented her patronage, had taken it upon herself to advise her lord and master on his first address from the pulpit. She evidently considered that new brooms should sweep clean. Thus it happened that so thorough was the new broom in its sweepings, and the Bishop in his denunciations of the Rajah's officials and their ways, that all present felt a fierce anger rising in their hearts. Although the Bishop impressed on them the burning desire he felt to bring his flock back to the fold and his congregation into leading better lives, the poor flock had really nothing to reproach themselves with, their lives having been quiet, simple and orderly. The Rajah himself was very much angered, and with good reason. The service over, he went his way home, and there and then wrote the Bishop a 'what-for' letter, in which he also touched on the many services he and his officers had rendered to the S.P.G. But 'Mrs. Proudie' was on the look-out and had made up her mind that the Bishop must remain—rightly or wrongly—paramount in Church affairs. The episcopal answer, prompted by her, added fuel to the flames, with the result that, for the time being, Church and State in Sarawak were torn apart. Of course the Rajah was perfectly right to act as he did, but Mr. and Mrs. Crookshank, who much disliked 'Mrs. Proudie,' did their best to widen the breach and prevent the unpleasantness being cleared up. For three years the feud went on, and only came to an end when the Crookshanks left Sarawak to settle in England.

It is rather amusing but somewhat disconcerting to realize how the members of almost any community of English men and women settled in out-of-the-way places take pleasure in having rows with one another, especially those who are ignorant of the world, who know nothing of Society with a big S, and who, suddenly finding themselves in a remote land, imagine that they are Somebody. They are apt to become pompous and silly, and to be jealous of those who receive more attention than they, when they revel in picking quarrels with those who may be their superiors. I used to think, when I heard of all these quarrels going on around me, how futile they all were.

Margaret Brooke, *Good Morning and Good Night*, Constable, London, 1934, pp. 50–5 and 62–4.

35
Outstation Squabbles in Indo-China

ROLAND DORGELES

Roland Dorgeles (Passage 22) noted that quarrels, similar to those in Sarawak described in Passage 34, were a feature of the small French outposts in Vietnam; and blamed the climate. He also noted that in times of crisis the solidarity of the European community was renewed and petty differences were forgotten. The evidence suggests that small European communities were prone to fractiousness wherever they were.

HUMAN beings may end by detesting one another simply because they are compelled to live perpetually together. When that happens, you find a wretched post in which the six Frenchmen who make up the whole white population never speak, never look at one another, do nothing but hate one another. Yet there they are, all stewing in the same pot. Heat, sultriness, and sleepless nights have strained their nerves to the breaking-point. A word, a posture, a look, will be enough to start a quarrel.

'Why did every one get angry,' wailed the resident's wife, a young Parisian with mournful eyes, who was telling me her troubles, 'because I invited the wife of the liquor-dealer to tea twice in succession and the surveyor's wife only once?'

As a result, the little French colony in that Annamese district seat had split into two factions, which incessantly reviled and endeavored to damage each other.

The trouble often arises in some such way, out of the vanity or jealous disposition of a woman. In another case, it is all on account of a duck, worth twenty cents, which a deputy insists that his neighbor the judge has stolen. Ridiculous quarrels! Village squabbles! Living on top of one another as they do, with never a breath of air from outside, nothing ever happening to divert their minds, they presently develop an obsession. They live only to detest one another. This lasts until a day of sudden danger or sickness. Then the enemies come running, forgetting everything else. After all, solidarity among colonials is something more than a mere name. But why rend one another in this fashion? The answer is the climate, the enervating atmosphere.

The Annamite makes no effort to resist but simply lets himself drift. It might be said that he lives at slow tempo; his everlasting relaxation rests him like sleep. The European on the other hand wants to have all his accustomed energy, and in the effort to surmount the mental lassitude that assails him, his nerves, if he is weak, give out.

The nights are not conducive to rest, and the middle of the day is simply unendurable. The torpor of the siesta hour, when all nature lies stunned under the terrible sun, is unimaginable. Not a sound, not a breath of air. Where are the murmuring forests of France? Birds sleep in the trees; even the leaves sleep. Not one thing stirs. Village hens and yellow dogs and black pigs take their rest too in a corner of the *cainha*. The shops and offices close in the cities, and the streets are deserted. A rickshaw feebly crawls past. Under the trees and the verandas the coolies stretch out by dozens, their thin legs overlapping and their rags mingled together. Not a European is abroad. Everybody sleeps with the fan turned on near the bed. Two hours of broken napping, bathed in perspiration, and you get up. Work begins again. You leave the house, still only half alive, jump into a rickshaw with a burning-hot seat, and remain shut up in office, factory, or shop until the end of the afternoon.

Roland Dorgeles, *On the Mandarin Road*, The Century Press, New York and London, 1926, pp. 210–11.

36
The 'Rijst-tafel' in Java

H. W. PONDER

The stolid Dutch burghers of Java enjoyed the pleasures of the table. In this passage, Mrs H. W. Ponder (Passage 16) describes the 'rijst-tafel', a centre-piece of Dutch colonial social life. Its nearest British colonial equivalent was the curry lunch.

I suppose that every one who has ever heard of Java has also heard of 'rijst-tafel,' the famous national dish of the country. It is really an adaptation—or perhaps it would be more correct to say an amplification—to Dutch tastes, of the native 'nasi besar,' or rice feast. Rice is the staple food of the people, and the foundation of every meal; and a feast, with them, is merely the addition of as many extra dishes as possible, to mix in the inevitable bowl of soft white grain.

But gradually it has come to be far more a Dutch than a Javanese custom. For the native only feasts on rare and special occasions, whereas to the Java Dutch it has become the standard midday meal. No hotel in Java, large or small, would dare not to serve it, and in the bigger ones, especially those that cater for tourists, it is a kind of ceremony, and a sight well worth seeing.

A long procession of table 'boys' is formed, led by the 'mandoer' (head boy), who bears proudly, rather like a Scotsman with a haggis, an immense bowl of rice, served boiling hot, but flaky and dry, as you get rice nowhere else but in the East.

From this the 'rijst-tafler,' if one may so call him, lays a solid foundation in a deep soup plate, and the fun begins. The procession approaches in single file (there may be any-thing up to twenty or twenty-five 'boys' in it), each carrying two dishes, from every one of which you are expected to help yourself. The first on the list is always vegetable curry; and after that, in bewildering array, come fried bananas, eggfruit, potato balls, curried chicken, fried chicken, fried duck, half a dozen varieties of dried fish (each more highly scented than the last), savoury rissoles, croquettes, pasties, sausages, fried eggs, baked eggs, liver, pancakes cut into strips, skewers full of scraps resembling cat's meat (but really

Serving 'Rijst-tafel'. From Thos. Cook & Son, Ltd., *Malaysia and Indo-China*, Singapore, 1929.

delicious), cucumber, chopped onion, grated coconut, chillies, 'zuurjes' (little pickles), and chutneys and peanuts, and a long list of other odds and ends. Last of all comes a dish of 'kroepoek' (great crinkly biscuits as big as plates, made of rice flour and flavoured with prawns) which are eaten with the mixture in place of bread.

To the visitor it is merely an amusing experience, a joke. But to the habitué it is a serious affair, with a technique of its own, a technique which, I regret to say, I have never been able to learn. I only know (from constant observation of my neighbours) that the various delicacies should be arranged on a definite plan, to which end several smaller plates are set round the central soup plate, like planets round the sun, so that each tit-bit may go to its appointed place. The dry ingredients are put on one plate, the liquid on another, and the greasy on a third, while certain items seem always to go into the central mixture direct.

The Dutchman's and Dutchwoman's capacity for this gargantuan dish is truly impressive. It is not at all unusual to see rijst-taflers of either sex summon the whole procession again when their plates are empty, and fall to a second time with equal gusto.' And finally, it must not be forgotten that the correct beverage with which to accompany the dish is beer, and in no niggardly spirit, either.

H. W. Ponder, *Java Pageant*, Seeley Service & Co, London, n.d., pp. 258–9.

37
Bachelor Boys in Java

HUBERT S. BANNER

In contrast to the Dutch inhabitants of Java, the English there in the 1920s, as described by Hubert Banner (Passage 17), were an irreverent and irresponsible lot. However, Banner was referring in particular to those employees of commercial companies who lived in a bachelor mess, were free of domestic ties, and eager for diversion.

As one of his anecdotes indicates, even Dutchmen could fall victim to ennui and desire excitement. From the style of writing one suspects exaggeration may well have crept in; perhaps, even, the apochryphal. However, a little embellishment to improve a good story may be forgiven. As we have seen in other passages, Europeans could be something of a law unto themselves while in the colonial environment.

HAVING now to the best of my ability described the main features of Java's institutions, it occurs to me that I may best bring my book to a close by dwelling for a little space upon its less serious side. Indeed, I think I may say without overstating the case, that the more flippant aspect of life in that 'Peerless Gem of the Tropic Seas'—I quote the guide-books—deserves to rank equally in importance with many a facet usually given more prominence. For in Java a vigorous sense of humour is a *sine qua non* in English people who would 'do their time' without succumbing to a premature decay both intellectual and moral. Beautiful though Java is, life there is characterized by a wearing 'sameness' that soon becomes an active *ennui*; and an enthusiastic welcome is accordingly given to any 'stunt' notion which may serve to break the chain of monotony, crazy though it may appear in the light of cold reason. There is ample evidence that this fact is often not sufficiently grasped by the home offices of business concerns in Java, and one hears of unimaginative people in London, Glasgow, and Manchester—most often this last dismal city, perhaps—heaping condemnation upon their representatives in the East for little 'steam-lettings' which, if they only knew it, enable the participants to attack their jobs with a fresh vigour. They seem never to have heard the old saying that 'All work and no play makes Jack a dull boy.'

But enough of this. Let me forget for a little while the existence of such wooden-heads, and narrate at random a few of the amusing recollections which come crowding into my memory.

It is perhaps only natural that the stolid Hollander provides a certain quantity of amusement for the British residents, though we are indisputably insular in our outlook. Apart from his digressions from our notions of sartorial correctness—I, for one, never got accustomed to the sight of a morning-coat worn in conjunction with a bowler hat, or, in extreme cases, a 'gents' straw boater' and brown boots—he never ceases to startle the newcomer by his habit of self-introduction. Up he marches with extended hand, and the announcement, 'My name is So-and-so' in Dutch. I have known a stranger to the country, in panic-stricken conviction that some customary *douceur* had been omitted, promptly press a coin into the outstretched palm.

The British community, which does not reach four figures throughout Java, is thrown very much on its own resources, and might be likened to the Athenians for its continual seeking after 'some new thing.' Three years ago, for example, it was quite spontaneously arranged to hold a 'fancy dress golf tournament' on the links at Chandi, the residential quarter of Samarang. Four holes were to be played, no club except a putter being permitted. Almost every Englishman and Englishwoman in the place took part, and a good many Dutch people into the bargain. The players, after being marshalled at a neighbouring Mess, were marched on to the links with putters at the 'slope,' headed by a brass band and Master of Ceremonies on horseback, wearing hunting 'pink' and a false nose. I have no hesitation in saying that everyone went to their work the next day refreshed in body and soul, but I am informed that certain soulless dolts in home offices not a thousand miles from Manchester were highly incensed to hear of the 'childish behaviour' of their Java representatives!

On another well-remembered occasion a bachelor Mess, bored with existence in general, suddenly decided to live a day of their lives backwards. Immediately on rising, accordingly, they took a final whisky-and-soda. This was followed, in the order mentioned, by coffee and liqueurs, dessert, pudding, roast meat, fish, soup, and a gin-and-bitters. At lunch-time they had tea, and at tea-time an excellent luncheon of curried chicken and rice. At the dinner-hour they began with toast and marmalade, continued with bacon and eggs, and concluded with porridge. After which they sipped their early coffee and munched their early fruit, 'and so to bed.' The experiment, so far as I know, was not repeated, but it had served to break the monotony....

* * *

The hospitality of the Java British community is of a high order, and is, moreover, a natural outcome of its joy at the advent of the stranger who comes to break the monotony of existence for it. Ask the visitors afterwards for their impressions, and in eight cases out of ten you will hear impassioned eulogies, not of the glories of Borobudhur, but of The Box, Batavia's British Club, or the Simpang Club at Surabaya. Let me quote the case of a certain gallant officer in one of His Majesty's ships which visited Batavia not so very long ago.

'And what do you think of this salubrious spot?' somebody asked him.

'Well,' was the answer, 'I haven't had an opportunity of judging with the naked eye, but it looks O.K. through the bottom of a tumbler!'

There is a famous little club at one of the towns on the north coast which, while nominally a Dutch institution, has usually had a majority of British on its committee, and has consequently shone in the matter of dances and other entertainment. In the 'bad old days'—not so long ago either!—its bachelor members had a great name for 'hitting it up' on Saturday nights, and bitter were the execrations of the peaceful citizenry inhabiting the bungalows immediately adjoining. One Dutch gentleman in particular was continually sending *chits* across complaining of the loss of his sleep, and threatening to appeal to the authorities. At last came a night of even more unholy racket than of wont, and one of the leaders of the revels chanced to glance in the direction of the uncomplacent one's house. Espying him violently gesticulating at the telephone, he drew his conclusions, which were speedily justified by the apparition of a police officer at the club entrance.

Before the official could even open his lips to broach his errand, he was seized and dragged to the bar, where neat brandy was administered in quantity. Nothing loth, he applied himself heartily to the stimulants, doubtless arguing that they would help him in tactfully performing an unpleasant duty.

'And now,' said his hosts, when they had got him thoroughly keyed up, 'away and do your duty!"

But the officer was by no means certain now just what that duty was.

'If you would add to your kindness, *goede Heeren*,' he begged, fingering his numbed brow, 'and just explain the circumstances to me once again....'

'What! *You're* a nice sort of policeman!' he was told. 'We ring you up to rid us of one who is ruining the peace of our little festivity, and you ask what your duty is!'

'I—I—The brandy—I blush to say I have forgotten,' faltered the representative of the Law.

'Well, well. Boys will be boys, and we don't want to be hard on you. Now then. You see that house over there—'

And presently the watchers had the wicked joy of beholding the unfortunate invoker of Authority being hauled down his own front steps in his gents' slumberwear. His protestations were of no avail. He spent the remainder of the night in the cells, where he doubtless had his wish for undisturbed peace.

On the occasion of another 'binge'—at a bachelor Mess in Surabaya this time, and quite recently—when the riot ran somewhat high, the police were got rid of by a different expedient. One of the revellers withdrew to a bedroom and reversed his collar and waistcoat, appearing a moment later on the verandah-steps. The remainder of the company somehow mustered the self-control to fall into a respectful silence on his arrival, and the pseudo-padre then proceeded to address the astonished officers with murmured blessings and benedictory gestures. They withdrew in abasement, one of them audibly protesting that 'if the *Dominie* was present, *of course* everything was in order'. Taking into consideration the fiendish quality of the din which had originally attracted the policemen's attention, I cannot help wondering what conception they must have subsequently harboured of the English clergy.

I think the dullest town, *in se*, that I have ever known was Cheribon, where for a considerable time I was the only Britisher. Indeed, it was in those days a place no self-respecting firm ought ever to have sent a white man to, though I believe things are better nowadays. Our Mess—I lived with an American and a young Dutchman—was ready to seize upon any idiotic excuse for a jamboree, and idiotic enough some of them were, in all conscience. I will content myself with one example. We had a stupendous colony of dogs, and in due course puppies began to be fairly constant arrivals. If I remember right we had come back one evening from the official opening of a new wing to the hospital, and were greeted with the news of a fresh litter of pups.

'I've got an idea!' suddenly exclaimed the American. 'We'll invite the neighbourhood to an official Opening of the Puppies' Eyes!'

And so it was done. Invitation cards were sent out, the house and garden were decorated with flags lent by a shipping agency, and a native brass band was engaged. All day that epoch-making festival raged, and great was the fame thereof from end to end of Java. Never, I will wager, did the bluest-blooded canine aristocrat of Cruft's form the nucleus of a greater stir than did that litter of miserable little mongrel pups.

It was Cheribon, moreover, which gave birth to, I think, *the* most utterly futile and inane incident in all my recollection. One Saturday afternoon there sat in the Cheribon club two very corpulent and very merry Dutchmen of middle age. They had dropped in for a *pahitje* (gin-and-bitters) before lunch, but time had flowed by and gin had flowed down, and it was now well after lunch time.

'*Kom, kerel*,' said one of them at last. 'It's time for *rijst-tafel* and a snooze.'

'Not a bit of it,' said the other. 'You and I are going to do something original this afternoon—something *really* original. We're going to climb the Cheremai and have a look into the crater.'

Now the Cheremai is a volcanic peak behind Cheribon, some 11,000 feet in height, and presenting steep slopes and patches of jungle scarcely suitable for the afternoon promenade of two gentlemen of years and avoirdupois. The scheme nevertheless found favour, and presently the expedition set forth. It included, besides bearers laden with tinned foods and a case of gin, a Chinese stonemason and a number of coolies staggering beneath the weight of a marble table-top 'borrowed' from the Club, whereon it was purposed to carve a suitable inscription on reaching the goal. It was never carved, however. For, sad to relate, the table-top was allowed to fall en route and shattered into fragments. But towards evening on the following day the perspiring heroes actually arrived within a hundred yards of the crater's lip. While admiring the spirit that had upheld them in their struggle, one is tempted to a sardonic conjecture as to that spirit's quality by the fact that there was now remaining a mere sup of gin out of the whole caseful with which the expedition had started out. This the two worthies sat down to demolish before staggering the last hundred yards.

'It is a truly original thing we do this day,' observed the one. 'Few men have climbed the Cheremai and viewed its crater.'

And then the other's face lit up with a great inspiration, and he let out an excited *godverdomme*—a naughty expletive much used by Hollanders in moments of stress.

'I have it!' he shouted. 'Anyone could climb the Cheremai and view the crater, but who would ever think of climbing it and then going home *without* viewing the crater? Come on!'

And believe it or not, they scrambled to their feet and started running down the slope without a backward glance, happy in the conviction that they were really and truly at last doing something original!'

As I mentioned before, some pretty 'queer birds' find their way out East, and there are many who will still remember one quaint individual who arrived in Java some years ago and provided a butt for a good deal of good-natured ragging. Let us call him R—. Simplicity shone from his large, vacant face and was reflected in his slow, deliberate speech. A couple of days after his arrival he received a typewritten communication in Dutch on highly official-looking paper, and hastened to get it translated by a clerk. Its tenor was something as follows:

'SIR,

Her Majesty's Minister of Public Hygiene has noted with displeasure that you have as yet failed to comply with *Stat. CXLIX. Cap. 9937. Par.* 423, which stipulates that all foreigners landing on these shores shall, within 24 hours, shave, or cause to be shaved, their hair to within millimetres 0.333 of the scalp.'

Off he rushed to take a senior's advice on this precious document, and was urged to disregard it.

'After all,' said the senior airily, 'they can't do more than jug you for five years, and you will have the satisfaction of being a martyr to the excellent cause of "Britons never, never, never shall be slaves."'

But R—turned up next morning as bald as a coot! Needless to say, the 'official' document had been fabricated in the office.

There used to exist until a few years ago a highly comic militia called the *Schutterij*, in which not only the young Dutchmen, but foreigners also, were compelled to serve. The uniform was stuffy and antiquated, the arms used were almost antediluvian, and the institution was cordially hated and despised by everybody who had anything to do with it, but especially by the British. The one nationality excepted from this conscription was the Japanese, doubtless because the Dutch were not over-anxious for their routine to be assimilated in that quarter. The Japanese, however, apparently hurt at the omission, petitioned to be included, and sooner than comply, Government promptly exempted all foreigners. The officers must have breathed a heartfelt sigh of relief, for the British had ever been a terrible thorn in their sides.

Not the simplest order but the English *schutter* would manage to make a hash of it. Ordered to 'right turn,' invariably he would swivel to the opposite direction. Bidden to 'order arms,' he would infallibly come to the slope. One bright spark, who explained his absence from a parade by saying his horse was dead—he was in the mounted section—was curtly informed that the excuse was invalid, and the official intimation even breathed a *soupçon* of mistrust as to its veracity. At the next parade, accordingly, the delinquent appeared on foot, followed by a bullock-cart, from which he presently tipped the carcase of his defunct steed at the colonel's feet. On another occasion a very ceremonial review—I think some foreign prince was present—during which the cavalry were to charge down the King's Plain at Batavia and rein in their horses before the saluting-base, was entirely ruined by reason of every single horse ridden by an Englishman unaccountably conceiving the project of galloping straight on to its stables instead of stopping. Curious!

Hubert S. Banner, *Romantic Java as It Was & Is*, Seeley Service & Co., London, 1927, pp. 266–74.

38
Singapore Thespians

CHARLES BURTON BUCKLEY

Colonial society was thrown on to its own resources when it came to entertainment. In British colonies, amateur theatricals were popular, while the more ambitious attempted to establish professional or semi-professional companies when the communities concerned appeared able to support them. In this passage, C. B. Buckley writes of early amateur theatricals in Singapore, quoting from the Singapore press of the day. After a first attempt at serious drama, the stress was on comedy, farce, and entertainment.

In the mid-nineteenth century, the theatre was not regarded as quite respectable and theatre-going met with opposition from the

Christian church. That men played female roles owed something to the lack of young European women in Singapore society but more to the feeling that respectable women did not go on stage. W. H. Read, who later in life became a leading citizen of the colony, appeared as an 'actress' in many stage performances in his younger days.

Sir Harry [Henry] Keppel, mentioned towards the end of the passage as playing leapfrog, was in 1846 renowned for his activities in Borneo in support of Rajah James Brooke and later rose to the rank of Admiral.

O N the 14th of March, 1844, there was a revival performance under the management of Vincent Crummles, who was Captain Calbeck of the Madras Army. The plays were *Charles the Second* or *The Merry Monarch* and *The Spectre Bridegroom*. In the second piece appeared for the first time Miss Petowker as Lavinia, and Mr. Johnson as Dickory. The theatre was in Dutronquoy's Hotel, then called the London, where the Adelphi now stands in Coleman Street. Miss Petowker for several years played ladies' parts. She had the smallest waist, and smallest

Members of an amateur theatrical group. Amateur theatrical performances were a popular form of entertainment.

foot, of any lady in Singapore, and was the envy of all the sex, for it was acknowledged she was the prettiest little chamber-maid on the stage and a clever little actress, and played every-thing she attempted most successfully. One night, after a performance, she was taken to the house of a lady friend, where there was a lady visitor, who talked to the actress for some time and seemed much impressed with her ladylike bearing, &c., when the pert little woman came out with a rather strong expression which aroused the old lady's suspi-cions; so she walked up to Petowker and said in tragic tones, opening her eyes as wide as she could, 'Why you naughty creature, you are a man,' and so it was—Mr. W. H. Read! Since that he has played important parts in his own character on another stage quite as successfully, but he probably often looks back with pleasure to the days when he tripped the boards in petticoats....

An incident occurred to show that the opposition then shown by some clergy to the stage was in full force. One of the cloth, a clergyman of the Church of England, preached a powerful tirade against the stage and actors in general, and said that no modest woman should appear in such a character as Portia. This Revd. gentleman was severely handled in the papers by several writers, and the result of the sermon is thus recorded in the *Free Press* of 25th July, 1844:—'One good resulted from the sermon on Sunday, although not the one exactly intended by the Revd. gentleman, viz., persons who never visited a theatre before, went on Monday, and the house was crowded!'....

On November 24th, 1864, was performed *Charles the Second*, with Dunman as *Captain Copp*, his last appearance; and the farce of *State Secrets*, in which Tidman played the *Tailor of Tamworth*, the principal character. With the exception of the acting of these two, the performance was a failure. Dunman, as has been said, never played again. Miss Petowker's last performance was as *Fantine*, a low lodging housekeeper, and she looked the part to perfection. Archie Spottiswoode was Miss Ledbrooke and made up and played ladies' parts excellently well. The late Mr. William

Rodyk, Registar of the Malacca Court, was the third female, and also played very well. One night when the *Dido*, Sir Harry Keppel's ship was here, after a performance, her Captain, Officers and amateurs, and Miss Petowker, played at leap-frog on the stage, and after their game adjourned for supper to the Navy House, which stood on the site occupied now by the Masonic Hall. The house belonged to Mr. Read's father.

Charles Burton Buckley, *An Anecdotal History of Old Times in Singapore*, Fraser & Neave, Singapore, 1902, 2 vols; reprinted in 1 volume by University of Malaya Press, Kuala Lumpur, 1965, pp. 742–3 and 747.

39
Acquiring a Mistress

LADISLAO SZÉKELY

Ladislao Székely (Passages 2, 10, 21, and 28) was familiar with the situation on the rubber plantations of Sumatra. In his novel, *Tropic Fever*, the narrator has been living on his own long enough to begin to dream of the girl, Elsa, whom he had left behind and to long for female company. One evening, he is visited by his friend Dwars, who sits with him on the veranda of his bungalow. What follows is an unromanticized account of the transaction which brings Kartinah into his house as servant and mistress. The power relationships between the white men and their male and female employees is clear. The narrator has his scruples, but circumstances and the apparently willing submission of the woman overcomes them.

FROM outside came the sound of shuffling feet.

'Tabeh, Tuan,' said a man's deep voice.

Dwars rose and walked to the banisters of the covered veranda. The yellow-red light of the kerosene lamp shone beyond the banisters. There, crouching, was an old Javan-Malay, about thirty-five to forty, and behind him squatted quite a young woman. Almost a child still. Bashfully she lowered her eyes and crept behind her husband's broad back.

'Tabeh, Pardi,' Dwars returned his greeting, 'I have something to say to you.'

'*Melinken*, Tuan, I am your servant from the tip of my hat to the sole of my sandals.'

'Pardi, the Tuan Besar and the Tuan Ketjil have given you this woman.'

'That is so,' came the low answer.

'The thoughts of man may turn, Pardi.'

'That is so, Tuan.'

'Your Tuan wants to have your woman.'

Pardi said nothing. The rain fell in torrents.

'Melinken, Tuan, I am your servant from the tip of my hat to the sole of my sandals.'

'But don't be sorrowful on that score, Pardi. As soon as a new transport of coolie women arrives you can choose one for yourself. Here are ten guilders for you, and now go home. The woman will stay here, she is to be nyay to the tuan.'

'Tabeh, Tuan.'

The shuffling steps withdrew to the kitchen. A woman's voice could be heard asking something, and a man's voice answered her with a grunt. Then the conversion passed to a whisper that was lost in the noise of the rain.

All during this time the woman had said nothing. But neither had she been asked anything.

'What was all that stuff and nonsense about?' I asked with annoyance.

'Now listen,' Dwars began, 'a man cannot live without a woman. He needs a woman for all sorts of things. One can't bring a white woman out here, at least we little tuans may not do so. In the first place our contract forbids it, and secondly, we can't keep a European woman on our salary, at least not one that is at all respectable. So there's nothing left for us but to take a black woman. And you'll see, they aren't so bad. One must just train them well. But you have to do that with the others too, not only with the black ones. A woman will keep your house in order, will cook and wash for you, and look after you; if you are sick, she will nurse you, if you are in a bad mood, you can beat her, if in a good mood, you can stroke her. A woman like that is grateful for everything, my friend. Even for a beating. Just try it. You won't regret it.'

Silence. Lost in thought, I stared in front of me.

'Ugh! What a vulgar traffic in human flesh. Woman traffic. To buy his wife from my own coolie for ten guilders! I thank you for your assistance, but that won't work. That isn't really human traffic, but meat traffic. We didn't even ask the woman, but just purchased her like a cow. For ten silver guilders. No, I can't swallow that.'

'Don't make such a fuss. We all felt that way about it at first. A few days of it, and you'll get accustomed to it. When I was in your position, the thing repelled me just as it does you. And today I wouldn't give up Sarinah for any woman in the world. It's all a matter of habit.'

I had to think of Elsa. Of Elsa's fragrant face, her desirable red lips.

'No, I can't do it, Dwars. Even if I wanted to, I couldn't.'

'Because you're a blockhead. If you don't want to, then leave it alone. I can't force you. But anyway, don't send her back tonight. That would mortally offend poor Pardi. He couldn't look his coolie companions in the face again if his master did not want his wife even for a night.'

'All right, she can stay here for tonight. She can sleep somewhere at the back.'

So we agreed on that.

Afterwards we chatted for a long time. The beer was beginning to taste better, and a bottle of whiskey was produced from Dwars' carriage. It was far into the night when Dwars took his departure. The rain had stopped, and the moon even pierced the clouds.

Whistling, I let down the mat partition and went into my bedroom. As usual, my lamp burned with the wick partially screwed down. Our talk had relieved me, and I started undressing in a happy mood. All of a sudden I happened to glance into the corner. A dark shadow was crouching beside the wardrobe.

'Who's there?' I asked in alarm and seized my revolver.

'Only I, Tuan,' a woman's voice whispered.

210

I had quite forgotten the woman. With a deep sigh of relief I put down the revolver. But what was I to do with the woman? Drive her out? Send her to the kitchen? Amat was already asleep. Where in the world was I to put her?

'What is your name?' I asked her in my first confusion.

'Kartinah is my name, Tuan,' she whispered with lowered eyes.

'Come over here.'

Slowly, with delicate movements, she rose and approached me timidly. When she had reached me, she immediately squatted again in well-mannered fashion.

'Get up.'

'Yes, Tuan.'

She had a beautiful, slim, sinewy figure. Her brown skin was soft as velvet, her hair smooth and coal-black. Her face, too, was not ugly. Large, black eyes she had, and a small red mouth. Her nose was not even flat. And she had a pleasant odour of woman. She raised her glance for a brief moment and looked at me with her large, shining eyes, then she lowered her eyelids with her long lashes. She wore a pretty, coloured Batik sarong and a snow-white bodice.

'Do you want to be my nyay?' I asked hoarsely.

'As the Tuan commands.'

'I'm not commanding now, I'm asking: do you want to be my nyay?'

She looked at me. Obviously she did not understand. In all her life she had never been asked whether she wanted anything. She had always been commanded.

'Melinken, Tuan. As the Tuan commands.'

'And if I do not command, but just say: stay here?'

Again she looked at me. Again she did not understand me. If a man said anything, that was a command. And especially if that man was a big tuan. With large, astonished eyes she continued to look at me.

'If the Tuan says I am to stay, then I stay.'

'And Pardi?'

She cast a quick glance at me. She had not yet understood that, but soon she grasped it:

'Pardi, too, is commanded by the Tuan. When I was given to him, it was the Tuan who commanded that, too. And if the Tuan takes me away from him, that is also a command of the Tuan.'

'Do you love Pardi?'

Now her glance had something roguish in its understanding.

'I was ordered to go to Pardi. I honour him because he is older and because he gives me food.'

'From now on I shall feed you. Wait a moment, I want to get my cigarette case.'

Trembling, I ransacked the other room for my cigarettes. I knocked against a chair, and it fell over with a crash. I set it up again and sat down on it. Where should I send the woman? But if I wanted to send her away, why did I first talk with her? Why did I promise her that she would from now on be fed by me? Was I completely crazy? Or did I really want to send her away? Tomorrow. Perhaps.... I lit a cigarette. The flaming match glowed red in my trembling hands.... Oh, why was I making such a fuss? Tomorrow she'd go home like a lamb, and that would be the end of it.

Returning to my bedroom, I found the Batik sarong and the white bodice lying on the floor. I opened the mosquito-netting. Like a warm, living statue cast in bronze, Kartinah lay on the white sheet.

* * *

'Bangon, Tuan, bangon!'

I jumped up. Beside my bed crouched a brown, child-like young woman with white teeth and black eyes. She held a tray with steaming coffee, a few bananas and a corn-cob. On the table lay a clean white suit, and in front of the bed stood my slippers.

How good that coffee was! That stupid Amat never gave me bananas in the morning. And how did the little woman know that I like corn?

There was a knock at the door:

'Tabeh, nyay, here's the hot water for shaving.'

Nyay? Amat's tongue had quickly accustomed itself to this respectful mode of address. But yesterday the woman was an orang-contract, a despised pariah. For one night she had slept with the tuan, and already she was a nyay. . . .

'Kartinah, who ever told you to bring me corn?'

'I imagined you liked it, Tuan. Last night you ate seven cobs.'

'Yes, and how do you know that?'

'I saw Amat take out the empty plate.'

'You certainly have good eyes! And how do you know that one needs hot water for shaving? Amat has been waiting on me for five months now, but he doesn't know that yet. This is the first time I've had hot water.'

'I served a white Mem in Java. There the tuan also shaved with hot water.'

She crouched by my bed and waited for me to seize the tray. She held her right wrist gripped in her left hand.

'Get up, put down the tray, then you may go.'

Light as a lizard she slipped out, without a sound she opened the door and disappeared into the dark. Hurriedly I dressed, the coolies were already assembling outside. It did not take me long to dress. I found my buttons in my suit, and notebook, watch and penknife laid out.

Ladislao Székely, *Tropic Fever*, Harper & Brothers, New York, 1937; reprinted by Oxford University Press, Kuala Lumpur, 1979, pp. 156–63.

40
Franco-Vietnamese Liaisons

HARRY A. FRANCK

In this passage the American traveller Harry A. Franck comments on what he saw of liaisons between French men and Vietnamese women and between Vietnamese men and French women in Indo-China in the mid-1920s.

A French novelist whose background is Indo-China rates its 'scourges' (*fléaux*) as—in the order of their appearance to the newly arrived colonial perhaps—sun, 'boy', *congaïe*, alcohol, gambling, opium, and madness. Most of these are self-explanatory. The 'boy' alone is sometimes enough to drive the exile to drink, if not to madness, and it is not infrequently he who more or less surreptitiously brings in the *congaïe*, perhaps his own sister, sometimes even his own wife. The *congaïe*—normally a perfectly respectable Annamese word for girl—is in colonial vernacular what in France is known as *petite femme*, and by many other names, some of them far less complimentary, in every land. As our own pretty but stupid girls go into the movies or the 'Follies,' those of Annam become the temporary wives of the French. There is a lot of romance about the *congaïe*, from those of the 'Madame Butterfly' temperament, until one finds that she is sometimes hired by the week, like a *bonne à tout faire*, and is often passed on to a successor with the furniture. Nor is she the Oriental doll she is painted by romantic Latin novelists, though during her first few terms of service she may have youthful charm and perhaps be pretty. Many Annamese mothers do not blacken the teeth of their daughters because they wish them to live with Frenchmen, especially if they are the daughters of other Frenchmen, which is said to make an ardent combination much sought after among colonial Lotharios. But the *congaïe* must love her François indeed if she eschews betel-nut for his sake; she is more likely to teach him the habit. There is little visible public opinion against these temporary matings, though it is said that the best class of Annamese look down upon the practice at least as much as do the most nearly prudish of the French. As in France, marriage is very difficult and its unofficial rival very easy; one may even take the *congaïe* back to France as a servant.

One sees half-breed children now and then even in thatched hamlets far from the centers, while there are plenty of both children and adults of mixed blood in any city. Wherever there is a Catholic community cynical French males suspect any one in the slightest degree off color as having French blood contributed by the 'missionaries.' The opposite combination, with the male Annamese the 'protector,' may sometimes be seen—a Frenchwoman in Annamese trousers in some wayside village or peering forth from some native den in the cities. There were several instances in Hanoï of Frenchwomen legally married to Annamese, most of them imported after the war. The wife of a furrier who won a gold medal and his French bride at the Marseilles exposition of a decade ago never went out, but stood looking through her *grille* like a captive animal. The Parisian wife of a barber in Haïphong lived in the not too large room of the barber-shop, with a bed off in one corner behind a bamboo screen that did not even conceal from observant clients that she was soon to contribute to the Eurasian population. The government is now refusing licenses for such marriages, but that naturally does not do away with similar unions as long as Frenchwomen are ignorant of the color-line or indifferent to it.

Harry A. Franck, *East of Siam: Ramblings in the Five Divisions of French Indo-China*, The Century Press, New York and London, 1926, pp. 237–9.

41
The Female Bond

MADELON H. LULOFS

For European women in South-East Asia, childbirth was often more frightening and lonely an experience than it would have been at home in Europe. In the mid-nineteenth century it was dangerous to the life of mother and child. In Sarawak, for example, Harriette McDougall lost four babies at, or soon after, birth and her own life was despaired of at least once, although her husband was a doctor as well as Bishop; while John Brooke Brooke, Rajah James's nephew, had both his wives die in childbirth. As medical science improved, the risks declined; but young wives were far from their own families and were often alone with strangers when the birth occurred. In this passage, Marian Versteegh's baby is delivered in the hospital run by the rubber company, some distance from the estate where her husband remains at work. She is attended to competently by the doctor and nurse, but it is from her servant Saima that she receives the comfort and care she craves.

SAÏMA was right. The child came sooner than they had expected. It was born early in the morning following the day when she was taken to the hospital.

'You got here just in time,' said Doctor Weisman, with a grin, bending his red kindly face over Marian as he felt her pulse. Then he patted her shoulder encouragingly and said: 'And now you've only got to keep calm and do exactly what I say, and then you'll see how short a time it takes us to bring the little chap into the world.'

Early in the new day, when it was still dark, he was born, Marian's son. She looked on quietly as the sister weighed him, washed him, and put him into the cradle in the corner of the room. All the while she had thought of but one thing: if only Frank had been there.

'And now you must sleep a little,' said the sister. 'The doctor has rung up Tumbuk Tinggih, and asked Mr. Van der Meulen to tell your husband.'

'Do you think he'll be able to come to-day, sister?' Her eyes were full of longing.

'Of course he'll come. I expect he'll be here this afternoon.'

As she talked, the sister quickly removed the instruments. She had still so much to do. The patient in room two was sure to be a case of dysentery. Then there were the two women in the native hospital who were in labour. She would have to go and have a look at them. Without interrupting her work, she drew her watch from a pocket in her apron. And the cook had to be told the menu of the day. The idiotic new Babu had of course again put all the mugs and basins in the wrong bathroom. The sister really had to run the whole establishment....

'Have a little nap now,' she said. 'I'll drop in again soon.'

Marian heard her going, her heels clattering along the

cemented passage. She looked round the bare hospital room. The walls were of coarse stone covered half-way up with a layer of dull green plaster. Above they were white. The grey cement floor smelt strongly of lysol. The windows on one side of the room were kept shut. On that side was the narrow garden which separated the annexes from the main building. The kitchen was there, and it was built in such a way that as he stood by the fire the Chinese cook looked straight at one's bed. Besides, it was better to keep the smell of cooking out.

Marian's hands lay limply by her sides. They were white hands with blue veins clearly marked. The child was quiet. Bobby! Her boy. It *was* a boy, as they had both wanted so much. This, then, was what it meant, to bring a child into the world. It had not been intolerable, and it had not lasted long—only a couple of hours. 'Jolly easy,' the doctor had remarked with his broad grin. She closed her eyes. She frowned. Then, carefully, she shifted one leg, just a little. God, how tired her muscles were!

She stared at the dull walls; a row of ants was marching up them in military fashion. 'Jolly easy!' and the sister had confirmed his verdict. I wish they could feel it, thought Marian. But that was not the worst. The worst was the lone-liness, the sense of desolation. Something as significant as that happened in your life, and there was nobody with whom to share the experience. You lay there by yourself for hours, alone with the doctor and the nurse whom you scarcely knew—they were simply two matter-of-fact persons who were glad that all was going well. And there was the same matter-of-factness when the child had arrived. Nobody gen-uinely shared your joy. Nobody really cared what kind of a child it was so long as it breathed. So long as there were no complications.

'A fine boy. My word, can't he yell!' the sister said with a laugh. She probably said the same thing of every boy that was born. 'And what's his name?'

'Bob... Bobby,' she whispered. It sounded so strange when she said the name for the first time; for her, until now, the name and the child had been two separate entities.

How could she rest with these abominable green walls round her? And with that row of ants, from which she could not keep her eyes? The low room was broiling hot. A smell of oil and of fish crept through the blinds. A glass of milk was on the table by her bed. It stood in a little bowl as a protection against the ants. The circles made by previous bowls still showed on the table.

The sister had not much idea of making things appetizing. There were no table cloths. It was a free hospital belonging to the company, and as for flowers, ... the sister had no time to see to that. She was everything here—nurse and house-keeper, and in the native hospital too. As for the doctor ... Marian smiled. He was a jovial, decent, soldiers' and planters' doctor, impatient of little pains and little complaints. How coarse his language was! For the last fifteen years, he had done nothing but heal wounded legs, and wounded stom-achs, bring dozens of coolie children into the world, and patch up half murdered coolies and assistants. In the course of those fifteen years he had forgotten that there was such a thing as a headache or nerves. Table cloths indeed!

Unheard, a little shadow had crept into the room. It was Saïma. Her first steps were towards the cradle. She cautiously lifted the curtain and stared for a long time at the child. Then she lifted a corner of the baby's napkin. A boy, she registered, and nodded approvingly. She closed the little curtain with the same cautiousness, and came towards Marian.

'Saïma rub, yes? Mim legs tired.' With slow movements she began to massage Marian's legs. 'Mim not say sister? Sister angry! Sister not know if not rub Mim can't walk. Sister fool-ish. Doctor also foolish. Doctor always cut. Always cut coolies. Saïma rather dead. When Allah say Saima must die ... Saïma die! But Saïma not contract coolie. If contract coolie, first cut, then die.'

Marian smiled. For Saïma everything began and ended with the question whether or not one was a contract coolie. She looked at Saïma's head bending low while her flexible brown hands massaged her legs with regular rhythmic move-ments. The brown faded face had an expression of intense devotion. Of a sudden Marian realized that here at last was the human-being who was not indifferent to what she felt: Here was a creature who had shown real interest in Bobby, a creature from an entirely different world, yet one who belonged to her, was a part of her life, and a part of the home at Tumbuk Tinggih. A beneficent rest filled her and under the soporific caress of Saïma's fingers she fell asleep.

Madelon H. Lulofs, *Rubber*, Cassell, London, 1933; reprinted by Oxford University Press, Singapore, 1987, pp. 100–7.

42
Racial Attitudes

HARRY A. FRANCK

Harry Franck (Passage 40) compares French colonials in Indo-China with their British and American counterparts.

AN old British captain, sailing the Far East for the past forty years, and familiar with most British colonies, insisted that, unlike his own people, the French do not coddle the natives of their possessions. England, he asserted, caters to the natives, gives them education and too much self-rule, and is all the more despised for it. Asiatics do not understand kindness and sympathy; therefore the French are respected. You must not mix sentiment with the ruling of inferior races, or for that matter of any other subject races, he went on; 'for instance, you do not seem to be having an entirely happy time in the Philippines.' The French themselves assert that there is more liberty under their form of colonial rule than under that of the British. I rather doubt it. Though the outward French attitude of equality irrespective of race or color may sometimes give that impression, in the end liberty in French and British colonies probably sums up to about the same total.

She—You know darling, I shall never learn this beastly language—Do ask the Boy for some matches.
He—Matches, Boy.

Learning the language.

It is true that the color-line is less tangible in Indo-China than in American or British colonies. French boys are deferential and even obedient to half-breeds, even to well dressed natives, such as an American or English boy brought up in a colony would scorn to glance at. Native and Eurasian boys of Indo-China act toward white boys as if they quite expected to be accepted as their equals, though that attitude does not exactly hold among adults. This freedom of intercourse has its good points—and certainly its bad. Yet the Frenchman is at heart no democrat; the line of cleavage is social rather than racial. There is every stratum of French society in Hanoï, from the haughty governor-general to the conscripts from manure-heap villages in rural France, and the common soldier is closer to the native rank and file than he is to the high officials of his own race, the governor-general socially more allied to high-class natives than to his own clerks and troopers. Yet on the whole it is better to be white. At the *guignol* near the tiger-cage in the big park about the palaces of the governor-general the Annamese policeman raps on the head native children who do not behave, but is very deferential to the white children who sit elbow to elbow with them. On the other hand the sweat-dripping French soldiers who come out of their cloth-inclosed cages between the acts of these popular outdoor Punch-and-Judy shows and smoke a cigarette before going back to their stifling duties as showmen again are regarded by the upperclass Annamese more as servants than as lords. There are not only French children with their amas in the front seats, and half-breed ones already posing as French, as they will through life, but purely native children as well; and not far away the adults sit or saunter and listen to the good band concert, or cluster before the monkey-house and other cages, without any outward evidence of that racial dissonance emphasized in our own or British colonies. The best hotels in the colony make no distinction between French and Annamese, or any combination of the two races; the Amamese wife of a Frenchman 'will be admitted to any circle in France to which the social position of her husband corresponds.' Yet Indo-China is almost the only place left where one still sees white men, and women, slap and otherwise manhandle their servants, and some Frenchmen speak to native railway men and the like in a way that in any other country would bring them the quite proper request to betake themselves forthwith to where it is reputed to be warmer than in the earthly tropics....

The French think that they cannot live in the tropics without a pith helmet, a cholera belt, wine, and a woman. One might add ice in the place of song. They have a curious belief amounting almost to a superstition that to take off *la casque* in the sun, even the reflected sun, be it only for the instant needed to mop the brow and sweat-band, will almost surely be fatal, so that every little while the thoughtless 'foreigner' is startled by raucous shouts of warning, and assailed with screams of dismay if he so much as thrusts his head out a window without his helmet on. Yet they constantly see the natives bareheaded, and either I must conclude that this, like the cholera belts with which even the women seem to torture themselves, is an unnecessary burden or that my own head is more *dure* than those of the notoriously hard-headed French.

Harry A. Franck, *East of Siam: Ramblings in the Five Divisions of French Indo-China*, The Century Press, New York and London, 1926, pp. 235–7 and 239.

Departure

ALTHOUGH numerous Europeans ended their days in South-East Asia, departure was as much a feature of European life and society in the region as arrival. European society was, in most cases, composed of transients, the Dutch providing the main exceptions: although everywhere there were those who 'stayed on'. Many others, of course, died, particularly in the period before the First World War, before improvements in medical knowledge and communications reduced risks and facilitated access to treatment. In the inter-war years, the shadow of premature death by disease or insurrection was largely lifted. The principal changes and fluctuations in European society were caused by arrivals and departures as people took up or completed their contracts and tours of duty and returned eventually to distant homelands.

Departure affected people in various ways, as the following passages reveal. In some cases people were pleased to leave a corner of the world into which they had not fitted—in which they had experienced much discomfort, loneliness, home-sickness, and separation from friends, family, and familiar pleasures. Others left with regret, having undergone experiences which altered their perceptions of themselves and their native societies. To many, their homelands were stranger and less welcoming than those corners of South-East Asia which had become their homes. In many cases they were returning to straightened circumstances and mundane lives among people who would never fully understand them and with whom they could rarely share their experiences. Life and work overseas had altered them and set them apart from those who had stayed at home. For this reason, many on their return formed or joined associations and clubs catering to returned expatriates and corresponded and met with old colleagues and friends in orgies of reminiscence.

We have only a few passages in this section. Most who wrote about their experiences did not dwell on departure: but there must have been few who did not, as their ships pulled away from the quayside of some tropic port, feel a pang of regret for what they were leaving behind. For Joseph Conrad (Passage 1 and 46), in the guise of Marlow, South-East Asia was forever associated with his youth and seen with the eyes of youth. Whatever experiences had dimmed his hopes had not dimmed the memory of that first arrival. Likewise, Harriette McDougall, whose last years in Sarawak had not been happy, remembered the romance and hope of her arrival (Passage 43). Archdeacon Sharp's departure from Sarawak was also hasty, but followed a more familiar pattern: farewelled by colleagues and friends, he was burdened with gifts and filled with emotion (Passage 44). However, it requires the skill and insight of a novelist to portray the complex feelings most Europeans experienced as they departed one life to begin a new, and so we turn to the conclusion of Madelon Lulof's novel, *Rubber* (Passage 45). Finally, as a coda, we end where we began, with Joseph Conrad, looking back to an experience which changed his life for ever.

43
A Mission Accomplished

C. J. BUNYON

Harriette McDougall (Passages 25 and 33) left Sarawak in January 1867, to recover her health on Penang Hill while her husband, as Bishop of Labuan and Sarawak, conducted a visitation to the Straits Settlements. The Settlements were to pass from Indian rule in April that year and to become a separate Crown Colony. McDougall had been arguing for a new diocese which would comprise the Settlements and the existing diocese of Labuan and Sarawak; and he hoped he would become its first Bishop. While in Singapore, McDougall decided rather hastily to take passage for England to look after his interests. The McDougalls half expected to return to Singapore, if not to Sarawak, but McDougall's health made this impossible.

The McDougalls had departed Sarawak without fanfare, but in a sense Harriette had already left. Worn out, unwell, disillusioned with Sarawak and the Brookes, desperately missing her family, she expressed her feelings in a letter to her brother in March 1866.

D OES it not seem a weary long time since we first came to Sarawak? When we were all young and enthusiastic and could give up even the beaten path of tranquil happiness for an idea! Could we have caught a glimpse of all these years, these sorrows and losses, the romance we cherished turned into so sober a reality, surely our hearts would have fainted and we could not have done it. I have not a doubt but that it was all right, and the years have borne their fruit to us and to others. The sober reality which remains is well worth cherishing and being very thankful for, by which I mean the mission and the native Church at Sarawak.

C. J. Bunyon, *Memoirs of Francis Thomas McDougall and of Harriette His Wife*, Longmans, Green & Co., London, 1889, p. 270.

44
Leaving Friends

ARTHUR F. SHARP

Illness caused Archdeacon Arthur Sharp to be ordered home from Sarawak in November 1910. He had served the Anglican mission for thirteen years, had been largely responsible for directing its effort amongst the Chinese community in Kuching. He had also taken a strong personal interest in the mission's work in an Iban community at Merdang, near Kuching, and had encouraged Asian Christians to assume greater responsibility within the church. His activities had not entirely pleased Rajah Charles, who disapproved of some of his methods and effectively blocked his becoming Bishop in 1908 after the retirement of the previous incumbent. Despite this disappointment, Sharp had stayed on to advise the new Bishop when he arrived in 1909 and retained the respect of the Rajah. The response of the Christian community he had served speaks for itself.

O NCE more I was to be saved from possible mistakes as to my call in the future. The incessant and widespread work of the past two years had used up much energy. Phlebitis, resulting from a fall in the jungle, compelled me to lie up. This, and varicose conditions had produced oedema, a kind of dropsy, which had spread upwards to such an extent that, in the doctor's opinion, a little further advance must be fatal. He urged that I must leave the Tropics at the shortest possible notice. He gave me a week in which to hand over my duties and start for home. Arrived there I must rest completely for a year, and then ask the Archbishop, who had promised me preferment, to put me in charge of the smallest and quietest living he could find. 'Oh, yes; I know what you would say. You would like to take a London living. But you will never do that as long as you live. Make up your mind to take the lightest work you can find. Settle down to it, and just be thankful that you are alive.'

This meant that no choice was left to me. I could give to the new Bishop only one of the two years the Archbishop had requested. It would require a fortnight to hand over, in order, all that I had been responsible for. The Bishop kindly made this possible, relieving me of duty as far as he could, and spreading the news of my early departure. The Resident of Kuching, knowing what a trial it would be to leave Merdang at this juncture, volunteered to accompany me on my last visit there, and by his encouragement and assurance of sympathy did much to cheer the people.

At Kuching, people came in from all sides to bid us a sad, and alas! sometimes a tearful farewell. Touching gifts and mementoes became almost a problem. The Chinese managed to get from China a great state banner in red silk and heavy gold letters, and symbolic figures embroidered in silk of various colours. Five humble Chinese friends made and brought us a heavy, handsome table in costly woods; the school sent a big gong on a stand of bilian carved into the coils of a snake. The same for over thirty years informed the neighbourhood in Hampstead when the Vicar was about to dine. This multitude of gifts poured in upon us, from the great banner to the carved silver egg-cup that our ricksha coolie presented on the breakfast table before we started. Only one more will I mention—the sole relic that I have of the small host that once adorned our home in England. It is an old Chinese 'grandfather's pipe,' its metal tarnished and its silk tassels faded and falling away with age. It was brought to me by my old, stalwart friend Ah Hang on the day before we left. It was his greatest treasure, and I could not bear to take it. But he was not taking no for an answer. He went away humbly, and I reckoned he would go to his home near Merdang.

The last night, we dined at the Residency, thoughtfully arranged for us then, because all our possessions had already gone to the ship that would sail in the morning. When Viva and I returned late that night, our empty home was occupied by the old pipe which Ah Hang had crept in to place there when no one could forbid.

Farewell functions crowded the last few days. I attended a banquet given by old boys of St. Thomas' School in their Club, and another given to Viva and myself in the Chinese Institute, and yet another by the officers of the Borneo

Company. Then there was a presentation given by the English community, and another that quite overwhelmed us from the Dyak tribes from far and near. The Rajah kindly sent a cheque for £200. On the morning of our departure there was a goodly crowd to see us off. Teachers and scholars mingled with the people who covered the wharf and gave us a cheer as we cast off. By then I had endured as much as I could stand up to, and I just remember a little daughter old enough to understand and to grip my hand out of sight on the forecastle. It felt like dying to all that one had lived wholeheartedly for during thirteen years. But the call now was just 'Westward Ho,' and faith has no time for repining. Yet my heart was sore, thinking of my brave Sister Caroline sticking faithfully to her post. We were always so much of one mind that it was like leaving a bit of oneself to 'carry on.'

Arthur F. Sharp, *The Wings of the Morning*, H. H. Greaves, London, n.d. [1953], pp. 218–20.

45
No Regrets

MRS CAMPBELL DAUNCEY

One European who did not feel the pangs of regret at leaving was Mrs Campbell Dauncey who had lived for less than two years at Iloilo on the island of Panay in the Philippines where her husband was employed in a sugar exporting firm. Watching the islands fade into the distance, she had no desire to return. England offered all the cultural pleasures of which she had been deprived. The following passage is extracted from two of her published letters, the first dated 14 August 1905, the second 25 August 1905.

O F course, in the temperate climes there are the inconveniences of dress, frost and drainage, but those are small when compared with art, books, good music, and intelligent fellow-creatures. Oh, you can't imagine the deadliness of the lives the white people lead here—the indifference, the stagnation, the animal round of food and sleep! I think if it had been my fate to stay on in the 'Island home and the Island life' for ever, if I had not become physically ill, I must have become mentally an invalid for the rest of my life.... I am afforded the delightful spectacle of one Philippine Island slipping past after the other into pale blue fluff, and I hope they will stay down under my horizon for ever.

Mrs Campbell Dauncey, *An Englishwoman in the Philippines*, John Murray, London, 1906, pp. 314 and 342.

46
Returning Home

MADELON H. LULOFS

At the conclusion of Madelon Lulof's novel, Frank and Marian Versteegh depart from Deli in East Sumatra where Frank has worked on the rubber plantation for nine years. The Depression has brought retrenchment and Frank has been dismissed, along with many others. His dream of staying on to make enough money for a decent retirement has been dashed and his future in Holland is uncertain. The son born to Marian (Passage 41) died in infancy. His is the little grave they leave behind. They now have a daughter, Tessa. The servant Saima has remained with them and has cared for Tessa since her birth. Something of the relationships forged during those nine years comes through in this passage, along with the emotions, fears, and hopes with which the Versteeghs make their departure. Although fictionalized, this passage is true to the experience of a very large proportion of ordinary Europeans as they prepared to leave for home after years living in South-East Asia.

MARIAN bent over the cabin trunk which stood in the empty veranda. Frank was sitting on the balustrade looking at the rubber garden. It was their last day, and the boat left to-morrow. The luggage for the hold had been sent on ahead. They were to spend the night with John. To-morrow he would drive them away in his car. He was deeply under the impression of their departure.

All their possessions had been sold—the car too. The sale had brought in very little. Who bought in these times?

Tessa was sitting on a cabin trunk playing with her doll. Saïma was squatting by her side stroking her little legs.

'Have you packed your things, Saïma?'

'Yes, Mim.' Saïma's wrinkled hand stopped. She looked at Tessa's small face with great attention.

'The doll's going too, Saïma,' said Tessa.

'Yes, nonnie.'

'On the big boat, Saïma.'

'Yes, nonnie.'

Nobody took any notice of these two. Marian was busy. Frank was reckoning once more how much interest he could get on his capital. He had solved this problem ten days ago and had since worked it out again and again. While he was thinking he saw Meesters, who had taken over his section, arrive through the garden.

'Hallo, Meesters! Do come in!'

'Hallo, people, I've just come to take leave! And I've got a big bit of news.'

Frank and Marian listened curiously.

'Vanlaer has been appointed inspector.'

'Well!' said Marian, clapping her hands with pleasure.

'I'm damned glad for him,' said Frank, and he meant it. He was pleased for John; but at the same time he could not help feeling a slight envy. There was a career that rose to the end, that crowned one's work. But dropping his painful thoughts, he said: 'But then one of the inspectors must have been made chief manager.'

'Yes, didn't you know? Van Hemert. Terheide has resigned on the spot!'

'Well, well, so it *is* Van Hemert!' It made Frank and Marian quiet for a moment.

'Well, people, I'm off now! The ton-tong will go for the

tappers in a minute. Not that it's worth much, what those rascals are bringing in. It's all loss, isn't it? Well, I can't complain. I'm off too next year. Aha, won't that be fine, to be able to drink real beer right to the day of my death? No more of that dirty bottled export stuff! And I'm taking my girl with me. I don't want any of those Dutch street wenches. Well, madam, all my best wishes! Versteegh, keep your tail up! Good-bye, little girl! Shake hands with your uncle.'

Tessa slipped down from her trunk and pushed her tiny hand into Meesters's big red fist.

'Well, good-bye, folks!' He walked through the rubber garden with big steps. Frank and Marian followed him with their eyes. Then, in the silent afternoon, the ton-tong went.

'That's the last time we'll hear it,' said Frank.

Marian looked at him tenderly. She heard the melancholy of his voice. These nine years, the best of their lives. They had grown to be one with the monotonous recurring rhythm of their existence. Nine years of good and bad days. And as she thought of the little grave they would leave behind, sudden tears dropped from her eyes on the balustrade. Frank put his arm round her shoulders.

'We've had a good time here,' he said hoarsely. 'We leave much behind us; but we're carrying much away too.' He indicated Tessa with a movement of his head.

She nodded. 'Everyone is given his little bundle to carry,' she said in a whisper.

John Vanlaer saw them off at the boat. They had found a corner of the smoking saloon. The boat was chock full—so many people were going back in these bad days. Conversation did not run easily. They were unconsciously waiting for the signal of departure. Saïma was standing near the bulwarks with little Tessa.

'Give my best greetings to all the folks, John. We had so little time for taking leave.'

'I won't fail you.'

'The Versteegh family?' The chief steward arrived with a gigantic basket of flowers.

'Yes, that's for us. Thank you. I say!' exclaimed Marian.

231

'How perfectly charming! It's from Van Hemert. How very, very charming of him!'

'Damned decent of him!' declared Frank. 'Do thank him for me, John. We'll write, of course. But will you thank him in advance?'

'I won't forget.'

They lifted their glasses. 'Here's to you, children, and much success in Holland!'

'And much success to you in your new position!'

They had nothing more to say. They thought of the years that had passed, that had tied them together and made them Deli people. The first syren rent the air. Marian started. A nervous trembling shook her.

'Let's go on deck,' she said. They rose and went to Saïma who held Tessa pressed in her arms. Continually she rubbed her broad, flat nose against Tessa's soft cheeks. She said nothing except: 'Nonnie! nonnie!' Tears ran down her shrivelled face. Marian put a hand on her shoulder.

'Don't cry, Saïma.'

'Yes, Mim.' Saïma rubbed the tip of her slendang along her nose. Then, with a quick gesture she took hold of Marian's hand and held it between hers. 'Saïma stays with the little sinyo, Mim.... Saïma carries flowers every month to the grave, Mim.'

Marian nodded mutely and pressed the old, faithful brown hand. Her eyes brimmed over. With trembling mouth, they all stood there, side by side. The second syren blew. A gong sounded. And then came the order: 'All non-passengers ashore, please!'

John seized Frank's hand.

'Well, good-bye, old chap! All will be well in the end.'

'Yes, I know. Thank you for everything.'

'Marian, I wish you strength. And happiness, much happiness.'

'Good-bye, John. Au revoir. Much happiness to you, too. And thank you. You've always been a faithful friend. Greet all of them for us. Don't forget, will you?'

'No, no! And greet the old white country for me.'

'Let me have little Tessa, Saïma.'

Saïma could not let the child go. She pressed her to her breast, she rubbed her little arms and her little legs.

'Tabeh, nonnie ... nonnie ... nonnie.' With her slendang before her eyes, she nervously presssed Marian's and Frank's hands. 'Tabeh, Mim. Tabeh, Tuan. Good-bye.'

'Good-bye, Saïma.'

A last handshake, and John went too. Behind him, like a blind animal, followed Saïma, stumbling and uncertain. The third and the fourth syrens sounded. Cables were cast off, the gang planks were drawn in, a shudder went through the ship as though it were a living thing, a narrow gap appeared between the pier and the boat, and widened. John was still waving, and Frank and Marian waved back.

'Au revoir! Tabeh, Saïma!'

The distance grew. Slowly the ship picked its way through the port. John looked after them and sighed. His thoughts went with them and flew ahead towards Holland. In three weeks they would be there, and he was left behind. He would have to stay two more years before his furlough. He was an inspector. A remarkable promotion at his age. And Frank was dismissed. Who had the better part? Had not they? They who returned to the change of the seasons, to the stormy skies of the cold lands, the dark autumn days, and the bursting spring? To the circle, the soil, the air of their child-hood world?

By the bulwarks, Frank and Marian still stood with Tessa. They did not speak. Their eyes rested for the last time on the low marshy coast and on the forest that lay broiling in the sun. Beyond, in his thoughts, Frank saw the work he was leaving behind, the work of nine hard years. Something of his soul he left there. A fresh breeze suddenly blew over the deck. Ahead lay the wide open sea.

'That's over,' sighed Frank.

Marian put her hand on his, and her voice was a sob and a laugh as she said: 'It'll be spring when we arrive, Frank! Spring for which we've been longing so, and now we'll have it!'

Then he stiffened his shoulders as though ready for a new burden and, putting her hand to his lips, he pressed a kiss on it.

Madelon H. Lulofs, *Rubber*, Cassell, London, 1935; reprinted by Oxford University Press, Singapore, 1987, pp. 309–14.

47
Looking Back

JOSEPH CONRAD

This last passage is from the concluding page of Joseph Conrad's short novel, *Youth*, with which we began this anthology. Although Conrad, in the guise of Marlow, speaks particularly of the sea, the sea may stand as a metaphor for the unfamiliar, the unpredictable, the alien—for an existence beyond that experienced by those who stayed 'on shore', at home. I imagine it speaks to, and for, many Europeans who in retirement return with nostalgia to the days when they were younger and South-East Asia was a world waiting to be explored and experienced.

In a sense, too, the story is a metaphor for the colonial experience, for nineteenth century imperialism which brought Europeans in large numbers to South-East Asia. Among the mixture of motives which carried men and women across the world there were the base and ignoble; but there were also courage, enterprise, a sense of adventure, a desire to achieve great things which, whatever the perceptions of those they governed or of later generations, gave their lives a purpose and a romance not entirely illusory.

'I have known its fascination since; I have seen the mysterious shores, the still water, the lands of brown nations, where a stealthy Nemesis lies in wait, pursues, overtakes so many of the conquering race, who are proud of their wisdom, of their knowledge, of their strength. But for me all the East is contained in that vision of my youth. It is all in that moment when I opened my young eyes on it. I came upon it from a tussle with the sea—and I was young—and I saw it looking at me. And this is all that is left of it! Only a moment; a moment of strength, of romance, of glamour—of youth! . . . A flick of sunshine upon a strange shore, the time to remember, the time for a sigh, and—good-bye!—Night— Good-bye . . . !'

He drank.

'Ah! The good old time—the good old time. Youth and the sea. Glamour and the sea! The good, strong sea, the salt, bitter sea, that could whisper to you and roar at you and knock your breath out of you.'

He drank again.

'By all that's wonderful it is the sea, I believe, the sea itself—or is it youth alone? Who can tell? But you here—you all had something out of life: money, love—whatever one gets on shore—and, tell me, wasn't that the best time, that time when we were young at sea; young and had nothing, on the sea that gives nothing, except hard knocks—and sometimes a chance to feel your strength—that only—what you all regret?'

And we all nodded at him: the man of finance, the man of accounts, the man of law, we all nodded at him over the polished table that like a still sheet of brown water reflected our faces, lined, wrinkled; our faces marked by toil, by deceptions, by success, by love; our weary eyes looking still, looking always, looking anxiously for something out of life, that while it is expected is already gone—has passed unseen, in a sigh, in a flash—together with the youth, with the strength, with the romance of illusions.

Joseph Conrad, *Youth; Heart of Darkness; The End of the Tether; Three Stories*, J. M. Dent & Sons, London, 1948, pp. 41–2.

Oxford Paperbacks for readers interested in South-East Asia, past and present

...ia

...kor and the Khmers
MALCOLM MacDONALD

Indonesia

An Artist in Java
JAN POORTENAAR

Bali and Angkor
GEOFFREY GORER

Coolie
MADELON H. LULOFS

Diverse Lives
JEANETTE LINGARD

Flowering Lotus
HAROLD FORSTER

Forever a Stranger and Other Stories
HELLA S. HAASSE

Forgotten Kingdoms in Sumatra
F. M. SCHNITGER

The Head-Hunters of Borneo
CARL BOCK

The Hidden Force*
LOUIS COUPERUS

The Hunt for the Heart
VINCENT MAHIEU

In Borneo Jungles
WILLIAM O. KROHN

Island of Bali*
MIGUEL COVARRUBIAS

Java: Facts and Fancies
AUGUSTA DE WIT

Java: The Garden of the East
E. R. SCIDMORE

Java: A Travellers' Anthology
JAMES R. RUSH

The Last Paradise
HICKMAN POWELL

Let It Be
PAULA GOMES

Makassar Sailing
G. E. P. COLLINS

The Malay Archipelago
ALFRED RUSSEL WALLACE

The Outlaw and Other Stories
MOCHTAR LUBIS

The Poison Tree*
E. M. BEEKMAN (Ed.)

Rambles in Java and the Straits in 1852
'BENGAL CIVILIAN' (C. W. KINLOCH)

Rubber
MADELON H. LULOFS

A Tale from Bali*
VICKI BAUM

The Temples of Java
JACQUES DUMARÇAY

Through Central Borneo
CARL LUMHOLTZ

To the Spice Islands and Beyond
GEORGE MILLER

Travelling to Bali
ADRIAN VICKERS

Twin Flower: A Story of Bali
G. E. P. COLLINS

Unbeaten Tracks in Islands of the Far East
ANNA FORBES

Witnesses to Sumatra
ANTHONY REID

Yogyakarta
MICHAEL SMITHIES

Malaysia

Among Primitive Peoples in Borneo
IVOR H. N. EVANS

An Analysis of Malay Magic
K. M. ENDICOTT

At the Court of Pelesu
HUGH CLIFFORD

The Best of Borneo Travel
VICTOR T. KING

The Chersonese with the Gilding Off
EMILY INNES

The Experiences of a Hunter
WILLIAM T. HORNADAY

The Field-Book of a Jungle-Wallah
CHARLES HOSE

Fifty Years of Romance and Research in Borneo
CHARLES HOSE

The Gardens of the Sun
F. W. BURBIDGE

Glimpses into Life in Malayan Lands
JOHN TURNBULL THOMSON

The Golden Chersonese
ISABELLA BIRD

The Malay Magician
RICHARD WINSTEDT

Malay Poisons and Charm Cures
JOHN D. GIMLETTE

My Life in Sarawak
MARGARET BROOKE, THE RANEE OF SARAWAK

Natural Man
CHARLES HOSE

Nine Dayak Nights
W. R. GEDDES

A Nocturne and Other Malayan Stories and Sketches
FRANK SWETTENHAM

Orang-Utan
BARBARA HARRISSON

The Pirate Wind
OWEN RUTTER

Queen of the Head-Hunters
SYLVIA, LADY BROOKE, THE RANEE OF SARAWAK

Six Years in the Malay Jungle
CARVETH WELLS

They Came to Malaya
J. M. GULLICK

Wanderings in the Great Forests of Borneo
ODOARDO BECCARI

The White Rajahs of Sarawak
ROBERT PAYNE

Myanmar

Faded Splendour, Golden Past: Urban Images of Burma
ELLEN CORWIN CANGI

Inroads into Burma
GERRY ABBOTT

Philippines

Little Brown Brother
LEON WOLFF

Singapore

Manners and Customs of the Chinese
J. D. VAUGHAN

Raffles of the Eastern Isles
C. E. WURTZBURG

Singapore 1941–1942
MASANOBU TSUJI

Travellers' Singapore
JOHN BASTIN

South-East Asia

Adventures and Encounters
J. M. GULLICK

Adventurous Women
J. M. GULLICK (Ed.)

The Architecture of South-East Asia through Travellers' Eyes
ROXANA WATERSON

Explorers of South-East Asia
VICTOR T. KING (Ed.)

Soul of the Tiger*
J. A. McNEELY and P. S. WACHTEL

Tropical Interludes
GRAHAM SAUNDERS

Wonders of Nature in South-East Asia
THE EARL OF CRANBROOK

Thailand

Behind the Painting and Other Stories
SIBURAPHA

Descriptions of Old Siam
MICHAEL SMITHIES

The Politician and Other Stories
KHAMSING SRINAWK

The Prostitute
K. SURANGKHANANG

Temples and Elephants
CARL BOCK

The Sergeant's Garland and Other Stories
DAVID SMYTH & MANAS CHITAKASEM

To Siam and Malaya in the Duke of Sutherland's Yacht *Sans Peur*
FLORENCE CADDY

Travels in Siam, Cambodia and Laos
HENRI MOUHOT

Vietnam

The General Retires and Other Stories
NGUYEN HUY THIEP

The Light of the Capital
GREG & MONIQUE LOCKHART

*Titles marked with an asterisk have restricted rights.